Contemporary Issues
in the **Early Years**

6TH EDITION

Edited by **Gillian Pugh** and **Bernadette Duffy**

Los Angeles | London | New Delhi
Singapore | Washington DC

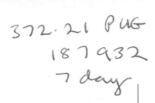

Los Angeles | London | New Delhi
Singapore | Washington DC

SAGE Publications Ltd
1 Oliver's Yard
55 City Road
London EC1Y 1SP

SAGE Publications Inc.
2455 Teller Road
Thousand Oaks, California 91320

SAGE Publications India Pvt Ltd
B 1/I 1 Mohan Cooperative Industrial Area
Mathura Road
New Delhi 110 044

SAGE Publications Asia-Pacific Pte Ltd
3 Church Street
#10-04 Samsung Hub
Singapore 049483

Editor: Marianne Lagrange
Assistant editor: Kathryn Bromwich
Production editor: Nicola Marshall
Copyeditor: Elaine Leek
Proofreader: Jill Birch
Indexer: Martin Hargreaves
Marketing manager: Catherine Slinn
Cover design: Naomi Robinson
Typeset by: C&M Digitals (P) Ltd, Chennai, India
Printed in India at Replika Press Pvt Ltd

First edition published 1992
Second edition published 1996
Third edition published 2001, reprinted 2002
Fourth edition published 2006, reprinted 2008
Fifth edition published 2010, reprinted 2010

Library of Congress Control Number: 2013930419

British Library Cataloguing in Publication data

A catalogue record for this book is available from the British Library

ISBN 978-1-4462-6640-3
ISBN 978-1-4462-6641-0

This new edition is dedicated to the memory of our mothers, Rachel Drayson (1922–2012) and Mary Duffy (1936–2012) and to Dominic Gareth Landau, Gillian's grandson, born in May 2013, and his mother, Carolyn.

Contents

About the Editors

Gillian Pugh has worked throughout her life in the children's sector, most recently as Chief Executive of the children's charity Coram, from which she retired in 2005. She has advised governments in the UK and overseas on services for children and families, was an adviser to the House of Commons Select Committee for children, schools and families and has published widely. Gillian recently retired as chair of the National Children's Bureau, as visiting professor at the Institute of Education, as President of the National Childminding Association and as a Vice President of Early Education. She was a panel member of the recent review into the Family Justice system, chaired the Advisory Committee for the Cambridge Primary Review and is a co-author of the final report, *Children, their World, their Education* (Routledge, 2009). She was awarded the OBE in 1996 and made a DBE in 2005 for services to children and families.

Bernadette Duffy is Head of the Thomas Coram Centre in Camden, one of the first to be designated as a children's centre and identified as a particularly successful school by Ofsted. Bernadette has contributed to a range of publications and is author of *Supporting Creativity and Imagination in the Early Years*. She was on the working parties which devised *Curriculum Guidance for the Foundation Stage*, *Birth to Three Matters* and the *Early Years Foundation Stage* framework. Bernadette is also a member of a number of advisory groups for the Department for Education, including Early Years Co-production, Early Years Workforce, Teaching Agency, Integrated 2 Year Old Review and the Evaluation of Early Education in England. She was on the advisory committee of the Cambridge University Primary Review. Bernadette is a Vice President of the British Association for Early Childhood Education and trustee of the Froebel Trust, and was made an OBE in 2005.

About the Contributors

Elizabeth Andrews has worked with services for children and young people with special educational needs and disabilities for over 30 years. She began her career as a teacher of deaf children and spent 10 years in universities as a lecturer and teacher trainer, before moving to the voluntary sector and, most recently, independent consultancy. Liz is a former Director of the Early Support programme, which was developed by the Department for Children, Schools and Families between 2003 and 2009 as the national programme for young children with disabilities and their families. She is currently a member of the Early Support Consortium appointed by the Department for Education as a delivery partner for service development associated with the Government Green Paper *Support and aspiration: A new approach to special educational needs and disability*.

Carol Aubrey is Emeritus Professor at University of Warwick and Visiting Professor at Birmingham City University. She trained as a primary school teacher and educational psychologist and spent a number of years in primary teacher education with a particular focus on the early years, first at University College Cardiff and then at the University of Durham. Her research interests lie in the policy-to-practice context of early childhood education and care, leadership, early learning and development, with a particular interest in mathematical development and inclusion/special educational needs.

Jacqueline Barnes is Professor of Psychology at Birkbeck, University of London and Honorary Senior Psychologist at the Tavistock and Portman NHS

Foundation Trust. She has conducted research focused on services for young children and their families for more than 30 years. Her particular focus has been on ways to prevent or reduce children's socio-emotional and behavioural problems and parenting difficulties.

Kate Billingham worked as a health visitor and children's nurse before moving into public health and policy. She has worked in government and led the introduction of the Family Nurse Partnership in England.

Rebecca Brown is a research associate at the Centre for Child and Family Research, Loughborough University. Her research interests include homelessness, and outcomes for vulnerable children. Recent publications include Ward, Brown and Westlake, *Safeguarding Babies and Very Young Children from Abuse and Neglect* (London: Jessica Kingsley Publishers, 2012). She currently takes a lead role in a major longitudinal study of professional decision-making and its consequences for infants suffering or likely to suffer significant harm, and is also working on an NSPCC funded study to develop a model for pre-birth assessment.

Caron Carter is a Senior Lecturer in Early Childhood at Sheffield Hallam University. Prior to her current post, she was an early years teacher and then a deputy head teacher in a nursery and infant school. She has recently completed her PhD focusing on children's friendships. Her other interests include children's participation and children's literacy.

Ann Crichton has a background in the voluntary sector and as a children's centre leader at the Chai Centre in Burnley, a combined children's centre and healthy living centre. She also led a health improvement team for NHS East Lancashire; the team acted as the bridge between mainstream health services and children's centres and provided infant mental health and substance misuse services at the centres. Ann was a founding member of the Children's Centre Leaders Reference Group in 2008 and chair of the group from 2010 to 2012. Ann is currently an independent consultant, working with Pen Green Research, Training and Development Base and Leadership Centre and teaching on MA and BA courses. She was awarded the OBE in 2011.

Mary Crowley has a background in adult education. She was Chief Executive of Parenting UK from 1999 to 2007 and led the development of the National Occupational Standards for Work with Parents and a number of European parenting initiatives. She was awarded the OBE in 2008 and is Chair of the International Federation for Parenting Education (www.fiep-ifpe.fr). Mary is Irish and has five children and four grandchildren.

Jan Dubiel is an early years specialist who has worked as a Nursery, Reception and Year 1 teacher, Early Years Consultant and Adviser. Recently he was programme lead for the Early Years Foundation Stage and EYFS Profile at the QCDA and is currently National Development Manager for Early Excellence.

Kathy Goouch is a Reader at Canterbury Christ Church University and co-director of The Baby Room Project with Sacha Powell. Kathy's research and publications are focused on babies and young children, and in particular early literacy.

Pauline Jones started her career in residential childcare. After qualifying as a social worker, she worked across the voluntary and statutory sectors. Crossing from social work to education she taught and tutored in Further Education, and developed the Diploma in Nursery Nursing for profoundly deaf students, before becoming head of a Child, Health and Social Care Department. Together with colleagues she wrote a series of textbooks to support early years training. In 2000 she joined the Sure Start Unit, ultimately becoming Regional Manager for Sure Start and Children's Fund in the East Midlands. In 2001 she was awarded an MBA in Educational Management; her final dissertation was on ensuring the quality and effectiveness of Sure Start Local Programmes. At the Children's Workforce Development Council Pauline led on developing Early Years Professional Status and the new Qualifications and Credit Framework early years qualifications. In 2012 she was awarded the OBE for services to early years education.

Perpetua Kirby is an independent researcher (www.pkrc.co.uk) working across the public and voluntary sector to support, research and evaluate the ways in which children and young people are listened to, engage in dialogue and influence decisions. She has published widely on the subject, including revising the Open University pack on *Listening to Young Children* and being the lead author on *Building a Culture of Participation*, the influential national research and handbook for child and youth services, published by the Department for Education and Skills in 2003.

Y. Penny Lancaster began her career as a primary school teacher in New Zealand and has since worked in a range of educational projects within Europe, the Middle East and Africa. She was formerly the director of the successful Coram project 'Listening to young children', which won the best education and training project in the 2005 Charity Awards. She is currently writing up her PhD thesis which focuses on children's perspectives of their Key Stage 1 classroom experience. She is particularly interested in understanding the way daily practices and relations of power within the classroom shape children's legal entitlement to 'express their views freely about matters that affect them'.

Sandra Mathers began her career as a primary school teacher, and is now a senior researcher and Principal Investigator at the University of Oxford. Her main research interest is the quality of early years settings, and the relationships between quality and children's developmental outcomes. Recent research studies have included the Evaluation of the Graduate Leader Fund, the Evaluation of the Early Education Pilot for Two Year Old Children, and 'Improving Quality in the Early Years', which explored the relationships between different measures for identifying and improving quality. Sandra is also a co-Director of A+ Education Ltd, supporting local authorities and early years practitioners in improving quality using the Environment Rating Scales (ECERS, ITERS and others).

Cathy Nutbrown is Professor of Early Education and Head of the School of Education at the University of Sheffield. She teaches and researches in the field of Early Childhood Education. Cathy began her career as a teacher of young children and has since worked in a range of settings and roles with children, parents, teachers, and other early childhood educators. Her research focuses on family literacy, inclusive education, the arts and childhood. In 2010 she contributed to the Tickell Review of the Early Years Foundation Stage and in June 2012 published her *Foundations of Quality*, known as the Nutbrown Review, an independent review of Early Education and Childcare Qualifications undertaken for the government. She is Editor-in-Chief of the Sage *Journal of Early Childhood Research* and author of more than 50 publications, including: *Early Childhood Education: History, Philosophy and Experience*; *Understanding Schemas and Young Children*; *From Birth to Three*; *Inclusion in the Early Years*; *Justifying Enquiry* and *Threads of Thinking*.

Sacha Powell is a Reader in Early Childhood at Canterbury Christ Church University. She co-directs The Baby Room Project with Kathy Goouch, which has generated opportunities for collaboration with colleagues interested in infants' education and care from other countries in Europe, North America, Australasia and Asia.

Julie Revels has 27 years of experience in the field of special educational needs, disability and early years. This has been a combination of school-based, central service and local authority strategic roles. She currently works as a tutor for the Institute of Education and delivers CPD for Early Support Consortium, National Association of Special Educational Needs (nasen) and the National Literacy Trust.

Fiona Roberts is a senior research officer at the University of Oxford. After studying psychology, she now works in the Families, Effective Learning, and Literacy research group in the Department of Education. Fiona's main research interest is in young children's literacy development and, more specifically, interventions to improve children's literacy through supporting parents. She is currently involved in a large randomised trial of such a programme: Supporting Parents on Kids' Education (SPOKES).

Iram Siraj-Blatchford is Professor of Early Childhood Education at the Institute of Education, University of London. Her recent research projects have included Evaluation of the Foundation Phase across Wales and she is principal investigator of the major DfE 16-year study on Effective Preschool, Primary and Secondary Education (EPPSE 3–16) Project (1997–2013) and of the Effective Pedagogy in the Early Years project. She is working on longitudinal studies as a principal investigator in a number of countries, including Australia and Ireland. She has always been particularly interested in undertaking research that aims to combat disadvantage and to give children and families from these backgrounds a head start. She is a specialist, early years adviser to governments and ministers in the UK, where she is conducting reviews of research on child outcomes for the Centre for Effectiveness and Outcomes and advises governments overseas.

Brenda Spencer has been a teacher, head teacher, and additional inspector leading inspections both in maintained schools and registered provision. She works as a freelance consultant in early years and primary education and has contributed to the work of the Standards and Testing Agency (formerly QCA and NAA), National Strategies and was a member of the Early Education Advisory Group.

Philippa Stobbs is Assistant Director of the Council for Disabled Children. Her professional background is in teaching and school inspection work. She leads the policy work for the Special Educational Consortium, national support to parent partnership services, and has led a number of developments in the education of children with SEND, particularly work involving partnerships. Philippa was recently seconded to the Department for Education where she managed the Lamb Inquiry and led national work on the development of SEN data on progression. She is part of the CDC team working as the DfE's strategic reform partner on SEN and disability and was part of the team developing initial teacher training and advanced level materials on SEN and disability for the TDA. Philippa trains, writes and provides consultancy on SEN and disability in schools and early years settings and in policy, both nationally and internationally.

Kathy Sylva is Professor of Educational Psychology at the University of Oxford. She has carried out many large-scale studies on the effects of Early Childhood Education and Care on children's development. She also studies ways to support early literacy through school and home based programmes. She has been a lead researcher on the Effective Pre-School and Primary Education (EPPE) study and also on the National Evaluation of Children's Centres. A dominant theme throughout her work has been the impact of education and care not only on 'academic knowledge' but on children's behaviour, self-regulation, and disposition to learn. She has been specialist adviser to the Parliamentary Select Committee on Education 2000–2009. She was awarded the OBE in 2008 for services to children and families. She was a member of the Tickell Review Expert Panel on the EYFS 2011.

Linda Uren has more than 30 years' experience working in social services and children's services at local and national level. With a social work background, she is currently Director of Children's Services in Gloucestershire. She worked previously for the Department for Education and Skills on Sure Start, in particular leading for the DfES on the 2004 Childcare Review. She is a member of the current government's Early Years Co-Production Group.

Harriet Ward is Research Professor and Director of the Centre for Child and Family Research (CCFR) at Loughborough University, UK and co-director of the government-funded Childhood Wellbeing Research Centre – a partnership between the Institute of Education, University of London, Loughborough University and PSSRU, University of Kent. She has more than 20 years' experience, both as a research director and field researcher, as an adviser to policymakers and service providers, and as a social work practitioner. Harriet has recently completed a major research study on infants suffering, or likely to suffer significant harm and she has co-authored *Safeguarding Children Across Services: Messages from Research on Identifying and Responding to Child Maltreatment,* the Overview of the Department of Health and Department for Education funded Safeguarding Children Research Initiative. She was awarded the CBE for services to children and families in June 2012.

Helen Wheeler is a Principal Officer in the Early Childhood Unit at the National Children's Bureau (NCB). Helen has many years' experience as a primary and nursery school teacher and worked as part of an ethnic minority achievement team in the London Borough of Ealing. She joined NCB to research and support the development of PEAL (Parents, Early Years and Learning) and currently leads on new developments for the Making it REAL (Raising Early Achievement in Literacy) project in partnership with the University of Sheffield.

Introduction

Bernadette Duffy

In this edition of *Contemporary Issues* we reflect the early years at a time of economic challenge, with the worst recession since the 1930s and significant cuts to public funding. In this climate the early years sector has the daunting task of maintaining the progress made during the previous years of public investment.

The Coalition government's first policy statement on early years expressed in *Families in the Foundation Years* (DfE/DH, 2011a) and *Supporting Families in the Foundation Years* (DfE/DH, 2011b) continued many of the messages about the importance of the early years that had evolved over the preceding decade. These documents responded to the independent reviews described by Gillian Pugh in Chapter 1. They recognised the strides that had been made by the sector, expressed ongoing support for integrated working, including children's centres, and strengthened the focus on parents and early intervention, though the Every Child Matters agenda was no longer the focus.

But nothing stands still, and January 2013 saw the publication of *More Great Childcare* (DfE, 2013) which sets out the new vision for early education and childcare. While the importance of quality early years provision to children's well-being now and success in the future is still emphasised, concerns about the cost of childcare for working parents and the taxpayer are to the fore. The roles of central government and local authorities are to be reduced; the focus is on sector-led improvement with all providers learning from the best and the sector deciding what is needed and how to address this. Improved qualifications and increased qualification levels are seen as key to increasing professionalism in the sector, with higher qualified staff meaning that there can be greater flexibility. This, it is argued, will enable central government to deregulate and trust providers, including childminders, to make decisions about issues including ratios and premises, which it is expected will reduce costs for parents.

While the proposed improvements to qualifications have been well received by most in the sector there are anxieties about deregulation. There are strong doubts that the flexibility to increase ratios will actually lead to reductions in the cost of childcare for parents and real concerns that one practitioner working with four babies under one year of age is a poor decision, however well qualified the practitioner.

Trusting the sector is welcome but can the sector take this level of responsibility? In comparison to schools, the early years is a young sector that has had significantly less investment and time to evolve. It is also much more diverse than schools, even with the introduction of academies and free schools, and is heavily dependent on private and voluntary providers where there are low levels of staff qualifications compared with schools. Are there enough high-quality and willing providers who are trusted across the sector to lead it?

There is good evidence for leadership within the schools sector supported by what was the National College for School Leadership. This shows that the strategy works well for operational issues, for example curriculum and teacher development, but evidence is lacking for success in strategic issues – whose responsibility is it to identify gaps, coordinate a response to address them and ensure that it works? *More Great Childcare* sees Ofsted as the sole arbiter of quality in the early years, with a strong focus on identifying underperforming providers, but this is a new role and it is not clear how the sector and Ofsted will work together to ensure the improvements needed.

While there are cuts, the country is still investing significant public money in early years services and the government needs to ensure that this is used to achieve the outcomes intended. Over the past decade we have gathered strong evidence about what works and improves outcomes for children and their families. If we know what high quality looks like should we not be ensuring that all children and their families have access to this? There is tension between giving providers the freedom to decide and ensuring that all children have access to high-quality services. As the Ofsted Annual Report for 2011/12 points out, the poorest provision is in disadvantaged areas where children are most in need of high quality (Ofsted, 2012). The Effective Provision of Pre-School Education project has shown that unless the provision is of high quality it is of little value to children and their families (Sylva et al., 2004).

The vision described in *More Great Childcare* depends on the early years sector having had the chance to mature into a strong sector with shared values and one that can lead its own development. The risk is that there is still too much fragmentation and insufficient capacity within the sector to take on this role and the progress that has been made in improving outcomes for children and families will be undone.

In this, the sixth edition of *Contemporary Issues in the Early Years*, we seek to reflect the achievements and progress that have been made in the early years but also the changes and challenges that a deep economic depression and a new government with its own priorities have brought. At a time of change and debate about early years services it is even more important that we address the major themes in this book: How can we work together better to meet the needs of young children and their families? How do we ensure that all children have equality of opportunity? How do we use what we know from research and practice to create early years services that truly put the child at the centre?

This book is divided into three sections. Part 1 looks at policy and research, Part 2 addresses putting policy and research into practice and Part 3 explores workforce issues.

The first five chapters focus on policy and research. In Chapter 1 Gillian Pugh charts the development of early years services and reviews the main developments in national policy in recent years. She provides us with a clear understanding of how we have got to where we are, the success we have achieved and the challenges that lie ahead in this difficult time. Gillian points out that the past 20 years have seen unprecedented expansion in the amount of early years provision, but opportunities to create a coherent early years strategy have not been taken and current economic constraints are putting both quantity and quality at risk.

In Chapter 2 Linda Uren describes recent developments in local authorities and shares one local authority's approach to the development of children's services and children's centres. At a time when the role of local authorities in ensuring quality is being questioned while the responsibilities for sufficiency remain this is a key chapter. Linda identifies the importance of thinking positively and of local areas continuing to innovate and collaborate to improve the quality of services and utilise increasingly scarce resources effectively.

Chapter 3 looks at the world picture. Sacha Powell and Kathy Goouch provide a valuable insight into the ways early years services are viewed in other countries and identify the lessons we can learn from them. They show that how early childhood provision is understood and constructed is dependent on societal aims, national politics and policy, and levels of investment.

Sandra Mathers, Fiona Roberts and Kathy Sylva's chapter looks at quality in early childhood education: what it is and how we can define it. The issues and challenges involved in measuring it, and the impact of different dimensions of quality on children's development over time are identified. They draw on the findings from research, including the Effective Provision of

Pre-School and Primary Education Project, and present the evidence for long term effects.

Ofsted is to be the sole arbiter of quality, and in Chapter 5 Brenda Spencer and Jan Dubiel consider their role and the implications of the recent changes to the inspection of early years services. They describe the new inspection frameworks and ask if they are likely to achieve their stated aim of improving the quality of provision for children.

In the second part of the book are nine chapters focusing on practice and showing how policies and research are being implemented by practitioners. Y. Penny Lancaster and Perpetua Kirby write the first chapter in this section. They define what it means to listen to young children within the context of Every Child Matters and the EYFS, explore our view of childhood and show how practitioners can enable young children to articulate their feelings, experiences and ideas.

Chapter 7 is written by Bernadette Duffy. She describes the recent development of the English early years curriculum and the revised Early Years Foundation Stage framework comparing it to frameworks elsewhere in the United Kingdom. The chapter looks at what we mean by the term 'curriculum' and includes theories that have influenced its development.

In Chapter 8 Caron Carter and Cathy Nutbrown explore the issue of assessment. They discuss the different forms of assessment, including the new 2-year-olds progress report and profile, and the purposes it can be put to. Cathy and Caron highlight the value and visions that need to underpin respectful assessments of young children and describe ways in which early childhood educators can use assessment to understand young children's capabilities and learning.

The number of children's centres has reduced by more than 400 through closures, amalgamations and reorganisations since the Coalition government was formed and those remaining have experienced funding cuts of a third in real terms (Leper, 2013). Ann Crichton's chapter is written in this climate. It describes the development of children's centres, including their new purpose: increased responsibility for disadvantaged families and less focus on providing early education and childcare. Ann identifies the challenges but also the opportunities, with examples of successful children's centres.

In Chapter 10 Kate Billingham and Jacqueline Barnes look at the key role of health in early years services. They identify the government's moves to greater integration in which health is seen as integral to wider services for young children. Kate and Jacqueline provide an overview of health in the early years and identify the issues that need to be addressed when health and other partners work together to promote children's health and well-being.

Diversity, inclusion and learning are the important themes for Iram Siraj-Blatchford's chapter, and in it she looks at practitioners' understanding of children's multiple identities. Iram challenges the hidden assumptions that disadvantage children on the grounds of ethnic background, gender or socio-economic class. She points out that it is essential that children learn social competence to respect of other groups and individuals, regardless of difference. Philippa Stobbs, Elizabeth Andrews and Julie Revels pick up these themes in Chapter 12 in relation to children with disabilities and special educational needs. They outline the landmark events for special needs in early years services and argue that there is a growing view that meeting children's special needs is an indivisible part of the children's services agenda. Recent developments and emerging practice in meeting special needs within inclusive settings are also addressed.

Many of the authors have included references to the key role of parents as part of their chapter. In Chapter 13 Mary Crowley and Helen Wheeler expand on this theme drawing on their experiences and the PEAL project. They give a brief history of the development of services for parents and current policy. Mary and Helen explore the ways that parents and practitioners can work together for the benefit of children, parents and practitioners, sharing examples of good practice from settings across the country.

Harriet Ward and Rebecca Brown have contributed a crucial new chapter looking at the importance of safeguarding children in the early years. They describe the impact of abuse and neglect on early childhood development, showing why early intervention is important, and point to the role of early years practitioners in identifying and responding to maltreatment, in preventing its recurrence and mitigating impairment.

Part 3 explores workforce issues at a time when government wants to increase qualification levels but local authority spending on training for childcare staff has been cut by at least 40% (Clayton, 2013). Pauline Jones, with help from Rob Nicholson, describes the early years workforce and stresses the importance of quality. Pauline questions the nature of the early years sector and discusses the findings of the Nutbrown Review (2012), in particular the roles of Early Years Professionals and teachers, and Level 2 and 3 early years qualifications. The chapter ends by looking at the way forward and the challenges still to be addressed if early years work is to become a career that is valued and recognised by society.

Finally, in Chapter 16 Carol Aubrey considers the background and development of multi-agency teams. The challenges of restructuring children's services and recent government policies are addressed. Carol looks at the leadership and working of multi-agency teams and explores the nature of leaderships and strategies to support leaders.

Almost all of the contributors to this book are nationally or internationally known for their contribution to the early years debate. All have been actively involved in the research, development of policies and improvements in practice that this book discusses. All share a commitment to the well-being of young children and their families, which comes across strongly in each of their chapters. It is a crucial time for the early years and there are many concerns about reduced funding and deregulation, but the sector has a history of innovation, creative responses to challenges and the ability to seize opportunities. We hope that this book will help practitioners to focus on what we know is vital for children and families and ensure that the gains the sector has made in recent years are maintained and enhanced.

References

Clayton, E. (2013) 'Councils slash childcare training by more than 40 per cent', *Children and Young People Now*, 11 January.

Department for Education and Department of Health (DfE/DH) (2011a) *Families in the Foundation Years – Evidence Pack*. London: DfE/DH.

Department for Education and Department of Health (DfE/DH) (2011b) *Supporting Families in the Foundation Years*. London: DfE/DH.

Department for Education (DfE) (2013) *More Great Childcare*. London: DfE.

Leper, J. (2013) 'Number of children's centres falls by more than 400', *Children and Young People Now*, 29 January.

Nutbrown, C. (2012) *Foundations for Quality. The Independent Review of Early Education and Childcare Qualifications: Final Report* (Nutbrown Review). London: Department for Education.

Ofsted (Office for Standards in Education, Children's Services and Skills) (2012) *The Annual Report of Her Majesty's Chief Inspector of Education, Children's Services and Skills 2011/12*. Norwich: TSO. www.ofsted.gov.uk/resources/annualreport1112. (accessed 28 June 2013).

Sylva, K., Melhuish, E. C., Sammons, P., Siraj-Blatchford, I. and Taggart, B. (2004) The Effective Provision of Pre-School Education (EPPE) Project: *Technical Paper 12 – The Final Report: Effective Pre-School Education*. London: Department for Education and Skills/Institute of Education, University of London.

Companion website

To access a variety of additional web resources to accompany this book please visit: **www.sagepub.co.uk/pughduffy**

The material includes:

- web links
- links to journal articles and current policies and frameworks
- videos of the editors discussing the current issues facing Early Years Education

PART 1

Policy and Research

CHAPTER 1

The Policy Agenda for Early Childhood Services[1]

Gillian Pugh

The past two decades have seen considerable developments in the availability and organisation of early childhood services as early childhood remains high on the policy agenda. This period has not been without its challenges, reflecting changing political priorities and economic circumstances, and opportunities have been missed to create a more coherent strategy for young children and their families. This chapter considers these changes and raises a number of issues that are considered further in the chapters that follow.

A brief history

Since the establishment of the first nursery school by Robert Owen, in Scotland in 1816, the development of early education in the United Kingdom was until recently remarkably slow by comparison to much of mainland Europe. In 1870 publicly funded education became compulsory at the age of 5 years, but from the earliest days children as young as 2 years were admitted to primary schools. During the course of the twentieth century successive governments supported the principle of free nursery education but seldom found the resources to fund it. Even with the gradual establishment of nursery schools and, during the 1914–18 war, some public daycare centres, the predominant form of early education in the United Kingdom was for 130 years state primary schools. The lack of appropriate provision within the education system led to two parallel developments during the second half of the twentieth century: on the one hand, the emergence during the 1960s through the voluntary sector of the playgroup movement; and, on the other, the growth of full daycare to meet the needs of working parents, initially through childminding and, additionally since the 1990s, through private sector day nurseries.

This legacy is important in understanding the state of early childhood services at the beginning of the twenty-first century. The second edition of this book, published in 1996, described services in the United Kindom as discretionary, with low levels of public funding compared with mainland Europe, with a heavy reliance on the private and voluntary sectors, with diversity of provision but little choice for parents, lacking in coordination between providers from different agencies, and with different services having different aims and purposes, and being used by different client groups – working parents, children 'in need' and parents able to use part-time nurseries (Pugh, 1996).

The levels of concern expressed here were reflected in a number of prestigious national reports published during the 1990s, notably the Rumbold Report *Starting with Quality* (DES, 1990), largely ignored by the government at the time, but very widely used subsequently as the basis for best practice in early years settings. During the 1980s and early 1990s there was a lack of political conviction that young children mattered and a view that children were the private responsibility of their parents. But there were also unclear and conflicting messages about what was required – should an early years policy be most concerned about preparing children for school, or with daycare for working parents? Should it provide stimulation for a developing brain, or equal opportunities for women? Was it about cost savings for employers, able to retain staff when they became parents, or about reducing the benefit bill for single parents, enabling them to return to the workforce? Or was prevention the main driver – whether of developmental delay in children or juvenile crime?

The tide began to turn in 1995 as additional funding for the education of 4-year-olds was announced but, controversially, the funding was to be made available to parents through vouchers that could be redeemed in private, voluntary or local authority nurseries. A pilot scheme was rolled out amid mounting criticism, but full implementation was stopped by the election of a Labour government in 1997. Fifteen years later the expansion of services for our youngest children has been considerable, and this chapter assesses the extent to which the vision of what was called for during the 1990s has been realised.

An integrated strategy for young children and their parents?

Throughout the years of the Labour administration (1997–2010) the expansion of early years services has to be seen within the context of the 2003 Green Paper *Every Child Matters* (DfES, 2003) – described by the Prime Minister, Tony Blair, at its launch as the most significant development for children in over 30 years – and the subsequent 2004 Children Act. The report took prevention as its starting point and accepted the view that to support all children better through well coordinated mainstream services was more likely to benefit those in need and at risk than a separate child protection service. Based on a review of relevant research and widespread consultation with professionals and young people, the five key themes of the Every Child Matters policy initiative were

- strong foundations in the early years
- a stronger focus on parenting and families
- earlier interventions and effective protection
- better accountability and integration locally, regionally and nationally
- reform of the workforce.

The overall aim of the Green Paper and the subsequent 2004 Children Act was to improve outcomes for all children and narrow the gap between those who do well and those who do not, through reconfiguring services around children and families. The focus was on entitlements for children through five main outcomes:

- Being healthy – enjoying good physical and mental health and living a healthy lifestyle.
- Staying safe – being protected from harm and neglect.
- Enjoying and achieving – getting the most out of life and developing the skills for adulthood.
- Making a positive contribution – being involved with the community and society and not engaging in antisocial or offending behaviour.
- Economic well-being – not being prevented by economic disadvantage from achieving their full potential in life.

The long-term vision that emerged through the Children Act and the implementation paper *Every Child Matters: Change for Children* (DfES, 2004) was the development of integrated education, health and social care, through children's centres, extended schools and improved services for young people; better support for parents provided by better qualified staff; and targeted services planned and delivered within a universal context.

At central government level, responsibility for most services for children, young people and families was brought within a single directorate at what is now called the Department for Education under the direction of a Minister for Children. Children's health remained within the Department of Health, although a parallel National Service Framework for children's health was developed (DH/DfES, 2004). In local areas, directors for social services and education were replaced by a director for children's services, and an integrated mechanism for planning and delivering services – Children's Trusts – were established. There was also a common assessment framework, an integrated workforce strategy, an integrated inspection framework (see Chapter 5) and a new curriculum framework (see Chapter 7). It was a huge and ambitious agenda.

Throughout three Labour administrations the increase in services for young children was driven by two parallel forces. The first was the commitment from both Prime Ministers and Chancellors to eliminating child poverty by 2020, a commitment which drove the increase of childcare as a means of enabling women to return to work and thus increase family income. There was also a growing awareness of the gap, in terms of overall well-being and achievement, between children who do well and their peers who do not.

The second was two growing bodies of research: neurological research suggesting that early learning contributes to the developing architecture of the brain – pointing to the importance of early learning; and evidence from developmental psychology that the earliest interactions between child and carers provide the cultural structure that underpins the development of intellectual schema – showing what kind of learning is best (Sylva and Pugh, 2005).

The Coalition government, whilst taking office at a time of severe economic restraint, has in many respects continued to support the development of early years services, as this and other chapters will illustrate. *Supporting Families in the Foundation Years* (DfE/DH, 2011b) sets out the government's vision for what it calls the foundation years and in so doing responds to a number of reviews commissioned during the early days of government: Marmot's review of inequalities in health (Marmot, 2010), Frank Field's review on poverty and life chances, which placed a strong emphasis on the foundation years (Field, 2010), Graham Allen's reports on early intervention (Allen, 2011a, 2011b) and the proposals for a revised Early Years Foundation Stage by Clare Tickell (Tickell, 2011). This vision includes:

- a strong focus on child development
- putting parents and families at the heart of services
- intervening early and using evidence-based interventions
- working with skilled professionals
- working in partnership with the sector.

The interweaving of these various agendas – the anti-poverty agenda driving the increases in 'daycare'; the research into child development and children's learning driving 'early education'; a strong focus on early intervention because it saves both human suffering and, hopefully, greater expenditure later; all within a context of severe cuts in the public expenditure budget – has led to considerable tensions between increasing the quantity of provision whilst ensuring that high quality is maintained.

Some policy milestones

The policy agenda in England since 1997 has been considerable:

- The initial National Childcare Strategy (DFEE, 1998) included an expansion of nursery education and childcare from birth to 14, together with the establishment of Sure Start Local Programmes and early excellence centres, and a programme of neighbourhood nurseries.
- The 10-year childcare strategy, *Choice for Parents, the Best Start for Children* (HM Treasury, 2004) aimed to increase the accessibility of good quality affordable childcare and other support for parents. It included extending paid maternity leave (nine months from April 2007 and 12 months by 2010); increasing the hours of free nursery education from 12.5 to 15 per week (from 2010); reforming childcare regulation and inspection; reforming the career and training structure of the early years workforce; and improving the childcare part of the Working Tax Credit to help low and middle income families with childcare costs.
- The 2006 Childcare Act brought together earlier provision in order to create some 3,000 children's centres, and placed a duty on local authorities to secure sufficient childcare for working parents, and to ensure services are integrated. Local authorities were also required to improve outcomes for children and to narrow the gap between those who do well and those who do not.
- The Early Years Foundation Stage was introduced in 2008 to create a framework from birth to the end of Reception year (DfES, 2007). A revised and 'slimmer' version was introduced in September 2012 (DfE, 2012a).
- From 2010 free nursery education has been extended to 2-year-olds in disadvantaged areas, with promises to rise to 40% by 2014, although there is some concern as to how this will be funded.

- Improved qualifications and training for early years workers was a priority for the Children's Workforce Development Council until it was closed in 2012. Nutbrown's report (2012) included recommendations for the expansion of this work, although many of her recommendations have been rejected by government (DfE 2013).
- An integrated inspection service for all early years services was set up within Ofsted.
- There has been a recognition that services must meet the needs of parents as well as children. The 2007 *Children's Plan* stated 'government does not bring up children – parents do – so government needs to do more to back parents and families' (DCSF, 2007: 5). *Supporting Families in the Foundation Years* sees parents and families as at the heart of services (DfE/DH, 2011b), and there is a strong emphasis on parenting programmes.
- The beginnings of better coordination with health, through an expansion of the Healthy Child Programme (see Chapter 10), proposals to combine the 2-year-old health review with the EYFS assessment, and the promise of more health visitors, particularly in children's centres.

Despite these very considerable developments in early years services, the current system has been described as fragmented, confusing, segregated, wasteful and riven with inequality (Moss, 2012), hardly a coherent strategy.

Availability, affordability and sustainability

From lagging well behind our European neighbours in the early 1990s, an OECD report in 2008 found that the United Kingdom was at that point the highest spender on pre-primary services in Europe (OECD, 2008). Nursery education in England, now available for 15 hours a week, is free and is accessed by 93% of 3-year-olds and 98% of 4-year-olds (DfE, 2012b).

The public funding for these places is available to nursery and primary schools in the statutory sector, as well as to private and voluntary sector nurseries so long as they meet nationally approved standards. Of a total of 2,011,400 childcare and early years places for children under 5 in England, more than a third are in maintained schools (802,000), nearly half of these in primary schools with Reception classes but no Nursery classes. The remainder are in the private and voluntary sectors: some 236,900 places with childminders, 251,000 in sessional daycare, and 721,000 in full daycare (DfE, 2012c).

This heavy reliance on the private and voluntary sectors has led to a mixed economy of private and state funding within early childhood services. The 2006 Childcare Act reinforced the role of the market, requiring local authorities to facilitate the provision of services and allowing them to provide them only as a last resort. This has been further strengthened by the Coalition government, which sees local authorities as having a strategic commissioning role, stimulating the local market of private, voluntary and independent providers in order to provide parents with greater choice (DfE/DH, 2011b). There has been a substantial increase in for-profit provision since 1997, and over 60% of full daycare settings are now privately run (DfE, 2012c). It is not surprising to find that a profit model is difficult to operate in the most disadvantaged areas, leading to both poorer provision and a lack of sustainability.

Despite the considerable additional expenditure for part-time nursery provision, it is clear that parents make the major financial contribution to the cost of services, particularly before and after the free nursery education, in holidays, and most provision for children under 3. Affordability remains a key problem, with annual daycare costs rising by 6% in 2012, to an average of £5,100 a year for a child under 2, at a time when wages remained stagnant (Daycare Trust, 2012). Working Tax Credit, introduced in 1998 to assist low-income families with up to 80% of their childcare costs, was reduced in 2011, leading to fewer families receiving this help. The Daycare Trust review found significant gaps in childcare availability across Britain, with a worrying lack of childcare for disabled children and for parents who work outside normal office hours. Over half of local authorities said that parents had reported a lack of childcare in the previous 12 months.

The precarious nature of the funding and of parents' ability to pay creates challenges for nurseries in the private and voluntary sectors. Despite fees in England being amongst the highest in the world, 12% of childcare providers are making a loss, and in the poorest areas the proportion is higher (DfE, 2012c). The government, concerned that regulations on staff-to-child ratios are a key driver of costs and that parents would pay less if they were relaxed, recommended an increase in the numbers of children per staff member (DfE 2013) but have subsequently dropped the proposal in the face of strong opposition from parents and providers. It is difficult to escape the challenge that this presents in terms of ensuring the quality and safety of the provision.

Joined up services?

It is clear from the official figures quoted above that government still sees a separation between childcare (mainly in the private and voluntary sector) and early education or early years (mainly in the maintained sector). This is not peculiar to the United Kingdom, as a recent UNESCO study (Kaga et al., 2010) has pointed out (see also Chapter 3). Many countries have split systems, reflecting – as in this country – the historical roots of provision, and how such provision reflects a nation's societal and policy aims. There have been attempts to create provision that integrates care and education – a task that would be eased if a satisfactory term could be found to describe this 'educare' provision. During the 1970s the first 'combined nursery centres' were established, followed some 20 years later by a small number of early excellence centres. But the most widely developed service was the targeted community-based Sure Start programme, originally established in 1998 with £540 million to fund 250 local programmes and soon extended to 520 communities (Glass, 1999; Eisenstadt, 2011). Targeted at children under 4 and their families in areas of high need, Sure Start Local Programmes (SSLPs) were enormously popular with local parents, and although the first major evaluation report showed – not surprisingly – modest outcomes (NESS, 2005) later reports found that the programme was improving the life chances of children in poor families in a number of key areas (NESS, 2008) and had particularly strong results for parents, with greater life satisfaction, less harsh discipline and a more stimulating home environment (NESS, 2010). Evaluation has, however, been difficult, largely because of the original design, which encouraged local communities to create their own schemes, and because of the length of time that it took to get local projects started (Eisenstadt, 2011).

In addition, the goal posts have been continually moved, with further expansion of the Sure Start concept through the establishment of children's centres rather than through separate Sure Start schemes (HM Treasury, 2004). Children's centres were less generously funded than early excellence centres, but they did have an additional emphasis on health, being required to provide a base for midwives, health visitors, and speech and language therapists (see Chapter 10), as well as information and support for parents, training and support for childcare workers and strong links with JobCentre Plus. By 2010 there were over 3,000 centres, for which the Coalition government pledged continuing support. However the funding for centres is now incorporated within an 'early intervention grant' which is not ring-fenced, there is a new focus on payment by results, and there is concern that cuts in public expenditure are leading to both closures and amalgamations (4Children, 2012). See Chapter 9 for a fuller discussion.

The original concept of children's centres envisaged an integration of early education and care, with support for parents and health involvement (Pugh, 1994; Makins, 1997). Very few are now in a position to provide early education as well as the outreach and family support services, and given the evidence on the key importance of high quality early education to improving outcomes for children, it is not perhaps surprising that the evaluation of Sure Start has shown such limited impact. As Eisenstadt has pointed out, if outcomes are to improve, then community services such as Sure Start must be linked to focused services and to high quality early education (Eisenstadt, 2011).

Within local areas, although local authorities continue to have a duty to ensure children have access to early education, the Coalition government has removed many of the more strategic coordinating duties of local authorities as well as removing the ring-fencing of funding for children's centres and other early years services. This is further discussed in Chapter 2.

Quality in service provision

Despite the arguments in the Rumbold Report (DES, 1990) of the importance of the context of learning and the process of learning – the way in which children acquire the disposition to learn – there were widespread concerns at the end of the 1990s that the National Curriculum and the national literacy and numeracy strategies were leading to pressure to formalise education at the earliest opportunity. It was therefore with some enthusiasm that working parties of early years experts developed both the *Curriculum Guidance for the Foundation Stage* (DfEE/QCA, 2000) for children aged 3 to 5, and *Birth to Three Matters* (DfES, 2002), a framework for all practitioners working with children under 3. Both of these documents were based upon clear and unambiguous statements of the principles that should underpin both learning and teaching and these principles have subsequently informed both the initial Early Years Foundation Stage (EYFS) Framework which became statutory in all early years settings in 2008 (DfES, 2007) and the revised EYFS which came into force in 2012 (DfE, 2012a). The EYFS creates a statutory commitment to play-based, developmentally appropriate care and education for children between birth and 5 years of age, together with a regulatory framework aimed at raising quality in all settings and amongst all providers. It recognises the central contribution that parents make to their children's development, and is underpinned by key principles recognising the unique nature of children, who are constantly learning, and the importance of supportive relationships and enabling environments. (See also Chapter 7.)

Although the revised Early Years Foundation Stage has been largely welcomed across the early years sector, there are concerns both about its implementation and about the interface between the Foundation phase and Key Stage 1, particularly in view of the government's focus on 'school readiness'. The cutting back of advisory support at both national and local level and a reliance on the sector to lead itself do not sound hopeful in a largely under-qualified sector. The interface with Key Stage 1 is of equal concern. The Cambridge Primary Review concluded on the basis of widespread research and practice in other countries that the principles governing the foundation years should be extended into primary schools until at least age 6. 'This would give sufficient time for children to establish positive attitudes to learning and begin to develop language and study skills which are essential to later progress' (Alexander, 2010: 491). There are fears that the current requirement to focus on phonics in the teaching of reading and the obligatory phonics test in Year 1 will have a deleterious effect and will lead to a skewing of the curriculum in early years settings.

The EPPSE research noted above, commissioned by government to inform its policymaking, has played a key role in ensuring that, despite the requirement to expand provision as quickly as possible, the needs of children are not lost. Key findings have been that the best quality has been found in settings in the maintained sector which integrate care and education, and that there is high correlation between well-qualified staff and better outcomes for children, with quality indicators including warm interactive relationships and a good proportion of trained teachers on the staff (Sylva et al., 2004, 2010; see also Chapter 4). These findings were reinforced by the Millennium Cohort Study (Mathers et al., 2007), by the evaluation of the Neighbourhood Nursery Initiative (Smith et al., 2007), and most recently in the Nutbrown Review (2012) on qualifications in the early years sector, which is noted below and in Chapter 15. There are concerns about the quality of provision for 2-year-olds as places for this age group are expanded, predominantly in the private and voluntary sectors.

Support for parents – or parents as supporters?

A recognition of the need for greater support for parents has featured strongly in government policy, from the Green Paper *Supporting Families* (Home Office, 1998), through the establishment of Sure Start programmes, and *Every Child Matters* (DfES, 2003) to the Coalition government's *Supporting Families in the Foundation Years* (DfE/DH, 2011b). Acknowledgement of the importance of the relationships between parents and their children, and a recognition that bringing up children is a challenging and sometimes difficult task for which help should be universally available before things start to go wrong (see Pugh et al., 1994) is finally leading to the establishment of a wider range of services, from informal through to the more structured parenting programmes (see Chapter 13). However, the current emphasis on improving outcomes for children has also reinforced the concept of parents as their children's first educators. Pulling together a wide body of research, and drawing particularly on EPPE, Desforges and Abouchaar (2003) confirmed the view that parental involvement in schools and early years settings, and above all the educational environment of the home, have a positive effect on children's achievement and adjustment. At its best this is building on partnerships between parents and professionals that have been central to good early years provision for many years, as for example in the PEAL project described in Chapter 13. But there is a danger that an instrumentalist view of parents as the key to better-behaved and more highly achieving children can also lead to undue pressure on parents at a time when they are also under pressure to return to paid employment.

Staff training and qualifications

As the EPPE research notes, the qualifications of the staff are a critical ingredient in securing good outcomes for children, and yet the early years sector has always suffered from low levels of qualified staff and of pay. The 2005 workforce strategy (DfES, 2005) and the Children's Workforce Development Council gave the early years a high priority and set a target of one graduate in every group setting by 2015 (two in disadvantaged areas). Although the qualifications levels of early years practitioners are improving, there are still only 84% of childcare staff with at least a level 3 qualification, and only 11% of this workforce are qualified at level 6 (graduate level) or above, though figures for early years staff in nursery and primary schools are higher (DfE, 2012c). Staff across the sector are still seen as having low status, pay is considerably lower than the national average, and even within the teaching profession early years teachers are seen as of lower status than secondary school teachers. There is also continuing lack of clarity over how the new Early Years Professional Status (EYPS) relates to qualified teachers, both in terms of their roles and in relation to differentials in pay, and it is difficult to see the rationale for two graduate-level practitioners rather than one. The current training of early childhood teachers is also of concern, for it is not well suited to the multi-agency role of children's centres, nor does it encompass the development and learning needs of children under 3.

Nutbrown's recent review of qualifications (Nutbrown, 2012) reinforced the importance of high quality staff, with the necessary skills, knowledge and understanding, if there is to be a lasting impact on children's later learning and achievements. She set a long term vision for a well-qualified and professional early years sector, seen as expert and recognised for the contribution it makes to society. She called for a more rigorous qualifications framework, for level 3 to be a minimum requirement for all who work in the sector, for stronger graduate leadership, and for a specialist early years route to QTS. This latter proposal was rejected by government in favour of calling EYPs 'Early Years Teachers' and seeing them as equivalent to qualified teachers (DfE 2013).

Can the gap be narrowed in the early years?

Given the huge impact of poverty on children's outcomes and the potential for positive intervention during the early years, are there ways in which early years services can support the government's commitment to 'narrow the gap'? For as a recent study has pointed out, it is not only the poorest citizens who are affected by an unequal society. Bringing together 30 years of research, Wilkinson and Pickett (2009) argue that the most unequal societies, which include the UK, impact negatively on almost everyone in them. Almost every modern social and environmental problem, from ill health to breakdown in community life, violence, drugs and obesity, is more likely to occur in a less equal society. In more unequal societies, they argue, parents from lower socio-economic backgrounds have lower aspirations and self-esteem, and find it hard to provide the caring and stimulating environment that their children need when they themselves are poor, or stressed or unsupported.

So what factors can contribute to narrowing the achievement gap? A recent overview by the Centre for Excellence and Outcomes (C4EO) (Coghlan et al., 2010) has revealed that although poverty had the greatest influence on children's outcomes, other factors were also significant – including ethnic background, English as a second language, health and safety, freedom from abuse, parental education and the home learning environment. This study, and an earlier one for the Narrowing the Gap project (Springate et al., 2008), identified a number of cross-cutting themes that related to successful practice, although there are considerable challenges in attempting to simultaneously improve educational progress for all children and narrow the gap:

- Involving parents in any interventions, particularly those that encourage parents to support their children's learning and create a positive home learning environment
- High quality early education, provided by well-trained staff, focusing on individual children's needs, and targeting literacy and language
- Interventions that build constructive relationships between adults and children, from early attachments in the early months of a child's life through to good relationships between early years practitioners and children in early years settings and an emphasis on developing social skills.

This focus can clearly make a difference, but it is no substitute for broader policies of wealth distribution and economic growth.

Some challenges

The achievements since 1997 are remarkable, and there is much to applaud in the expansion of services and the attempts to improve quality across all sectors. The Coalition government has continued to invest in the early years and to emphasise the importance of parents, and the rhetoric points to the importance of high quality services run by well-qualified staff. But the reality is that rising costs within a weak economy are leading to a strong emphasis on the creation of markets, on decentralising control, and reducing regulation, whilst the gap between rich and poor is growing and the poorest children and families continue to be most at risk.

It is only high quality services that improve outcomes for children, particularly the most disadvantaged. As the expansion continues but the funding reduces, it is difficult to see how this quality be maintained and improved. Not only are staff being cut back, and less well qualified staff employed, but local authorities are having to reduce their support services and the ring-fencing of much early years funding has been removed.

Linked to this is the issue of sustainability and affordability, and of whether sufficient public funding can be secured to expand nursery education to more

2-year-olds as well as continuing with the 15 hours a week for 3- and 4-year-olds without further reductions in children's centres. It is already evident that, with the exception of this 'nursery education' funding, the move towards a universal entitlement for integrated care and education for all children is heavily dependent on parental purchasing power and on their subsidising a service that is provided largely through the voluntary and private sectors.

The challenges of recruiting, training and remunerating a workforce fit for the early years services of the future are also considerable, both in terms of front-line staff but, equally importantly, for the leaders, the heads of services and centres who will have to drive the agenda forward. There is also the issue of pay. Whilst Nutbrown (2012) outlines a clearer framework for early years qualifications and greater opportunities for training, the workforce will not attract or retain high calibre staff unless they can earn comparable wages to the other professionals they are working alongside.

We must also ask where early years services fit within the overall pattern of provision for children, and particularly how they relate to schools – what could be described as the 'L-shaped dilemma'. As the horizontal at the foot of the L (all services for children under 5) expands and the extent of the funding and staffing challenge becomes more apparent, the question arises as to whether early years services are the first part of the education system (the upright of the L, going from 0 to 19) or part of a completely different system. Although one-third of all under 5s and almost all 4-year olds are actually in Nursery or Reception classes of primary schools, the government describes early years settings as either 'childcare' or 'early years provision'. The new proposals for EYPs to be called Early Years Teachers but without qualified teacher status (DfE 2013) exacerbates the separation of early years from primary education. As Nutbrown says, one form of inequality is being replaced by another (Nutbrown, 2013: 7). If the Early Years Foundation Stage is to be really effective, this should be revised to cover the years from birth (or whenever a child starts in out-of-home care) to 6 years, including both reception and Year 1 in primary school, and this should be seen as the first stage of the education system.

Finally, is it possible to devise a policy that meets the needs of both parents and children? Many parents currently feel torn by the dual messages coming out of government – return to work in order to earn your way out of poverty, on the one hand, but parenting is the most important role that you will play and your child's future depends on the quality of your relationship, on the other. Balancing work and family life is a challenge for parents of children of all ages, but is particularly acute for parents of young children.

As the services continue to evolve in the face of economic constraint, it will be important to ensure that quality of service provision is maintained as the quantity increases, that children's needs remain paramount, and that parents really do feel that they have choice.

Key points to remember

- The past 20 years has seen unprecedented expansion in the amount of early years provision, but opportunities to create a coherent early years strategy have not been taken and current economic constraints are putting both quantity and quality at risk.
- Early years services are still poorly coordinated: whilst 3- and 4-year-olds have access to free part-time nursery education provision, full daycare is largely provided by private and voluntary sector providers and is costly to parents.
- Early years services have the potential to improve children's life chances but only if they are of high quality.

 Points for discussion

- Should priority be given to extending provision, for example for 2-year-olds, or to improving the quality of existing provision?
- What further measures would improve the integration of care and education in early years settings?
- Has government struck the right balance between parents being encouraged to return to work and caring for their young children?

Reflective task

- What policy initiative do you think would have the greatest impact on improving outcomes for the most vulnerable children?

Note

1 This chapter predominantly focuses on policy in England. Although there are many similarities in developments in Scotland, Wales and Northern Ireland, there are also differences, including the legislative framework. Government websites are listed below. A summary of current policies can be found in *Early Education*, 66, Spring 2012, pp. 4–7 or on the Early Education website www. early-education.org.uk.

Further reading

Department for Education and Department of Health (DfE/DH) (2011) *Supporting Families in the Foundation Years*. London: DfE/DH.
Miller, L. and Hevey, D. (2012) *Policy Issues in the Early Years*. London: Sage.

Useful websites

The following websites provide the most up-to-date information on early years policy in England, Scotland, Wales and Northern Ireland:

www.education.gov.uk/schools/teachingandlearning/curriculum/a0068102/early-
   years-foundation-stage-eyfs
www.scotland.gov.uk/Topics/People/Young-People/Early-Years-and-Family/
   early-years-collaborative
www.wales.gov.uk/topics/educationandskills/earlyyearshome/?lang=en
www.deni.gov.uk/search.lsim?sr=0&nh=10&cs=iso-8859-1&sc=&sm=0&mt=1&ha=
   deni-cms&qt=early+years

To access a variety of additional web resources to accompany this book please visit: **www.sagepub.co.uk/pughduffy**

References

Alexander, R. (ed.) (2010) *Children, Their World, Their Education. Final Report and Recommendations of the Cambridge Primary Review*. London: Routledge.

Allen, G. (2011a) *Early Intervention: The Next Steps*. An Independent Report to Her Majesty's Government. London: Cabinet Office.

Allen, G. (2011b) *Early Intervention: Smart Investment, Massive Savings*. London: HM Government.

Coghlan, M., Bergeron, C., White, K., Sharp, C., Morris, M. and Wilson, R. (2010) *Narrowing the Gap in Outcomes for Young Children through Effective Practice in the Early Years C4EO Knowledge Review 1*. London: C4EO.

Daycare Trust (2012) *Childcare Costs Survey 2012*. London: Daycare Trust.

Department for Children, Schools and Families (DCSF) (2007) *The Children's Plan: Building Brighter Futures*. Norwich: TSO.

Department for Education (DfE) (2012a) *Statutory Framework for the Early Years Foundation Stage 2012: Setting the Standards for Learning, Development and Care for Children from Birth to Five*. Runcorn: DfE Publications.

Department for Education (DfE) (2012b) Provision for Children under Five Years of Age in England. Statistical First Release, January 2012. www.education.gov. uk/rsgateway/DB/SFR/s001074/sfr13-2012.pdf (accessed March 2013).

Department for Education (DfE) (2012c) Childcare and Early Years Providers Survey 2011. Released September 2012. www.education.gov.uk/rsgateway/ DB/STR/d001088/index.shtml (accessed March 2013).

Department for Education (DfE) (2013) *More Great Childcare*. London: DfE.

Department for Education and Department of Health (DfE/DH) (2011a) *Families in the Foundation Years – Evidence Pack*. London: DfE/DH.

Department for Education and Department of Health (DfE/DH) (2011b) *Supporting Families in the Foundation Years*. London: DfE/DH.

Department for Education and Employment (DfEE) (1998) *Meeting the Childcare Challenge*. London: TSO.

Department for Education and Employment(DfEE)/Qualifications and Curriculum Authority (QCA) (2000) *Curriculum Guidance for the Foundation Stage*. London: QCA.

Department for Education and Science (DES) (1990) *Starting with Quality: Report of the Committee of Enquiry into the Quality of Education Experience Offered to Three and Four Year Olds* (Rumbold Report). London: HMSO.

Department for Education and Skills (DfES) (2002) *Birth to Three Matters: A Framework to Support Children in Their Earliest Years*. London: DfES.

Department for Education and Skills (DfES) (2003) *Every Child Matters*. Green Paper. Cm 5860. Norwich: TSO.

Department for Education and Skills (DfES) (2004) *Every Child Matters: Change for Children*. Nottingham: DfES Publications.

Department for Education and Skills (DfES) (2005) *Children's Workforce Strategy*. Nottingham: DfES Publications.

Department for Education and Skills (DfES) (2007) *The Early Years Foundation Stage*. Nottingham: DfES Publications.

Department of Health and Department for Education and Skills (DH/DfES) (2004) *National Service Framework for Children, Young People and Maternity Services*. London: DH Publications.

Desforges, C. and Abouchaar, A. (2003) *The Impact of Parental Involvement, Parental Support and Family Education on Pupil Achievements and Adjustment: A Literature Review*. Research Report 433. London: Department for Education and Skills.

Eisenstadt, N. (2011) *Providing a Sure Start*. Bristol: Policy Press.

Field, F. (2010) *The Foundation Years: Preventing Poor Children Becoming Poor Adults. The Report of the Independent Review on Poverty and Life Chances*. London: Cabinet Office.

4Children (2012) Sure Start Children's Centres Census 2012. www.4children.org.uk/Resources/Detail/Sure-Start-Childrens-Centres-Census-2012 (accessed March 2013).

Glass, N. (1999) 'Sure Start: the development of an early intervention programme for young children in the UK', *Children & Society*, 13 (4), 257–65.

HM Treasury (2004) *Choice for Parents, the Best Start for Children: A Ten Year Strategy for Childcare*. London: TSO.

Home Office (1998) *Supporting Families*. London: Home Office.

Kaga, Y., Bennett, J. and Moss, P. (2010) *Caring and Learning Together: A Cross National Study of the Integration of Early Childhood Care and Education Within Education*. Paris: UNESCO.

Makins, V. (1997) *Not Just a Nursery: Multi-Agency Early Years Centres in Action*. London: National Children's Bureau.

Marmot, M. (2010) *Fair Society, Healthy Lives. Post-2010 Strategic Review of Health Inequalities in England* (Marmot Review). London: Department of Health.

Mathers, S., Sylva, K. and Joshi, H. (2007) *Quality of Childcare Settings in the Millennium Cohort Study.* DCSF SSU/2007/FR/025. London: DCSF.

Moss, P. (2012) 'Integration of childcare and early education services is long overdue', *Nursery World*, 3 September.

NESS (National Evaluation of Sure Start) (2005) *Early Impacts of Sure Start Local Programmes on Children and Families.* Report 013. London: HMSO.

NESS (National Evaluation of Sure Start) (2008) *The Impact of Sure Start Local Programmes on Three Year Olds and Their Families.* Report 027. London: HMSO.

NESS (National Evaluation of Sure Start) (2010) *The Impact of Sure Start Local Programmes on Five Year Olds and Their Families.* RR 067. London: Department for Education.

Nutbrown, C. (2012) *Foundations for Quality. The Independent Review of Early Education and Childcare Qualifications: Final Report* (Nutbrown Review). London: Department for Education.

Nutbrown, C. (2013) *Shaking the foundations of quality? Why childcare policy must not lead to poor quality early education and care.* Sheffield: University of Sheffield.

OECD (2008) *Education at a Glance.* Paris: Organisation for Economic Cooperation and Development.

Pugh, G. (1994) 'Born to learn', *Times Educational Supplement*, 11 November.

Pugh, G. (ed.) (1996) *Contemporary Issues in the Early Years*, 2nd edn. London: Paul Chapman.

Pugh, G., De'Ath, E. and Smith, C. (1994) *Confident Parents, Confident Children.* London: National Children's Bureau.

Smith, T., Smith, G., Coxon, K. and Sigala, M. (2007) *National Evaluation of the Neighbourhood Nurseries Initiative.* DCSF SSU/2007/FR 024. London: DCSF.

Springate, I., Atkinson, M., Straw, S., Lamont, E. and Grayson, H. (2008) *Narrowing the Gap in Outcomes: Early Years 0–5.* Slough: NfER.

Sylva, K., Melhuish, E. C., Sammons, P., Siraj-Blatchford, I. and Taggart, B. (2004) The Effective Provision of Pre-School Education (EPPE) Project: *Technical Paper 12 – The Final Report: Effective Pre-School Education.* London: Department for Education and Skills/Institute of Education, University of London.

Sylva, K., Melhuish, E., Samons, P., Siraj-Blatchford, I. and Taggart, B. (2010) *Early Childhood Matters. Evidence from the Effective Pre-School and Primary Education Project.* London: Routledge.

Sylva, K. and Pugh, G. (2005) 'Transforming the early years in England', *Oxford Review of Education*, 31 (1), 11–27.

Tickell, C. (2011) *The Early Years: Foundations for Life, Health and Learning. An Independent Report on the Early Years Foundation Stage to Her Majesty's Government* (Tickell Review). London: Department for Education.

Wilkinson, R. and Pickett, K. (2009) *The Spirit Level: Why More Equal Societies Always Do Better.* London: Allen Lane.

CHAPTER 2

Facing Austerity: the Local Authority Response

Linda Uren

Chapter contents

- Impact of the Coalition government agenda on local areas
- Thinking positively
- What practitioners should expect
- Challenges and opportunities – how local areas are responding
- Issues to grapple with

One enduring feature of early years services is that they tend to be local, very much part of local neighbourhoods, enjoy significant support from communities and depend on some strategic coordination and planning to reach families who need their services. Although there have been significant changes since the publication of the last edition of this book, many of the issues will be familiar.

This chapter therefore focuses on clarifying the roles and responsibilities of local councils, considers the way in which local partnership working is developing and identifies the challenges faced at the local level in the light of new government policy and significant financial constraints. Individual practitioners may feel that this broader context is less relevant for them but the importance of the wider context cannot be over emphasised, particularly in identifying and supporting our most vulnerable children. When a child is identified as needing additional support for whatever reason early years practitioners need to be confident in their ability to mobilise other professionals and act effectively; local authorities play a key role in ensuring the right infrastructure is in place.

Impact of the Coalition government agenda on local areas

The local landscape in terms of early years services has been transformed since 1997 with universal nursery education for 3- and 4-year-olds, a network of children's centres and information and support for childcare. The 2004 Children Act gave local authorities responsibility for leading multi-agency working in the local area focused on improving outcomes – the shorthand for this was often 'Every Child Matters'. Whilst every local area is different, all were expected to establish a local partnership called a Children's Trust and produce a local plan – the Children and Young People's Plan – which every organisation working with children was expected to cooperate with. Every area also put arrangements in place for coordinated assessments through the Common Assessment Framework, which all agencies and professionals were expected to use to provide joined up support for children as soon as additional needs emerged. For early years the 2006 Childcare Act formalised the role of local authorities in improving outcomes for children under 5, providing advice, information and training and sufficient childcare. There have been parallel developments in both Wales and Scotland – the Welsh Flying Start programme is aimed at targeting the most vulnerable children and in Scotland an Early Years framework has been developed that draws together a wide range of plans to improve outcomes for young children; it is one of three frameworks that aim to establish a 'coherent and long term approach to addressing the disadvantages in Scotland and breaking the intergenerational cycle of inequalities' (Scottish Government, 2011).

The new Coalition government, elected in 2010, has maintained the commitment to the importance of early years services; evidenced by important policy statements such as *Supporting Families in the Foundation Years* (DfE/DH, 2011) and the continued investment made at a national level, including a major commitment to fund nursery education for 40% of the most disadvantaged 2-year-olds. However, the context within which local areas are working has changed significantly and these are impacting on early years services across the country. One key feature of the new government's policy is localism, which can be summarised as less prescription and more local freedom – all government departments aspire to this and early years policy is no different. This is not the place for a wider discussion as to how far central government is really willing to delegate authority and responsibility to local areas but the implications for early years services so far have been:

- The statutory framework for early years (and children's) services remains intact with some notable exceptions
- There is no longer a requirement for a local Children and Young People's Plan; expectations of Children's Trusts have disappeared
- Statutory guidance has been reduced and simplified, e.g. guidance on children's centres, Working Together
- Encouragement for local communities to take on service delivery
- Loss of ring-fenced budgets.

At the same time the major reforms in education and health services are both impacting on the local authority role. In education as schools become increasingly autonomous, the role of the local authority is changing rapidly. Most councils are welcoming the return of public health responsibilities after a gap of 30 years; this is very significant for early years services since responsibility for commissioning public health nursing services will also transfer from 2015. This is important because one of the most significant Coalition government commitments has been to significantly increase the number of health visitors working in England – key professionals working with all young families and highly skilled in helping the most disadvantaged.

This is all at a time when public sector budgets are reducing significantly and demand for some services increasing, e.g. for child protection and support for older people. Councils nationally are seeing a reduction of around 28% in their budgets from 2010 to 2014 and this is likely to continue beyond 2015. All councils want to protect services, especially for vulnerable people, but the scale of these savings means many early years services have seen reductions in funding, e.g. 60% of children's centres surveyed by the charity 4Children (2012) stated that they were facing significant budget reductions. The most visible reductions will be those that have a direct impact on front line delivery such as children's centres, but there have also been significant reductions in staff supporting initiatives and partnership working. This is having an impact on local early years providers and professionals because the capacity to support workforce development, coordinate local projects or help schools and nurseries to work together has often reduced or ceased.

Thinking positively

The context described above is challenging for everyone but that should not prevent local areas continuing to innovate and collaborate to improve the quality of services and utilise increasingly scarce resources effectively. Taking a longer term view, early years practitioners today have a number of advantages compared to just 10 years ago:

- A stronger sector identity – most local areas will still have arenas where early years professionals and groups come together to learn and develop services
- Stronger evidence about what works and the importance of the early years of life
- Established children's centres now looking at consolidating their role
- A secure niche in local children's services
- Understanding about the importance of quality standards and workforce development
- Many examples of excellent partnership working with health, education and social care professionals.

Inevitably less national prescription means that local patterns of service are beginning to look very different and professionals moving between local authority areas may find greater differences. At the same time this should encourage innovation and collaboration in local areas – whilst public sector funding may become more targeted there is always room for enterprise and early years has long traditions of parent- or community-led support. The drive for savings has also resulted in greater support for early intervention and evidence-based programmes. The Allen Report (Allen, 2011) typifies this, arguing strongly for innovative ways of financing evidence-based interventions, which will save money in the long term. Given the strong evidence base about the benefits of intervening with very young children, early years services can only benefit from this debate.

Local authorities have also signed up to 'sector-led improvement' as a model of driving better performance and innovation by utilising expertise within the sector rather than external inspectorates and advisers. In children's services this led to the creation of a Children's Improvement Board (CIB), which coordinated mechanisms within regions and centrally to provide challenge and support to individual local authorities. Early years was part of this process with the CIB leading on some aspects of payment by results for children's centres and supporting a small number of early years 'demonstrator sites' to share learning and practice. Government funding ceased unexpectedly in 2013, but local authority commitment is likely to see many elements of the programme maintained.

What practitioners should expect

Before we examine some of the challenges and ways in which local areas are responding to the new context it is important to set out what arrangements all early years practitioners should expect to be in place wherever they are working. Local authorities continue to have a range of responsibilities in respect of early years provision and identifying and supporting vulnerable children. They must:

- Ensure children at risk of significant harm are identified and action taken to address their needs
- Ensure a system is in place to identify additional needs
- Make arrangements for assessing and meeting special educational needs
- Ensure children's centre services are available to every community and that those services support all early years providers
- Ensure children have access to early education and school.

All settings and schools must ensure that staff are trained in basic child protection expectations and what to do when there are serious concerns about a child. It is often more challenging to access support for a child where concerns do not meet child protection thresholds or where special needs may only be emerging. Local authorities will vary but most will support groups of professionals in neighbourhoods or local areas to put a package of support in place. Where there are concerns about a child that are greater than a single agency can support, the most appropriate professional should undertake a common assessment, working with the child and their parent or carer to identify their needs and a simple plan of support. Some families need a range of support, e.g. speech therapy for a child, practical family support for a parent and a parenting programme. Professionals should work together forming 'A team around the child', sometimes known as a TAC, reviewing their work and making necessary changes in cooperation with the family.

Where children have emerging special needs or disabilities, the same process should be adopted as described above. If the child's needs become more complex, he or she may need a formal special educational needs assessment in order to ensure they receive the appropriate level of support as they move into school. This is a formal process managed by the local authority but early years professionals have a crucial contribution to make in helping to understand a child's needs and taking action to support a child's learning. All local authorities should have published arrangements for this process. This is an area where great change may be expected – the Coalition government is legislating to create a new responsibility for a health, education and social care plan for 0–25-year-olds with SEN and entitle families to personal budgets (DfE, 2011a). Early years staff are likely to be at the forefront of these changes; the example below shows how new approaches are already being developed:

Example: Gloucestershire Early Start Project

Starting from a very small pilot in January 2011 this has now been extended to all early years children in the county since April 2012. The approach offers an assessment (based on the common assessment) and then a plan with a small personal budget for families.

Between June 2011 and July 2012, 162 appropriate referrals were received and there are 116 active individualised support plans in operation, with the remainder in process. Parent evaluations show improvement in health and well-being, child development and school readiness and parental involvement. The most significant improvement is showing in parents' assessments of access to services and empowerment.

Challenges and opportunities – how local areas are responding

The earlier parts of this chapter have explained the context and challenges faced by local areas; they are not peculiar to early years – local councils and their partners face challenges on all fronts. For children's services in particular this is driving a search for greater efficiency but also the holy grail of investment in programmes, which will work and, crucially, result in reduced demand for expensive services in the future. Nevertheless, hard decisions have to be made and where alternatives cannot be found local services will experience funding reductions. There is a clear challenge to early years services in all this – to prove impact and value for money.

Early years services have a strong history of innovation and of adapting to the context – from early health visitors (or lady sanitary inspectors) responding to concerns about the conditions in which poor children were growing up, nurseries providing childcare to enable women to work during the Second World War onto more recent attempts to integrate education, health and care provision. Much innovation has been developed locally and then adopted at a national level – children's centres themselves were born out of examples of family centres, early years centres, nursery centres, all created at a local level. The challenge to the sector in the twenty-first century is to continue to adapt and find opportunities as well as managing the threats that the serious financial context brings.

Issues to grapple with

Local authorities and children's services

The Labour government in many ways consolidated the central role of local authorities in respect of children's services; it drove the establishment of new departments with specific responsibilities to coordinate local partners as well as bringing key services in social care and education together. This agenda was enthusiastically embraced by local government and still is, in many quarters; nevertheless the financial context is driving much greater diversity as councils seek to develop new service models and manage increasing demand with fewer resources to provide services.

There are two major trends – rationalisation of departmental arrangements by bringing together children and adult services in new combined departments and moving to a commissioning rather than a provider of services model. Most local areas are adopting elements of both approaches.

Combining the roles of Director of Children's Services (DCS) with the Director of Adult Service (DASS) is becoming increasingly common as part of a rationalisation of senior officer teams. It also reflects concerns that families suffer from artificial divides between adult and children's services. These issues most come to light when considering transition arrangements for young adults with additional needs and, the issue of most concern to early years practitioners, ensuring that vulnerable adults receive effective support when they are parents. The desire to tackle pressures on services for adults with long term conditions also requires action across the life course, e.g. tackling obesity.

At one level structural arrangements should not be a major preoccupation for the early years sector – supporting young families requires services and professionals to work together in an integrated way; young children will not develop unless their parents and carers are well supported. Indeed there are opportunities for parents to be more effectively helped if mental health professionals, for example, understand the importance of early help and impact on child development. Links with other services with a primarily adult focus such as employment advice and support, benefits advocacy and the criminal justice system all have the potential for more effectively supporting vulnerable families. Integrating services with health is a particular issue addressed below.

The other approach being driven by many local authorities is a focus on the council as commissioner rather than provider of services. This drive is supported by central government which sees commissioning as having the potential to focus on long term planning, outcomes and value for money – it defines commissioning as 'the cycle of assessing the needs of people in an area, designing and then achieving appropriate outcomes. The service may be delivered by the public, private or civil society sectors' (Cabinet Office, 2011). The government is particularly keen to see commissioning driving innovation, diversity and new forms of public sector service delivery, with greater community ownership (Localism Act 2011).

A few local authorities are more formally separating commissioner and provider functions but nearly all are building up their capacity to commission services, this includes a community leadership role – facilitating and influencing the pattern of services rather than directly managing provision. This is very relevant to the early years sector with its continued wide and diverse pattern of provision, strong traditions of community involvement and potential for joining up support for families across professional silos. Although the word may not have been used, many councils have always adopted a commissioning approach to leading and developing early years provision in their local areas – supporting new services, stimulating the market and encouraging workforce development. As they extend this approach across other parts of their business there is an opportunity to connect early years and childcare with, for example, economic development or general provision of advice, support and guidance.

If commissioning is about driving better forward planning and clarity about outcomes, it must also manage the tensions between commissioning evidence-based programmes and encouraging innovation. Another part of the government agenda is to drive diversity and choice in provision, encouraging small business and mutuals to develop; or members of the local community to take up opportunities to run services (the community right to challenge/ right to provide – see Localism Act 2011; Community Right to Challenge, 2012). In practice the early years sector has much to teach other parts of the economy on these issues having long embraced this diverse market. Commissioners, however, need to ensure that diversity does not lead to fragmentation such that families cannot access the childcare or early years provision that they need – securing sufficient early education and childcare remains a statutory duty.

Partnership working

Partnership working still remains a cornerstone for early years services at a number of different levels – at child and family level, in local neighbourhoods or areas and, more strategically, across local authority or regional areas.

The main changes at a strategic level relate to the role of Children's Trusts and the emerging Health and Wellbeing Boards; the changing role of the local authority in relation to schools also needs to be considered. Although there is no longer a statutory requirement for Children's Trusts to exist most local areas continue to retain a local Children and Young People's Plan which sets out agreed priorities based on analysis of need. Opportunities have been taken to develop more flexible partnership working arrangements with an emphasis on maintaining working relationships rather than bureaucratic 'boards'.

Health reforms following the 2012 Health and Social Care Act have significant implications at a local level. GP-led Clinical Commissioning Groups (CCGs) are making key decisions about priorities and funding in the local health economy. It is to be expected that NHS providers will continue to develop over time with a greater variety of models – a number of key community health services such as health visiting and school nursing are now managed by social enterprise companies for example. Local Health and Wellbeing Boards have a broad remit to ensure there is a good understanding of their local community's needs, agree priorities and encourage more joined up and integrated services. Membership will vary but must include senior local councillors, representatives of Clinical Commissioning Groups (CCGs) and Healthwatch (the consumer or customer voice) and Directors of Adult and Children's Services. Directors of Public Health are also statutory members and will play a key leadership role locally, especially in developing the local strategic needs analysis and strategy. The needs of young children and their families (including maternity) should be a high priority for most Boards because of the importance of intervening early and the vulnerability of very young children. Boards are likely to take a keen interest in children's centre services and how well health, education and social care provision is integrated. Nevertheless the early years sector may have to work hard to ensure local boards do prioritise this work because the ever pressing issue of increasing demand for care from older people and adults with long term conditions is likely to be at the forefront of most Board members' minds.

The other key relationship locally is with schools both as providers of early years services themselves and as vital partners in improving outcomes for children and supporting families. The current government has driven greater choice and diversity through its academy and free school programme, which further reinforces the independence and autonomy of schools from local authorities. Nationally with the majority of secondary schools now academies and a good proportion of primaries following suit, there is much debate about the future role of the local authority in education with a wide range of views about how school improvement will be managed in the future. Early years practitioners will continue to work in schools and other settings and will want to make strong connections at local level – good communication as children transfer into the Reception year from other early years settings will continue to be essential. This agenda will, though, mean that arrangements at a local level for involving schools in children's services are likely to differ considerably from area to area – in some places collaborative working will remain a strong feature, in others primaries may begin to work together in federations or as part of academy chains – early years settings and children's centres will need to be flexible to accommodate new relationships and ensure engagement in early years issues.

Despite these changes, local authorities will continue to maintain a strong leadership role in children's services, bringing the wide range of stakeholders together to focus on priorities and maintaining support for the wide network of early years provision.

The case for early intervention

Other chapters in this book set out the now extensive evidence about the importance of intervening early on and the dividends that can be reaped from high quality interventions when children are young. One significant advance has been the acceptance by policymakers that investing in early intervention makes sense economically, i.e. it could potentially reduce spending on expensive, specialist services in social care, health and education and indeed in the criminal justice system. This acceptance has moved the debate on to which interventions are most likely to have the desired impact and how to fund such interventions at a time of national austerity. Local authorities are generally enthusiastic about this and keen to support evidence-based work.

The belief in early intervention and, particularly, in early years investment underpinned much of the last government's policy on Sure Start; but a political consensus has been reached with work led by the now Secretary of State for Work and Pensions, Iain Duncan Smith, through the Centre for Social Justice. Uniquely, Iain Duncan Smith and Graham Allen, the Labour MP for Nottingham, published a report in 2008 (Allen and Duncan Smith, 2008) arguing for a cross-party consensus to take action to transform parenting skills and revitalise the upbringing of the poorest children to break the cycle of disadvantage. Graham Allen has subsequently conducted a review (Allen, 2011) into early intervention looking at which evidence-based programmes have most impact and at funding mechanisms, e.g. through devices such as social impact bonds where private investment is attracted to support early intervention services, with a reward being paid if results are achieved. It has to be said that it is very early days for this sort of development. A number of local authorities have been working on these issues and have signed up to be Early Intervenors working with Graham Allen. Other interventions are Community Budgets (www.communities.gov.uk), which aim to pool local funding and respond to families and communities in different ways; local government has long argued that more effective use could be made of public sector funding in a local area if decision-making was delegated to the local level.

One of the most well supported evidence-based programmes is the Family Nurse Partnership model, which has been implemented in a number of local areas across the United Kingdom and is described in more detail in Chapter 10. Adapted from the United States, it offers an intensive home visiting programme to young first-time parents, provided by highly skilled and trained nurses.

Whilst some of these ideas are controversial – there is considerable debate over the evidence used, much of which comes from the United States – they further strengthen the argument for investing in support for young children. As Graham Allen says in his report: 'There is abundant evidence … to suggest that the first three years of life create the foundation in learning how to express emotion and to understand and respond to the emotions of others. Lessons learnt in this period can last a lifetime, and prepare an individual to progress physically, mentally and emotionally at every stage of life – especially in becoming a good parent.' They also emphasise the importance of focusing on parenting issues as well as children's education and development; other government initiatives such as the Department of Communities and Local Government's Troubled Families programme (DCLG, 2012) build on this by targeting families with multiple problems by coordinating support provided.

A major preoccupation for most local authorities is the child protection system. The review of safeguarding practice led by Professor Eileen Munro (Munro, 2011) has been universally welcomed. Professor Monro's recommendations included the simplification of processes and systems and a call for social work practitioners to refocus on reflective practice, reinforcing a continuous pattern of learning and improvement across the system. This is a major agenda for local councils and it needs to be remembered that young children are the most vulnerable in the child protection system (approximately 43% of children subject to child protection plans in March 2011 were under 5 years old – DfE, 2012a) and improving practice with confident early decision-making is vital to improve outcomes. The Munro Report recommendation that there should be an effective early help offer in every local area further reinforces the messages about prevention and intervening early. Planning in local areas will now take account of new Ofsted inspections (Ofsted, 2012) of child protection practice, focusing on the child's journey and testing the quality of early support.

If the case for early intervention has mostly been accepted, the challenge remains securing and sustaining the 'up front' investment when budgetary pressures are so severe. Many local areas are finding this challenge daunting as budgetary pressures increase.

Money, money, money – children's centres

By the time of the 2010 general election local authorities had responsibility for a network of over 3,000 children's centres. Although there appears to be a political consensus that these services should be maintained, the budget cuts, increasing local autonomy and economic recession have all challenged the sustainability of many centres.

Following the 2010 emergency budget, local authorities had to manage immediate budget reductions in funding that covered children's centres. This was followed by the public sector spending review and budget announcements which set local councils a challenge to lose 28% of their budgets over a four-year period – with the largest cut in 2011/12. Local authorities have long been effective at implementing government policy and have responded efficiently to this challenge. For a long time early years budgets have been ring-fenced by government and therefore protected at local level from changes; the shift to local autonomy has meant that early years budgets have not enjoyed any particular national protection from budget savings.

Although it is hard to estimate the total impact of savings, government reports suggest that by July 2012 there were 281 fewer children's centres (Hansard, 2012). Campaigners fear that many more centres are operating on reduced hours or that fewer services are available. It is likely that local campaigns supported nationally by organisations such as the Daycare Trust (2012) and strong support for individual children's centres may have modified proposals and resulted in some level of protection. How long services can be protected will depend on a range of factors at local level, including other budgetary pressures, local politics and government decisions about funding overall.

The government has now published revised children's centre statutory guidance which, although much shorter, is arguably stronger in setting out expectations on local authorities although it is much less prescriptive about how centres should be run and the service offer. In particular, it introduces a new duty to consult in a situation where closure of a children's centre is being contemplated.

Another feature of current government policy is an emphasis on payment by results. The Department for Education proposed a payment by results regime in respect of children's centres (DfE, 2011b; NCB/NFER, 2011). However this has not been rolled out, presumably due to the complexity of such a system. Nevertheless the challenge is to ensure funding of services, incentivising providers to target their efforts on the areas where most change is needed.

The government is also interested in different delivery models, in particular where parents and staff are more directly involved in designing and running services – children's centres are seen as providing good opportunities for local communities to take more control. There can be tensions here, however, with local authorities' commissioning intentions. Many local authorities will be seeking greater efficiencies and savings in how children's centres are run, which has resulted in a trend to cluster centres together for management purposes. This can also make service delivery more flexible and able to respond to changes in demographics.

All of this can create tensions locally and will require good commissioning skills in councils, in particular working with local providers to develop the market. Local authorities will take different views about the role of children's centres – emphasising their role as a key element of universal provision or preferring a more targeted model with a focus on the most vulnerable families or communities. This debate is likely to continue at a national and local level for some time.

To return to a point made earlier in this chapter, early years services (and local authorities) have always been noted for their ability to respond and flex in response to the changing context and children's centres need to become part of this tradition. Local Health and Wellbeing Boards will want to ensure that maternity and community health services are integrated or at least linked into children's centres and the increased investment in health visitors delivers better outcomes. Nevertheless, the outlook is uncertain, and whilst children's centres are undoubtedly here to stay local decisions will shape their exact role and greater diversity is to be expected over the coming years.

Early education and childcare

Local areas continue to coordinate a complex pattern of early years provision, to provide early education for all and childcare for working parents/carers. The government has maintained the universal offer of nursery education for all 3- and 4-year-olds, with nearly all rising 4-year-olds now in school Reception classes. The choices available to families before school vary considerably and are still, to some extent, dependent on long standing traditions in local areas, e.g. some local authorities invested heavily in maintained (school) nursery education in the 1980s (typically, but not exclusively, more urban areas); in these areas nursery classes and schools continue to be a significant feature, many now offering care across the working day. In other areas the emphasis remains on private and voluntary provision. Nationally early years provision still reflects a diverse pattern – across private daycare, maintained schools, voluntary sector and childminders. As the economy has retracted working patterns have changed and inevitably some childcare providers have been impacted on – in particular there has been a fall in the amount of childcare provided by children's centres (4Children, 2012). Local authorities should be monitoring the sector closely because they retain their duty to secure sufficient high quality nursery education places where parents want it; the importance of ensuring this provision can also meet families' broader childcare needs has never been greater.

The challenging issues about quality and workforce development are dealt with elsewhere in this book but all local areas will want to challenge themselves as to whether the free offer is having a long term impact on educational outcomes and benefiting the most vulnerable. The government has recently published benchmarking data that allows local areas to compare their spend and performance in comparison with each other. One issue of concern is that take-up of the full free offer – 15 hours per week – still seems to be lower in more deprived areas (DfE, 2012b). Government has changed its funding mechanisms to establish a level playing field across schools and other providers but there continue to be issues at a local level about the equity of funding with some providers feeling that they have to effectively subsidise free entitlement hours by charging more for additional care. The government is now changing its approach to funding the free entitlement at local level by creating a separate funding 'block' within the main school funding grant that will be ring-fenced to early years (DfE, 2012c). This may shine a light on value for money issues, the funding formula used and over-all impact of early years education that is now a considerable investment.

Local authorities are now focusing on delivering the new government offer of a free early education place for the 40% most disadvantaged 2-year-olds (DfE, 2012d). Pathfinder local areas have provided this offer on a limited basis from 2009; the offer is now being rolled out rapidly to cover 40% of the 2-year-old population by 2014/15. This is a very significant expansion of service given the context but it brings challenges with it. Given the research evidence that children will benefit from early education at this young age but only if it is of high quality, many local areas are a consider-able way from having sufficient, high quality places for the numbers of children who will need them. Secondly, some learning from early pilots is that this early education offer works best when it is accompanied by sup-port for parents and from other professionals such as speech therapists to really address emerging problems before they become entrenched. This logically gives children's centres a strong role in delivering the 2-year-old offer but many of the places will necessarily be in other provision. The rapid roll out at the same time as councils have reduced their core capacity for development will be a major challenge to the sector. The challenge is likely to be met because failure to deliver would be a betrayal of trust and loss of a major opportunity to make a sea change difference to vulnerable children.

Conclusion

The pattern of early years provision at a local level has been transformed over the past 15 years; it has benefited from strong evidence about its importance, from the dedication and enthusiasm of the workforce across different sectors, and a political consensus about its importance. Local councils continue to play a leading role in coordinating and planning delivery relying on a diverse range of providers across the statutory, private and independent, school and voluntary and community sectors. The economic context potentially increases families' need for support at the same time as public sector funding is being constrained.

Opportunities still exist but as the sector matures more will be expected and early years professionals must continue to contribute to local debates about priorities and practice and work across disciplines to respond flexibly to need.

Key points to remember

- Local areas have a long history of innovation and development of services to support families with young children.
- Current government policy is driving increasing diversity and early years practitioners need to ensure they are familiar with local arrangements for coordinating support for children.
- The shape of local authority children's services is changing rapidly but the central importance of high quality nursery education is now accepted across the political spectrum.
- The evidence for intervening early is compelling; practitioners need to ensure interventions are informed by evidence and have impact.
- As public sector funding is squeezed local communities will need to extend their role, especially in relation to 'open access' family support and childcare.

 Points for discussion

- How can local authorities make the case for investment in high quality early years services at a time of financial constraint?
- How should local areas target investment and services so that vulnerable families benefit?
- Given the increasing diversity in patterns of provision how can local partners work together to provide good support to local families?

Reflective tasks

- Given the economic context and the major policy changes described in this chapter consider what the key ingredients are of a local system that effectively identifies and supports the most vulnerable children.
- All local areas have a range of early years provision – children's centres, day nurseries, childminders, community groups – and professionals. In some local areas partnership working is effective and strong but not always. Some of our most vulnerable children have not been effectively supported as many enquiries into child protection failures have shown. Consider what leaders – in the local authority and in early years settings – can do to ensure families benefit from high quality services.

Further reading

HM Treasury (2004) *Choice for Parents, the Best Start for Children: A Ten Year Strategy for Childcare*. London: TSO.

Laming, H. (2009) *The Protection of Children in England: A Progress Report*. London: TSO.

Thane, P. (2011) The history of early years child care based on a presentation at the Department for Education on 6 October 2011. www.historyandpolicy.org/docs/pat_thane_early_years.

Useful websites

Centre for Excellence and Outcomes in Children and Young People's Services (C4EO): www.c4eo.org.uk

Children's Improvement Board: www.local.gov.uk/CIB

Ofsted – inspections of local authorities: www.ofsted.gov.uk

Research in Practice – digest of wide range of research evidence, much used by local authorities: www.rip.org.uk

Scottish Government policy: www.scotland.gov.uk/Topics/People/Young-People/Early-Years-and-Family

Welsh Government: www.wales.gov.uk/topics/childrenyoungpeople

For details of local practice, use local authority websites, usually found at www.<nameofplace>.gov.uk

To access a variety of additional web resources to accompany this book please visit: **www.sagepub.co.uk/pughduffy**

References

Allen, G. (2011) *Early Intervention: The Next Steps*. An Independent Report to Her Majesty's Government. London: Cabinet Office.

Allen, G. and Duncan Smith, I. (2008) *Early Intervention: Good Parents, Great Kids, Better Citizens*. London: Centre for Social Justice.

Cabinet Office (2011) *Modernising Commissioning*. Green Paper. London: Cabinet Office.

Community Right to Challenge (2012) The Community Right to Challenge (Expressions of Interest and Excluded Services) (England) Regulations 2012. Statutory Instrument No. 1313. www.legislation.gov.uk/uksi/2012/1313/made. (accessed 28 June 2013)

Daycare Trust (2012) *Save Our Children's Centre Campaign*. London: Daycare Trust.

Department of Communities and Local Government (DCLG) (2012) Helping troubled families turn their lives around. www.gov.uk/government/policies/helping-troubled-families-turn-their-lives-around (accessed March 2013)

Department for Education (DfE) (2011a) *Support and Aspiration: A New Approach to Special Educational Needs and Disability.* Green Paper. London: DfE.

Department for Education (DfE) (2011b) Letter to Directors of Children's Services, June 2011, from Children's Improvement Board. www.local.gov.uk/cyp-improvement-and-support (accessed 28 June 2013)

Department for Education (DfE) (2012a) Characteristics of Children in Need in England: year ending March 2012. Statistical First Release. www.education.gov.uk/researchandstatistics/datasets/a00215043/characteristics-children-in-need (accessed 28 June 2013)

Department for Education (DfE) (2012b) Foundation Years Benchmarking Tool. www.education.gov.uk/childrenandyoungpeople/earlylearningandchildcare/delivery/b00211546/foundation-years-benchmarking-tool (accessed 28 June 2013)

Department for Education (DfE) (2012c) *School Funding Reform: Next Steps Towards a Fairer System.* London: DfE.

Department for Education (DfE) (2012d) Extending free early education to more two-year-olds. Consultation July 2012. www.education.gov.uk (accessed 28 June 2013)

Department for Education and Department of Health (DfE/DH) (2011) *Supporting Families in the Foundation Years.* London: DfE/DH.

4Children (2012) Sure Start Children's Centres Census 2012. www.4children.org.uk/Resources/Detail/Sure-Start-Childrens-Centres-Census-2012 (accessed March 2013)

Hansard (2012) House of Commons Written Answers for 10 July 2012: Sarah Teather – Column 173W. Online: www.publications.parliament.uk/pa/cm201213/cmhansrd/cm120710/text/120710w0003.htm#1207111001493 (accessed March 2013)

Localism Act 2011. www.legislation.gov.uk/ukpga/2011/20/contents (accessed 28 June 2013)

Munro, E. (2011) *The Munro Review of Child Protection: Final Report. A Child-Centred System.* Cm 8062. London: TSO.

NCB/NFER (2011) *Feasibility Study for the Trials of Payment by Results for Children's Centres.* London: NCB.

Ofsted (Office for Standards in Education, Children's Services and Skills) (2012) *Proposals for the Joint Inspection of Multi-Agency Arrangements for the Protection of Children.* London: Ofsted.

Scottish Government (2011) *Early Years Framework: Progress So Far.* Edinburgh: Scottish Government.

CHAPTER 3

International Snapshots of Provision for Babies and Young Children

Sacha Powell and Kathy Goouch

Chapter contents

- Introduction to the idea that how early childhood provision is understood and constructed is dependent on societal aims, national politics and policy and levels of investment
- The relationship between state provision and private investment in countries around the world
- Globalisation and the development of indiscriminate 'borrowing' of aspects of policy across nations
- The connection between international economic challenges and the increase in the demand for daycare provision
- The different, and sometimes conflicting, aims for early childhood education and early childhood care and the consequences of these in relation to the nature of practitioners and pedagogy employed in the sector.

It would be presumptuous of us to claim in this chapter that we are able to offer a fully formed image of the ways in which young children are understood and cared for across the entire world! Instead, we aim to offer snapshots of research, policy and practice garnered from international literature, networks and visits as well as our own contextual knowledge.

It is difficult to understand other nations' early childhood education and care policies and practices without first exploring the shared understandings of members of that society (David et al., 2010). Rosenthal (2003) has suggested that what is thought appropriate for young children depends on the role assigned to early childhood in a particular society. She argues that in societies where the community is seen as more important than each individual the needs of that community will take precedence and adults, seen as superior to children, will pass on rules and knowledge and group members' interdependence is stressed. In individualistic societies, on the other hand, children are regarded as of equal importance to adults; their ideas, thoughts and independence are encouraged. While the intention of a national policy may be the development of a particular kind of society, ranging from highly community oriented to highly individualistic, the ways in which policies are enacted in practice will vary owing to the assumptions and traditions of local cultures and staff in different contexts (see David, 2006). Urban and Dalli claim that the English education system serves contemporary political incentives, stating that 'English education is [more] interested in forming children into useful members of society, their usefulness being determined by the assumed future needs of the labour market' (Urban and Dalli, 2012: 167). Further, national family policy, especially policies relating to parental employment, impinge on early childhood education and care (ECEC) provision. In countries with high rates of female employment outside the home, or aspirations to encourage mothers of young children to enter the workforce, care provision may be heavily emphasised. How the 'child' and 'childhood' are constructed is both informed by and informs national economic policies and the ways in which daily social practices are structured and shaped (Woodrow and Press, 2008: 88).

In exploring international ECEC provision it is helpful to raise questions connected to two key areas – policy and practice – and, while this chapter will not attempt to answer all of these questions, they draw attention to a wide range of possible issues that help to develop an understanding of a broad world picture:

Questions relating to policy issues: What national attention is being given to the ways in which babies and young children are cared for? What are the aims of the provision? What do different societies provide as education and/ or care services for young children and why does provision take this/these forms? Which government department is responsible for policy at national level? Are policies for young children dealt with in isolation or are they linked to family policy and education policy? Do the policies imply that babies and young children are seen as strong, capable people/citizens who have agency?

Questions relating to practice issues: What understandings about how young children learn are held in different societies? What are the origins of these understandings? What implications for staff education and conditions of service have been recognised and acted upon? Can influences from other countries/cultures be detected? Is play accented and, if play approaches are emphasised, how are play and learning interpreted? Who is monitoring and regulating practice?

At first glance

The United Nations Children's Fund (UNICEF, 2008: 1) has argued that around the world, '[t]oday's rising generation is the first in which a majority are spending a large part of early childhood in some form of out-of-home childcare'. In many countries this childcare is provided formally by public, private and voluntary sector organisations, although informal arrangements exist and are used. Enrolment in formal provision by a 'majority' of young children is certainly the case in many economically developed nations, but this does not apply to all countries or even all rich countries. Between 1999 and 2007 the world average for 'pre-primary' service enrolment rates increased from 33% to 41% respectively. In some countries the existence of services and enrolment rates are lower. For example, seventeen states in sub-Saharan Africa had enrolment rates below 10% in 2007, but these had increased by 82% since 1999, which was a rate of growth that outstripped many other regions or countries with comparatively low enrolment rates and higher national wealth (UNESCO, 2010).

These headline figures prompt questions about the near-universal increase in early childhood services reported in recent years; and what might lie behind the sizeable differences in enrolment rates, if indeed such data are to be trusted.

Significantly, this chapter is being written in the midst of the 'deepest economic downturn since the Great Depression ... national education budgets are coming under intense pressure [and] ... low-income countries ... find it difficult to protect spending on education, let alone to scale up investment' (UNESCO, 2010: 15). As the crisis touches lives around the world, what happens to young children becomes a more pressing question than ever. Intensive international action is needed to protect the basic human rights, including the rights to education and care, of babies and young children. This begins with an awareness and understanding of issues young children and their families face in different communities and the policies and provisions made by different societies and governments.

Concerns have been raised about making international comparison without due regard for methodological problems or specific national circumstances. As already intimated, to describe a global picture of the principles, policies, pedagogies and practices of ECEC is impossible, although some trends and commonalities may be found. Nevertheless, a steady creep of internationalisation and globalisation of ideas from minority world countries to those of the majority world can ignore culturally specific childcare and family circumstances that reduce the perceived need or desire for formal services or ideas about what is valued (DeLoach and Gottlieb, 2000; Dex and Ward, 2007). Consequently there have been criticisms of acritical transmission or transplant of ideas from one context to another. Bryan and Goouch (2006) have suggested that exploring and seeking to understand other countries' educational provision can only enhance one's own pedagogy if 'teacher travellers' possess strong personal–professional philosophies, clearly articulated in policy and practice; but the absence of a guiding set of beliefs can lead to superficial and inappropriate 'cut and paste' models of others' ideas and practices.

As well as great heterogeneity between nations' approaches to any provisions for young children (and indeed what constitutes this age group varies across the world), there can be huge regional variations within a country, particularly one as geographically large, economically varied and culturally diverse as China, for example. There is wide disparity in what happens while children are too young for compulsory education and inequalities persist in the accessibility of education for many girls, disabled children, migrant and refugee children and those who are economically disadvantaged and/or from minority groups.

> [I]nformal discrimination is widespread. It is embedded in social, economic and political processes that restrict life chances for some groups and individuals. Marginalisation is not random. It is the product of institutionalised disadvantage – and of policies and processes that perpetuate such disadvantage. (UNESCO, 2010: 135)

Nevertheless, when taken with some caution, cross-national, comparative studies as well as examples of other countries' provisions offer some evidence of increasing interest in young children around the globe and prompt questions for critical exploration and dialogue. Casting out for a 'world view' hinges on the location of the observer; as observers, we are the products of our own cultures no matter how far our travels may take us. Rather than attempting to 'control' for cultural bias or decontextualise our viewing platform, we need to reflect on how it positions us and influences the lenses we consciously or unconsciously select (or neglect) as tools to examine what others think and do.

The focus on early childhood

The global increase in ECEC provision and enrolment are often attributed to evidence from psychological and neuroscientific studies that have emphasised the importance of the first years of life for laying foundations for later physical and mental health and well-being. Longitudinal studies of involvement in ECEC programmes (such as the Perry Preschool Project in the United States that began in the 1960s) have also claimed improved, long-term economic prospects for the individuals and benefits for the nations in which they live (African Child Policy Forum, 2010).

A growth in the percentage of women in the workforce, particularly in economically richer nations, has been matched by increasing demand for childcare for babies and young children (Bennett, 2003). In 2008, 30% of children under 3 were enrolled in childcare facilities in member states of the Organisation for Economic Cooperation and Development (OECD) where data were available, with a wide range across those countries, with, for example, 'less than 10% in Chile, the Czech Republic, Hungary, Mexico, Poland and the Slovak Republic, more than 50% ... in Denmark, Iceland, the Netherlands and Norway' (OECD, 2011: 1). The research evidence that suggests the early years provide a critical or sensitive time in brain development and learning has led to greater investment in programmes that offer early education as well as care. The balance of emphasis may depend on the current governance of services, concomitant policy goals and their subsequent interpretation in practice, all of which are influenced by their historical maps and cultural traditions. In their 'path-dependency' approach to discussing the development of childcare and pre-school services in Europe, Scheiwe and Willekens ask:

- whether the ways of organising public childcare chosen ... in the past have shaped the later development of child-care policies;

- how competencies regarding childcare are divided between state and church;

- whether decision making on childcare issues is centralised on the state level, decentralised towards lower levels of the polity or entirely left to private initiative;

- whether public care for children under school age is defined as a matter of education, of protection or of emancipation of women.

(Scheiwe and Willekens, 2009: 2)

In England, the Sure Start programme exemplified a 'compensatory' approach to early childhood development, as did its US counterpart, Head Start. Both have targeted disadvantaged groups, providing interventions in the form of ECEC and a range of family support services. Such approaches have been supported with specific investment grants by the World Bank for country-focused compensatory programmes. In Mexico, the 'development objective of the Compensatory Education Project is to improve access to Early Childhood Education (ECD) services and learning outcomes of children in the most marginalized municipalities of Mexico' (Holland, 2010: 1). The underlying approach that seeks to promote social equity and inclusion is not without its critics. In England, as the Sure Start programme expanded in the last decade of the twentieth century, Gewirtz (2001: 372) argued that the government's plans were, 'replete with references to "community capacity building", a 'desire to universalise (a particular version of) middle-class values and approaches to education' within a broad system that continued to exacerbate hierarchical structures and unequal opportunities. Eisenstadt's account of the Sure Start programme in England begins with her assertion that traditional divisions between government departments were so entrenched and responsibility for education and childcare split such that innovation for inter-departmental working was only made possible by the particularly close working relationship between the Prime Minister of the time, Tony Blair, and his Chancellor of the Exchequer, Gordon Brown (Eisenstadt, 2011).

Nevertheless, widening the reach and availability of (affordable, accessible and good quality) ECEC provision is an issue that continues to be raised by the European Commission, along with extensive debate about what may constitute 'quality'. In 2011 it was argued that 'there is clear evidence that universal access to quality early childhood education and care is more beneficial than interventions targeted exclusively at vulnerable groups' (Burton, 2012: 6) and many countries have been attempting to ensure sufficiency to meet rising demand. Cost–benefit analyses have been used to argue for universal provision (UNICEF, 2008; Ben-Galim, 2011). In England, as early education and childcare continue to attract political attention, it was recently suggested that changes to the system could offer 'a single childcare support to be paid to the parents' to help ensure that 'children from deprived backgrounds (who already receive extra funding) could be matched with high quality provision' (Truss, 2012: 1).

The drive for universality (whether funded or unfunded) extends into Asia too. In China, for example, a wide discrepancy in the availability of places throughout the country has been one of the challenges facing the country's government in recent years (Zhu, J. 2010). Here, enrolment rates in towns and cities far exceed those in rural areas (Zhao and Hu, 2008); while in England, an entitlement to free early education for the 20% 'most disadvantaged' 2-year-olds from September 2013 has challenged providers to find or create many new places while attempting to maintain good quality provision for all young children. 'Good quality' is a contested concept but relies on a match between the aims and goals of policies and practice. This is problematic in a sector dogged by a historical split between 'education' and 'care' and dominated by a discourse focused on economic gain.

Provision: educating or caring?

The language employed to describe provision matters at many levels but different terms are sometimes conflated and cause conceptual confusion. It is not uncommon to read about early years education, pre-primary education, childcare or early childhood education and care/care and education (ECEC/ECCE). However, and despite popular usage, as Kaga claims, 'Given their distinct historical roots, "childcare" and "early education" services … embody different visions and understandings of children, programme goals, approaches and contents' (Kaga et al., 2010: 15). These terms may be used specifically to imply variation in structures, goals and professional responsibilities; or they can be deliberately integrated – conceptually, structurally and in practice. Writing about the 'lottery' of childcare provision in Scotland, Burton (2012: 4) states that, 'The reality is that care and education are not separate in terms of the benefits they can bring for children and families, but are separate in our systems of funding, provision and staffing.' Similarly, it seems unlikely that babies and very young children classify their experiences as 'care' or 'education', although some may have strong views about why they attend out-of-home provision and what they think it is for. But while the benefits of good quality education and care may not be separate, it seems clear that disadvantages can stem from this bifurcated system because ECEC for children aged 2 and above tends to attract greater investment than services for babies. Ackerman and Barnet (2009) considered the effects of increases in pre-school education in the United States for children aged 3 and older on the provision of childcare for younger infants and toddlers. Unexpectedly, they found that increases in provision of the former appeared to have led to increases in the latter but lacked policy attention to quality, which they found to be generally poor. In January 2012, the 'biggest reform of Australian childcare' began a 'new era of early childhood education and care that focuses on what is best for children, helping them to grow and learn' (Early Childhood Australia, 2012).

The Perry Preschool Project mentioned above and similar large-scale, longitudinal studies such as the Effective Provision of Pre-School Education (EPPE) project in the United Kingdom have been influential in shaping ECEC policies and provision. Primarily, these studies sought to demonstrate impact on children's cognitive and social/behavioural development and outcomes of their involvement in ECEC programmes. Both studies showed that there could be statistically significant gains for children from low socio-economic backgrounds if they attended 'good quality' ECEC provision. The methods used in these studies, which conformed to strict criteria for rigour and reliability, demanded within their particular paradigms, have impacted on ideas for ECEC curricula. In 2006, reviewing international literature about early years education, Stephen noted that, '[f]indings from the EPPE and REPEY projects support the general approach taken in the Curriculum Guidance for the Foundation Stage (QCA, 2000) with its emergent approach to learning and attention to intellectual growth' (Stephen, 2006: 17).

Where early education is intended to be a preparatory phase for compulsory schooling and interpreted as a narrow pedagogic emphasis on developing cognitive and behavioural skills, there can also exist a simultaneous lack of educational or developmental support in services whose primary goal is providing childcare while parents go out to work. Concerned about such polarised positions, Bennett (2006: 144) has suggested that the two major studies of ECEC services across OECD member states (OECD, 2001, 2006) yielded useful principles of (1) focusing on each child's agency and learning strategies and (2) a pedagogy of listening, project work and documentation to underpin work with children as a means to 'counter the tendency of seeing the school as the benchmark and of imposing external targets and skills on young children'.

When Phillips and Lowenstein (2011: 483) reviewed the literature about the impacts of ECEC they concluded that 'the quality of adult–child interactions in ECE settings is the most potent source of variation in child outcomes, although the amount of exposure to these settings also plays a role, perhaps especially with regard to social-emotional development … Some children, notably those growing up in poverty, appear to be more vulnerable to variation in the quality of ECE settings than do other children.' With the benefit of this finding, it is important to note evidence gathered in the Day in the Life Project, which illustrates that the ways in which practitioners view and understand the 'socio-historical and political contexts' in which they practise is reflected in the everyday realities of their interactions with children. For example, a practitioner in:

> *Australia*: rejected 'trappings of professionalism' – such as branded centre clothing – and instead identified a 'lived professionalism' in her leadership and moral purpose;
>
> *New Zealand*: demonstrated a 'reflective, articulate and agentic style of practice [which appeared] to conform to the structural and societal expectations for her role';
>
> *Sweden*: focused on 'working from an ethical base of respect … in line with the democratic values embedded in the Swedish preschool curriculum. (Miller et al., 2012: 5)

Such mature constructions, however, can only hope to exist within a frame of national policies that offer mature guidance, a considered system of regulation and monitoring and a level of investment. Where narrow, rigid structures exist, or inconsistent or very little guidance or support is offered, together with challenging conditions of work, then this kind of authentic commitment is more difficult to find (Powell and Goouch, 2012). Finland, which emphasises a social welfare/social pedagogy approach for the 70% of 3- to 5-year-olds in ECEC, has highly qualified staff with ongoing access to professional development (Miller et al., 2012). By implication it seems to matter less whether the policy emphasis is on care or education but significance lies in the qualification levels and commitment to ongoing professional development by the practitioners interpreting policy. Highly qualified 'carers' will produce the same positive outcomes as their equivalent highly qualified 'educators'. But, particularly in English-speaking countries, 'carers' tend to be less well qualified as a result of the lack of public investment and interest in services for the youngest children, which in England has applied historically to children up to three. In this debate, history is as important as geography. Tobin et al. (2009) note that:

> In 1985 and 2005 Chinese and American early childhood educational goals and practices were dramatically unalike, with China emphasising control and regimentation and the US play and choice. Twenty years later, China's early childhood educational goals have shifted towards child-initiation and creativity while early childhood education in the US has shifted in the opposite direction, toward more emphasis on academic outcomes and the teacher's role in instruction. (Tobin et al., 2009: 232)

Within this debate there is great variation in provision for maternity and/or paternity leave across countries, meaning that some women may have greater need for childcare than others, particularly where they do not have access to informal care provided by family or friends or neighbours. Statistics suggest that Croatia, Sweden, Denmark and Norway are the most generous in terms of a mother's leave after childbirth (one year's leave with 100% or 80% of salary) followed by Albania (one year's leave with 80% and 50% of salary), which contrasts sharply with Bahrain, for example, where women are offered 45 days' leave on full pay (UN Statistics, 2011). But these figures need cautious treatment and close attention to local beliefs and circumstances rather than a cursory presumption that one system is more generous than another. According to Lewis (2009: 74), the historical roots of policies for incentives to engage in paid work and paid or unpaid care are important considerations. She argues that only the United States and Nordic countries' policies are grounded in assumptions that men and women will undertake paid employment, although operating differently, the United States having a 'fiercely gender-neutral, equality-defined-as-sameness adult worker model', which many Western European countries have begun to adopt, while some (United Kingdom and the Netherlands) have simultaneously brought in policies designed to encourage lone mothers to find paid employment. But despite broad similarities in approaches, differences that appear to emerge from cultural traditions continue to abound. Consequently, while Sweden offers some of the most generous maternity leave entitlements it also has the highest number of women senior managers in Europe, whereas work disruption resulting from maternity leave and caring for young children has been found to hinder many women's career trajectories in the United Kingdom (Brewer and Paull, 2006). Furthermore, it should not be assumed that a country's headline statistical information can reflect the many different attitudes, beliefs and circumstances of its multi-cultural citizens. Some may be hampered by family circumstances regardless of national policy intent; they may prefer not to go out to work while their children are young; or they may face financial obstacles to accessing formal ECEC services (Bryson et al., 2005; Dex and Ward, 2007; Campbell-Barr and Garnham, 2010). In some countries attention has begun to turn to the education and care of children under 3. In England, the publication of a non-statutory framework, *Birth to Three Matters* (DfES, 2002), started a process of highlighting support for the learning and development of babies and toddlers, which was later subsumed within the first statutory framework for children from birth to 5 (DCSF, 2008).

Pedagogy and practitioners

Although pedagogy and curricula vary, after surveying services in 20 countries, the OECD identified eight key elements characterising successful ECEC policy for its member states, which were:

a systemic and integrated approach to ECEC policy

a strong and equal partnership with the education system

a universal approach to access, with particular attention to children in need of special support

substantial public investment allocated to services and infrastructure

a participatory approach to quality improvement and assurance

appropriate training and working conditions available for all staff

systematic attention to data collection and monitoring

a stable framework and long-term agenda for research and evaluation. (OECD, 2006: 3–4)

These key elements can be used while exploring the ECEC policies of any government. Twenty years ago the United Kingdom's responses to all the above elements would, almost certainly, have been negative, demonstrating the need to understand both a nation's developments as well as the reasons why developments have occurred (or not). In England ECEC for children up to 3 years of age is largely a private matter (excluding those children aged 2 from families who have been targeted for the new early education entitlement). The historic split between education and care is notable when babies and very young children's daycare is investigated. Babies as young as 6 weeks may spend 50 hours a week in day nurseries or with registered childminders. Although the adult–child ratio is higher than it is for older children, the qualifications requirements for staff who work in baby rooms are comparatively low. The drive to 'upskill' England's ECEC workforce with more graduates and leaders qualified to Early Years Professional Status (EYPS) has had little impact and reached few people who work with babies and toddlers. Indeed the gap appears to have widened as a result of this drive (Goouch and

Powell, 2013). Similarly in Scotland, sufficiency of childcare places for babies and children up to age 2 is also an issue and staff availability is linked to pay and conditions, where currently 'many of those working in the childcare sector are among the working poor themselves. They are often self-employed or on short-term contracts, and paid minimum wages' (Burton, 2012: 4). Additionally, it has been argued that there is an inherent and sad irony that the British government's attempts to meet 'the needs of the working mother fail to incorporate the needs of the nursery worker, who might also be a mother' (Osgood, 2012: 44). In times of increasing austerity, rising unemployment and economic hardship for families, Burton has reported that the costs of childcare have been rising while provision in Scotland has been diminishing. She says that, 'when families are pulling out of care provision – care providers cut staff working hours, perhaps pay and then jobs. Ultimately nurseries close and childminders give up their businesses. At a time when the population of under 5s has increased by 5%, the official number of providers of care for this age group has gone down by 3%' (Burton, 2012: 5). The provision of ECEC by a sector dominated by private enterprises means that most services are at the direct mercy of market forces while simultaneously constrained by requirements of the legislative framework within which they must operate.

Currently, in New Zealand, questions are being raised about the kind of care for children under 2 that is in the child's best interests, while at the same time acknowledging that the need to work and to care for infants and very young children is a complex issue, and that more support should be given for parental care of those children under 12 months (Carroll-Lind, 2011). In a report for the Ministry of Education in New Zealand, two of the key requisite factors for determining high quality early childhood education for children up to 2 years of age are that staff should be qualified to 'degree-level, [with] specialised training for work with infants and toddlers and ongoing professional development that takes into account new knowledge' and that 'attuned caregiving across the curriculum may be supported by teachers who have the capacity to engage in in-depth caregiving relationships with infants and toddlers, who have expert, specialised knowledge and the capacity to reflect and review their practice' (Dalli et al., 2011; see also Meade et al., 2012). These high level requirements coincide with the findings from the recent Nutbrown Review (see also Nutbrown 2012b and 2013), whose interim report recommended that:

> Good qualifications, taught well, ensure that those training to enter the early years workforce, and those already working with babies and young children, can be supported to develop the right blend of theoretical knowledge and practical skills. When these are combined with the commitment and passion evident across the sector we can expect to see better outcomes for children, in the early years phase and in their later life as well. (Nutbrown, 2012a: 5)

The notion of a 'qualification', however, also requires deconstruction. In New Zealand, for example, the term 'qualified' refers to those who have graduated through a degree programme. In England, 'qualified' currently refers to a National Vocational Qualification (NVQ), and generally nursery workers are qualified to NVQ level 2 or level 3, which is lower than a degree on a hierarchical qualification framework.

What seems to be most important, however, in all geographical contexts, is that rather than 'a preoccupation with satisfying the regulatory gaze' (Osgood, 2010: 130), a demand is made of all of those working with young children that they are guided by a 'sense of professionalism, hard work and concern for children' (Tobin et al., 2009). If it can be claimed that there are 'universal' features of early childhood care and education, one significant feature would be that the people who are involved with babies and young children matter to them (David et al., 2003) and that, equally, babies and young children matter to those caring for them (Gopnik, 2009).

Key points to remember

- There is a global increase in early childhood services, despite parental leave becoming more widespread.
- Provision for young children depends on how children, childhood and families are constructed and valued in different societies.
- This leads to a difference in the aims of particular kinds of daycare services and the amount of national and parental investment in early childhood education and care;.
- There are wide disparities in the kinds of qualifications required by different countries for those engaged in work in early childhood education and care.
- Private enterprise seems now to be dominant in the provision of early childhood services, particularly in English-speaking countries.

 Points for discussion

- Why does it matter whether provision for babies and young children is labelled 'education' or 'care'?
- Daycare is becoming increasingly expensive, and some say unaffordable, for families in some countries, including England. Who should provide and pay for childcare and how can the service be afforded?
- Research from New Zealand provides evidence that where 100% of practitioners in a setting are fully qualified (i.e. with an appropriate degree) there are recognisable benefits to the children, particularly those under 2 years of age (Meade et al., 2012). Discuss the implications of these findings.

Reflective task

- How can we learn from each other, across nations and cultures, without simply transplanting models?

Further reading

Meade, A., Robinson, L., Smorti, S., Stuart, M., Williamson, J. with Carroll-Lind, J., Meagher-Lundberg, P. and Te Whau, S. (2012) *Early Childhood Teachers' Work in Education and Care Centres, Profiles, Patterns and Purposes.* Wellington: NZ Childcare Association. Available at http://nzca.ac.nz/assets/RelatedDocuments/ Early-Childhood-Teachers-work-in-education-and-carecentres-web-090812.pdf.

Miller, L., Dalli, C. and Urban, M. (eds) (2012) *Early Childhood Grows Up: Towards a Critical Ecology of the Profession.* Dordrecht: Springer.

Tobin, J., Hsueh, Y. and Karasawa, M. (2009) *Preschool in Three Cultures Revisited.* Chicago, IL: University of Chicago Press.

Useful websites

www.africanchildforum.org/site/
www.earlychildhoodaustralia.org.au/
www.educationscotland.gov.uk/earlyyears/prebirthtothree/nationalguidance/ conversations/index.asp
www.literacytrust.org.uk/talk to your baby
www.cfs.purdue.edu/ITSI/default.php
www.unesco.org/new/en/education/themes/leading-the-international-agenda/ efareport/reports/2007-early-childhood/

To access a variety of additional web resources to accompany this book please visit: **www.sagepub.co.uk/pughduffy**

References

Ackerman, D. J. and Barnet, W. S. (2009) *What Do We Know About the Impact of Publicly Funded Preschool Education on the Supply and Quality of Infant/ Toddler Care?* New Jersey: NIEER. www.nieer.org/resources/research/ ImpactOfPreschoolExpansion042309.pdf (accessed June 2012).

African Child Policy Forum (2010) *The African Report on Child Wellbeing 2011 Budgeting for Children. Ethiopia.* Addis Ababa: African Child Policy Forum.

Ben-Galim, D. (2011) *Making the Case for Universal Childcare.* London: Institute for Public Policy Research.

Bennett, J. (2003) 'Starting Strong: the persistent division between care and education', *Journal of Early Childhood Research*, 1, 21–48.

Bennett, J. (2006) 'New policy conclusions from Starting Strong II: an update on the OECD early childhood policy reviews', *European Early Childhood Education Research Journal*, 14 (2), 141–56.

Brewer, M. and Paull, G. (2006) *Newborns and New Schools: Critical Times in Women's Employment*. London: Department for Work and Pensions. Research Report 308.

Bryan, H. and Goouch, K. (2006) 'Pedagogical connections, boundaries and barriers: the place of travel in teachers' professional development', *NZRECE Journal*, 9, 81–90.

Bryson, C., Bell, A., La Valle, I., Barnes, M. and O'Shea, R. (2005) *Use of Childcare Among Families from Minority Ethnic Backgrounds and Among Families with Children with Special Educational Needs*. Nottingham: DfES Publications.

Burton, S. (2012) Address to Scottish Trades Union Congress by Sarah Burton, Policy Development Manager, Children in Scotland at the Annual Conference of the STUC, Inverness, Monday 23 April 2012. www.stuc.org.uk/files/Womens20page/childreninscotland.doc (accessed 23 July 2012).

Campbell-Barr, V. and Garnham, A. (2010) *Child Care: A Review of What Parents Want*. London: Equality and Human Rights Commission Research Report 66.

Carroll-Lind, J. (2011) 'Through their lens: an inquiry into non-parental education and care of infants and toddlers', *The First Years*, 13 (1), 39–44.

Dalli, C., White, E. J., Rockel, J., Duhn, I., with Buchanan, E., Davidson, S., Ganly, S., Kus, L., and Wang, B. (2011) *Quality Early Childhood Education for Under-Two-Year-Olds: What Should It Look Like?* Literature review. Report to the New Zealand Ministry of Education. www.educationcounts.govt.nz/publications.

David, T. (2006) 'The world picture', in G. Pugh and B. Duffy (eds), *Contemporary Issues in the Early Years*, 4th edn. London: Sage.

David, T., Goouch, K., Powell, S. and Abbott, L. (2003) *Birth to Three Matters: A Review of the Literature*. Research Report 444. London: Department for Education and Skills.

David, T., Powell, S. and Goouch, K. (2010) 'The world picture', in G. Pugh and B. Duffy (eds), *Contemporary Issues in the Early Years*, 5th edn. London: Sage. pp. 33–46.

DeLoach, J. and Gottlieb, A. (2000) *A World of Babies. Imagined Childcare Guides for Seven Societies*. Cambridge: Cambridge University Press.

Department for Children, Schools and Families (DCSF) (2008) *Statutory Framework for the Early Years Foundation Stage: Setting the Standards for Learning, Development and Care for Children from Birth to Five*. London: DCSF.

Department for Education (DfE) (2012) *Statutory Framework for the Early Years Foundation Stage 2012: Setting the Standards for Learning, Development and Care for Children from Birth to Five*. Runcorn: DfE Publications.

Department for Education and Skills (DfES) (2002) *Birth to Three Matters: A Framework to Support Children in Their Earliest Years*. London: DfES.

Dex, S. and Ward, K. (2007) *Parental Care and Employment in Early Childhood.* London: Institute of Education.

Early Childhood Australia (2012) www.earlychildhoodaustralia.org.au/.

Eisenstadt, N. (2011) *Providing a Sure Start. How Government Discovered Early Childhood.* Bristol: The Policy Press.

Gewirtz, S. (2001) 'Cloning the Blairs: New Labour's programme for the re-socialization of working-class parents', *Journal of Education Policy*, 16 (4), 365–78.

Goouch, K. and Powell, S. (2013) *The Baby Room: Principles, Policy and Practice.* Maidenhead: Open University Press.

Gopnik, A. (2009) *The Philosophical Baby.* London: The Bodley Head.

Holland, D. (2010) *Implementation Status & Results. Mexico Compensatory Education* (P101369). Report No: ISR5229. Washington, DC: The World Bank.

Kaga, Y., Bennett, J. and Moss, P. (2010) *Caring and Learning Together. A Cross-National Study on the Integration of Early Childhood Care and Education Within Education.* Paris: UNESCO.

Lewis, J. (2009) *Work–Family Balance: Gender and Policy.* Cheltenham: Edward Elgar.

Meade, A., Robinson, L., Smorti, S., Stuart, M., Williamson, J. with Janis Carroll-Lind, Patricia Meagher-Lundberg and Sissie Te Whau (2012) *Early Childhood Teachers' Work in Education and Care Centres: Profiles, Patterns and Purposes.* Wellington: NZ Childcare Association. Available at http://nzca.ac.nz/assets/RelatedDocuments/Early-Childhood-Teachers-work-in-education-and-carecentres-web-090812.pdf (accessed March 2013).

Miller, L., Dalli, C. and Urban, M. (eds) (2012) *Early Childhood Grows Up: Towards a Critical Ecology of the Profession.* Dordrecht: Springer.

Nutbrown, C (2012a) *Review of Early Education and Childcare Qualifications: Interim Report* (Nutbrown Review). London: Department for Education. www.education.gov.uk/nutbrownreview (accessed 14 March 2012).

Nutbrown, C. (2012b) *Foundations for Quality. The Independent Review of Childcare and Early Education Qualifications. Final Report.* London: DfE.

Nutbrown, C. (2013) *Shaking the Foundations of Quality. Why 'Childcare' Policy Must Not Lead to Poor-Quality Early Education and Care.* University of Sheffield.

OECD (2001) *Starting Strong: Early Childhood Education and Care.* Paris: Organisation for Economic Cooperation and Development.

OECD (2006) *Starting Strong II: Early Childhood Education and Care.* Paris: Organisation for Economic Cooperation and Development.

OECD (2011) *PF3.2 Enrolment in Childcare and Pre-Schools.* Paris: Organisation for Economic Cooperation and Development. Family Database. www.oecd.org/els/social/family/database (accessed 28 November 2011).

Osgood, J. (2010) 'Reconstructing professionalism in ECEC: the case for the "critically reflective emotional professional"', *Early Years*, 30 (2), 119–33.

Osgood, J. (2012) *Narratives from the Nursery. Negotiating Professional Identities in Early Childhood.* London: Routledge.

Phillips, D. A. and Lowenstein, A. E. (2011) 'Early care, education, and child development', *Annual Review of Psychology*, 62, 483–500.

Powell, S. and Goouch, K. (2012) 'Whose hand rocks the cradle? Parallel discourses in the baby room', *Early Years*, 32 (2), 113–28.

Rosenthal, M. (2003) 'Quality in early childhood education and care', *European Early Childhood Research Journal*, 11 (2), 101–16.

Scheiwe, K. and Willekens, H. (2009) 'Path-dependencies and change in child-care and preschool institutions in Europe – historical and institutional perspectives', in K. Scheiwe and H. Willekens (eds), *Childcare and Preschool Development in Europe. International Perspectives*. Basingstoke: Palgrave Macmillan. pp. 1–22.

Stephen, C. (2006) *Early Years Education: Perspectives from a Review of the International Literature*. Edinburgh: Scottish Executive Education Department.

Tobin, J., Hsueh, Y. and Karasawa, M. (2009) *Preschool in Three Cultures Revisited*. Chicago, IL: University of Chicago Press.

Truss, E. (2012) *Affordable Quality: New Approaches to Childcare*. London: Centre Forum.

UN Statistics (2011) Table 5g. *Maternity Leave Benefits*. New York: United Nations Statistics Division. www.unstats.un.org/unsd/demographic/products/indwm/ (accessed June 2012).

UNESCO (2010) *Education for All*. Global Monitoring Report 2010. Paris: UNESCO.

UNICEF (2008) *The Childcare Transition*. Innocenti Report Card 8. Florence: UNICEF Innocenti Research Centre.

Urban, M. and Dalli, C. (2012) 'A profession speaking and thinking for itself', in L. Miller, C. Dalli and M. Urban (eds), *Early Childhood Grows Up: Towards a Critical Ecology of the Profession*. Dordrecht: Springer.

Woodrow, C. and Press, F. (2008) '(Re)Positioning the child in the policy/politics of early childhood', in S. Farquhar and P. Fitzsimons (eds), *Philosophy of Early Childhood Education, Transforming Narratives*. Oxford: Blackwell.

Zhu, J. (2010) *Curriculum Implementation Challenges and Strategies in China*. Report to OECD EDU/EDPC/ECEC/RD (2010)47. Paris: Organisation for Economic Cooperation and Development.

Zhao, L. and Hu, X. (2008) 'The development of early childhood education in rural areas in China', *Early Years*, 28 (2), 197–210.

CHAPTER 4

Quality in Early Childhood Education

Sandra Mathers, Fiona Roberts and
Kathy Sylva

Chapter contents

There are few who would deny that the quality of early years education and care
is important. But what is quality, and how can we define it? In this chapter, we

- set out different ways of defining quality;
- explore the issues and challenges involved in measuring it;
- and consider the impact of different dimensions of quality on children's development over time.

The chapter is deliberately broad, and provides an introduction to some of the
important themes relating to quality in early childhood education, as well as
suggestions for more in-depth study and further reading.

One of the most common ways of conceptualising quality is to distinguish
between process, structure and outcome. *Process* quality is a dynamic concept
relating to children's actual experiences, such as the warmth and responsiveness of their interactions with staff, and the activities they experience. *Structural* quality includes the more stable aspects of the environment, for example

adult–child ratios, group sizes or qualifications. Research shows that it is process quality which is most strongly predictive of child outcomes (Howes and Brown, 2000). However, it is difficult and time-consuming to measure because it requires in-depth observation. Structural quality characteristics, although less strongly related to child outcomes, are still important. They are also much easier to assess, as they can be clearly defined and consistently measured across different types of early years settings. For this reason, they tend to be popular with policymakers because they are easily adopted and regulable (Peisner-Feinberg and Yazejian, 2010). Structural and process descriptions of quality are often highly correlated: good things tend to go together. For example, the large-scale National Institute of Child Health and Human Development (NICHD) study of childcare in the United States reported that early childhood settings rated as safer, cleaner and with better adult–child ratios (better structure) tended to have more sensitive caregivers who provided more cognitively stimulating experiences (better classroom processes) (NICHD, 1999). Quality is sometimes considered in terms of its eventual outcome (i.e. children's developmental progress) but, although these longer term consequences of early years provision are relevant to quality, they are not part of its definition (Munton et al., 1995).

In this chapter we consider some of the different tools available to measure process quality, and some of the research which has explored the effects of process quality on children's development. We also describe which structural features of early years environments are most associated with high process quality. The majority of studies have used systematic observational measures, such as the Environment Rating Scales (e.g. ECERS and ITERS), to assess process quality, and also gathered information on structural characteristics such as ratios and staff turnover.

The empiricist/objectivist approach on which tools such as the ECERS and ITERS are based argues that quality can be defined as a 'collection of measurable characteristics in the childcare environment that affect children's social and cognitive development' (Siraj-Blatchford and Wong, 1999). However, others have argued that quality cannot be considered universal (i.e. true for all children within all contexts) and that research tools developed within one social and cultural context are not appropriate for others, where the desired outcomes for children might be different (e.g. in different countries). As Peter Moss and Gunilla Dahlberg (2008) point out, one response to this viewpoint has been to redefine quality as a 'subjective, value-based, relative and dynamic concept'. Under this relativist approach, definitions of quality aim to take into account the local social and cultural context, and incorporate the perspectives of multiple stakeholders (e.g. parents, children, practitioners and policymakers). Moss and Dahlberg themselves go even further, suggesting that the very concept of quality is constructed, and therefore restrictive, in that it assumes 'the possibility of deriving universal and objective norms based on expert knowledge' and that services such as early education and care can be evaluated to assess their conformity with these norms. They claim that quality is 'a language of evaluation that fails to recognise a multilingual world and, in so doing, denies the possibility of other languages'. In a paper directly responding to Moss and Dalberg's assertions, Siraj-Blatchford and Wong (1999) argue that, while quality should reflect the values of particular societies and stakeholders, many aspects of quality can be agreed upon by stakeholders across contexts, and can therefore be measured and used to inform research and practice.

As Sylva and Roberts (2009) suggest in a previous edition of this book, these different approaches to identifying quality (e.g. observational measures, stakeholder views, outcome measures) are all valid, but rest on different sources and standards of evidence. There is a lively ongoing debate about which tools are the most effective for measuring quality, and some of these issues are introduced within this chapter.

Measuring process quality

The Environment Rating Scales

The majority of studies in England over the past 15 years have used a set of tools known as the Environment Rating Scales to measure quality. These standardised quality assessment scales are used in many countries around the world for research, regulation and quality improvement. The three most commonly used are:

- the Early Childhood Environment Rating Scale – Revised Edition or **ECERS–R** (Harms et al., 2005), designed to assess centre-based early years provision for children from 30 months to 5 years;
- the Early Childhood Environment Rating Scale – Extension or **ECERS–E** (Sylva et al., 2003), designed to assess curricular provision for children aged 3 to 5 years;
- the Infant Toddler Environment Rating Scale – Revised Edition or **ITERS–R** (Harms et al., 2003), which assesses provision for children from birth to 30 months.

These tools consider the quality of the learning environment in its broadest sense, that is, the physical, pedagogical, social and emotional contexts in which learning and development take place. Each item in the Environment Rating Scales is scored through observation, and rated on a 7-point scale (1 = inadequate, 3 = minimal, 5 = good, 7 = excellent). Observers complete items and assign scores by rating specific statements or 'indicators' of quality. To score a 5 (good) on the 'Nap/rest' item, for example, observers must see evidence that '*children are helped to relax*' and that '*space is conducive to resting'*. This provides a measurable profile of quality across the various different dimensions.

The ECERS and ITERS sit strongly within the empiricist/objectivist tradition in that they aim to assess universal aspects important for children's development. They have been shown in many studies, both in the United Kingdom and elsewhere, to be reliable, valid and related to children's developmental outcomes (e.g. Hopkin et al., 2010; Sylva et al., 2010; Burchinal et al., 2011). Soucacou and Sylva (2010) have argued that objective measurements such as the Environment Rating Scales are implemented within 'communities of practice'. This suggests that their implementation may vary somewhat across cultures because of their different traditions but that the majority of items are agreed across many different countries.

Research studies on the relationship between process quality and children's developmental outcomes

In this section we outline a number of the key research studies which have explored process quality, and its effects on children's outcomes. From the United Kingdom, we discuss the Effective Provision of Pre-School, Primary and Secondary Education (EPPSE) project and the evaluation of the Early Education Pilot for Two Year Old Children. From the United States, we consider the large-scale longitudinal NICHD research, and a recent meta-analysis[1] of studies by Margaret Burchinal and colleagues. We use these to draw conclusions on the ways in which process quality shapes children's later development, and also consider two further examples of quality assessment tools.

Evidence from England

The Effective Pre-School, Primary and Secondary Education study (EPPE/ EPPSE; Sylva et al., 2010) is the largest longitudinal study in Europe on the effects of early education and care on children's development. EPPE assessed the process quality of 141 settings using the ECERS–R, ECERS–E and the CIS (Caregiver Interaction Scale; Arnett, 1989). A sample of 2,800 children who attended the 141 settings was followed longitudinally at ages 5, 6, 7, 10, 11 and 14 years. The quality of pre-school settings attended by these children was a significant predictor of children's developmental outcomes at all ages, even after controlling for earlier attainment and for both individual and family characteristics. The EPPSE study has shown that different dimensions of quality (as measured by the ECERS–R, ECERS–E and CIS) can have different effects on children's development over time. For example, higher quality scores on all these measures were associated with positive cognitive and social-behavioural outcomes at age 5. However, at age 11, while quality as measured by the

ECERS–R and the ECERS–E predicted children's social-behavioural development, only scores on the ECERS–E were related to children's national assessment scores in English and mathematics. The EPPSE study is unusual in that it continued to investigate the effects of pre-school quality on the developmental outcomes of young people to the age of 14 years. Although the strength of the effect was weaker, quality measured by the ECERS–E remained a significant predictor of young people's national assessment grades well into secondary school.

The EPPE study began when children were 3 years old, and so focuses on the effects of quality experienced by pre-school children. Another recent study in England used the ITERS–R to evaluate provision for children under the age of 3, and reaffirmed the importance of quality for very young children. The UK government funds an ambitious programme offering free early education places to disadvantaged 2-year-olds, to prevent risk of later developmental delay. The study in question was an evaluation of the pilot early education programme, which ran between 2006 and 2008. The findings demonstrated benefits for children attending the pilot places, both in terms of vocabulary at age 3 and improved parent–child relationships. However, these benefits were only seen for those attending high quality settings (Smith et al., 2009).

Evidence from the United States

Turning now to the US evidence on the relationships between process quality and child outcomes, we will consider the NICHD study, which developed its own tool for rating the quality of the child's care environment.

The Observational Record of the Caregiving Environment (ORCE) (NICHD ECCRN, 1996, 2000a) was developed as part of the NICHD Study of Early Child Care and Youth Development, a major longitudinal study designed to explore the relationships between different childcare experiences and children's developmental outcomes. The NICHD research team developed their own instrument because there was no existing tool that could be used to assess the quality of an individual child's caregiving environment across different types of setting (i.e. home-based as well as centre-based care) and across a wide range of ages (the ORCE is used from 6 to 54 months in the NICHD study).

The ORCE differs in three important ways from the Environment Rating Scales, which are designed to measure the global quality of a whole setting: it has a narrower focus on *specific* process indicators; it focuses on the caregiving experience of *individual children*; and it can be used to evaluate *parental* as well as professional care. The ORCE provides a detailed assessment of the sensitivity and responsiveness of the adult towards the child, and also records the child's behaviour. It makes use of both frequency counts, recording the occurrence or quantity of certain behaviours (the *behaviour scales*), and also ratings of the quality of parent/practitioner behaviour towards the child regardless of frequency (the *qualitative ratings*).

The ORCE has good validity, demonstrating relationships with expected structural measures such as ratios (e.g. NICHD ECCRN, 1996, 2000a, 2002). There is much evidence from the NICHD research demonstrating a lasting relationship between process quality, as measured by the ORCE, and children's developmental outcomes across a range of domains. Controlling for demographic and parenting variables, ORCE quality ratings (overall, but in particular language stimulation) were found to be related to scores on child cognitive language measures at 15, 24 and 36 months (NICHD ECCRN, 2000b). A more responsive and stimulating childcare environment was related to positive peer interactions and school readiness at 36 months (NICHD ECCRN, 2001) and to scores on cognitive and language assessments at 54 months (NICHD ECCRN, 2002, 2003). Considering even longer-term effects, higher quality care as measured by the ORCE has been shown to relate to better academic skills in third grade (NICHD ECCRN, 2005), better language skills in fifth grade (Belsky et al., 2007), and is still predictive of better achievement on assessments of vocabulary, reading and maths at age 15 (Vandell et al., 2010). The NICHD evidence emphasises features such as caregiver responsiveness, the language used by practitioners, and the appropriateness of activities, as the key elements of quality that are important for children's outcomes.

One final quality measurement tool to be considered is the Classroom Assessment Scoring System (CLASS; Pianta et al., 2007). The CLASS also focuses primarily on adult–child interactions and can be used from pre-school through to secondary school. The Pre-Kindergarten (Pre-K) version considers three main aspects in its assessment of overall pre-school classroom quality: emotional support provided by the teacher (e.g. positive/negative climate, teacher sensitivity), quality of instruction (e.g. concept development) and classroom organisation (e.g. behaviour management, productivity). There are 10 domains of interaction altogether and each is rated on a 7-point scale. Like the ECERS/ ITERS and the ORCE, the CLASS has been used in studies considering the relationship between process quality and child outcomes. For instance, Howes et al. (2008) found that the instructional quality ratings in pre-kindergarten programmes were positively associated with gains in children's language and literacy skills. Similarly, Mashburn et al. (2008) demonstrated a relationship between higher quality instructional interactions and better academic and language skills, as well as between higher quality emotional interactions and children's higher social competence and lower problem behaviour.

In summary then, many studies have explored the relationships between process quality and children's outcomes, using a range of different measurement tools to define and assess quality. In a recent meta-analysis, Margaret Burchinal and colleagues (2011) drew together the findings of the NICHD and many other – primarily American – studies on the relationships between early childhood quality and outcomes for children aged 2 to 5 years. Their starting point was that much of the evidence used to make policy decisions in the United States is based on analysis of a relatively small number of experimental studies (i.e. studies where children are randomly assigned to a 'treatment' or 'control' group), which assess the impact of specific and often quite intensive early childhood programmes. In contrast, their meta-analysis focuses on descriptive or quasi-experimental studies that do not involve specific interventions or projects but describe the effects of early years provision in a more naturalistic context. The authors restrict themselves to studies with a robust methodology and which employ widely used measures of quality and outcomes, including the ECERS, the CLASS and the ORCE. They conclude that higher quality is associated with higher language, academic and social skills and fewer behavioural problems, i.e. quality matters. However, they also note that the associations were quite modest. Therefore, although quality matters, it does not have a very strong relationship with children's outcomes. The authors consider several reasons for this, including the possibility that the effects of quality are in reality quite small. Since this would contradict the findings from experimental studies, which show large and lasting effects of quality on outcomes, they conclude that in fact the problem is in the *measurement* of quality. They recommend, for example, the use of more specific measures which focus on the precise aspects of quality expected to influence a particular child outcome.

Overall, the evidence suggests that process quality makes a modest contribution to children's developmental outcomes. One element in particular that seems to be key to children's progress is the quality of interactions in a setting. The evidence also tell us that quality matters more for specific groups of children, with the EPPSE research suggesting it can make a particular difference for boys, for children with special educational needs and for children experiencing multiple disadvantages (Sylva et al., 2010).

Structural characteristics – which features of early years environments are the most important for quality?

If it is true that process quality characteristics are most strongly related to children's outcomes, then why should we concern ourselves with structural characteristics such as ratios, qualifications and group sizes? Although the evidence for process quality is stronger, there is evidence that structural characteristics *do* influence child outcomes. For example, the EPPE study found that children made more progress in pre-school centres where staff had higher qualifications, particularly if the manager was highly qualified (Sylva et al., 2010). There is also evidence that structural characteristics have an *indirect* effect on children's outcomes via their effects on process quality.

That is, structural characteristics such as ratios and qualifications influence process quality, which in turn influences child outcomes (LoCasale-Crouch et al., 2007). The NICHD study found, for example, that higher levels of practitioner training and better staff–child ratios were associated with higher quality of staff–child interactions, which in turn were associated with improved cognitive outcomes for children (NICHD, 2002).

If structural quality characteristics can influence process quality, then they can also provide us with a means of improving it. Howes and Brown (2000) make a good case for improving quality via what they term 'structural remedies', pointing out that they are more easily changeable via regulation and policy. They also argue that, where early years funding and training are lacking, amendments via structural means are necessary before process quality can be improved. However, to be effective in improving process quality via structural means, we need to know which characteristics of early years settings are most closely related to process quality. In this section we focus on some key research studies that have considered the relationships between structural and process quality.

Staff qualifications and staff–child ratios are two of the characteristics most consistently identified as important. Looking first at qualifications, Siraj-Blatchford et al. (2006) note that having a 'well trained and qualified staff with a good understanding of child development and pedagogy' is a key component of high quality. Particularly important are specialised or sector-specific qualifications with a focus on early care and education, and graduate level qualifications (Burchinal et al., 2002; Fukkink and Lont, 2007; Sylva et al., 2010).

One of the most recent studies in England to explore the effects on quality of staff qualifications was the Evaluation of the Graduate Leader Fund (GLF; Mathers et al., 2011). This evaluation was designed to assess the impact of the graduate level Early Years Professional Status (EYPS)[2] on quality in the private, voluntary and independent sectors, and it also explored the effects of other early years qualifications. The research team used the ECERS–R, ECERS–E and ITERS–R scales to assess quality in over 238 early years settings at two time-points. Information was also gathered on the characteristics of the settings, including the qualifications of the whole staff team. Changes in quality between the baseline and follow-up time-points were analysed to compare the progress made by settings that gained an EYP during that time and settings that did not (whilst controlling for other possible influences on quality).

The findings showed that settings that gained an EYP during the course of the study made statistically measurable improvements in quality for pre-school children (as measured by the ECERS–R and E) compared with settings that did not. EYPs were found to improve the quality of support for children's communication, language and literacy, their reasoning and thinking skills, and their scientific understanding. Other gains were seen in the provision of developmentally appropriate schedules for children, and the way in which their individual needs were catered for. EYPs questioned as part of the study reported that the Early Years Foundation Stage (EYFS) had acted as a catalyst for many of the improvements in child-led learning and meeting the needs of the individual child.

Evidence from the EPPSE research also highlights the importance of graduate leadership; the research team found that having qualified trained teachers working with children in pre-school settings (for a substantial proportion of time, and most importantly as the pedagogical leader) had the greatest impact on quality, and was linked with better child outcomes in pre-reading and social development (Sylva et al., 2010).

Although graduate leadership is important, teachers and other leaders do not work in a vacuum, and the qualifications of the broader staff team will make a difference as well. Both the review of the EYFS (Tickell, 2011) and Cathy Nutbrown's recent review of early years qualifications (Nutbrown, 2012) acknowledge that the bar needs to be raised for the qualifications of the workforce as a whole. In support of this, evidence from both the GLF and the EPPSE studies found that the higher the overall qualification level of the staff team, the more developmental progress the children made.

As well as considering the qualifications of their workforce, leaders of settings should also carefully consider staff deployment in order to achieve maximum quality gains. For example, research shows that both quality and children's outcomes (e.g. language skills, social skills and secure attachments) are better where ratios are higher, and there is particularly convincing evidence that ratios are important for under 3s (e.g. Burchinal et al., 2000; NICHD ECCRN 2000a, 2002; Munton et al., 2002). In the GLF evaluation, rooms with fewer children per staff member offered higher overall quality, as well as higher quality personal care routines and a more appropriate and individualised schedule for infants and toddlers.

In addition to the overall ratios of staff to children, the deployment of the most highly qualified staff must also be considered. For example, the GLF evaluation found that EYPs were more influential on the quality of practice in their own rooms than in rooms in which they did not work; and the more time they spent working hands-on with children, the greater impact they had on quality. While this finding is perhaps not surprising, and reflects the role of EYPs as leaders of practice, it does highlight the importance of making sure that staff with the knowledge and abilities to disseminate good practice are able to do so across the setting, rather than restricting their leadership to specific rooms or age ranges. One striking finding was that, while 91% of EYPs taking part in the study worked in the pre-school rooms observed as part of the research, only 44% worked in the infant/toddler room observed. The low number of EYPs working with under 3s was cited as a possible reason for the lack of identifiable impact of the EYPS on quality for this age range.

While we might search for a simple solution or formula for high quality provision, the truth is that no single regulable characteristic – not even qualifications – guarantees high quality (Cryer et al., 1999; LoCasale-Crouch et al., 2007). As Scarr and colleagues wisely note 'what actually happens in classrooms ... is not adequately captured by most variables one can legislate and regulate' (1994: 149). Many of the factors that lead to high quality, such as good leadership, a positive ethos, a committed staff team, high quality staff support and professional development, are both harder to measure and harder to regulate for. However, the research evidence shows that, while we cannot rely on structural measures such as qualifications and ratios to ensure quality, they can provide a strong underpinning, enabling staff to make the most of their skills and providing the bedrock for high quality provision.

A final note of interest is provided by the GLF evaluation, and relates to the way in which we plan for improvement, and make changes designed to raise quality and outcomes. Many of the settings visited as part of the research made significant changes designed to improve quality between the baseline and follow-up assessments, for example physical changes to the building (e.g. a new layout or outdoor environment), changes in management (e.g. a new manager), or different ways of dividing up the children (e.g. a move to family groupings). In other settings, changes had occurred which might be considered as detrimental to quality, for example a large recent turnover of staff. The analysis showed that, whatever the purpose of the change, this measure of 'upheaval' was one of the strongest predictors of quality; settings that had experienced a greater number of changes were of lower quality. This finding that change can be disruptive in the short term reminds us that settings need to devote time and energy to settling in following a large change (even where this change is ultimately for the better) and that constant change might make it more difficult to provide a consistently high quality environment for children. It also highlights the importance of planning when implementing changes, in order to ensure the least disruption for staff and children.

Choosing appropriate quality measures

We have seen that the quality of early education and care matters, not only because it affects the everyday experiences of children but because research suggests that investing in high quality early years provision in the formative years of a child's life makes a significant difference to their long term life chances. Both process and structural quality have a role to play in shaping children's development, although studies suggest the positive effects are stronger for process quality than for structural quality.

The goal, then, is to work towards improving the quality of provision experienced by young children. As set out in the introduction to this chapter, in order to improve quality we must first be able to define it, and also to measure or evaluate it. Many different tools exist to measure both process and structural quality, several of which have been discussed in this chapter.

The choice of tool for evaluating quality is absolutely fundamental because, as Pianta notes, 'what gets measured gets done' (2012: 7). That is, the aspects or dimensions of quality included in a measure will ultimately be the aspects that are focused upon in efforts to improve practice. Therefore, in order to do the best job in terms of improving quality we must ensure that our measures capture the aspects of quality which are important.

One key criterion is that measures capture the dimensions of quality that are predictive of children's development (i.e. they are validated by research). However, as we saw earlier in this chapter, it is also important that measures reflect the local context and the perspectives of different stakeholders. Each stakeholder group will have their own concept of what quality looks like, and of which aspects are particularly important. Each will also have a different role to play in improving quality, and therefore have slightly different needs in terms of the measures they use. For example:

- researchers need effective tools to support them in identifying which aspects of quality shape specific child outcomes, in order to inform policy and practice;
- policymakers in central government need to be able to identify where investment is needed in order to improve outcomes for young children;
- local authorities need to be able to prioritise funding, support and training using evidence-based decisions, and to encourage providers in quality improvement;
- providers need effective tools to identify their own strengths and possible areas for development, in order to improve the quality of the provision they offer; and
- parents need tools to help them to select high quality provision for their children.

Zaslow and colleagues (2011) argue that the measures we choose for improving quality will depend greatly on our role and context, and that the choice of measure should be informed by the purpose for which it will be used. In essence, different tools are needed for different jobs. A researcher exploring the relationships between individual aspects of quality and children's outcomes may need a very specific measure, while a setting manager wishing to evaluate and improve quality may need a more global and comprehensive measure covering many different dimensions. The authors acknowledge that there may be great advantages in using one quality measure for several purposes, but warn that care should be taken when using a single tool for multiple purposes. For example, a parent wanting to choose an early years setting for their child may be overwhelmed by the amount of information provided by a tool developed for research, or one that is designed to provide settings with detailed information to guide improvement.

A recent research study considered some of these issues within the English context, focusing on the most common quality measures used for regulation, quality improvement and research, including Ofsted inspection reports, the Environment Rating Scales (ECERS and ITERS), and quality assurance schemes (Mathers et al., 2012). One of the primary goals was to establish how well these measures captured quality, and how useful they were to different stakeholder groups. No single measure reflected all the aspects of quality valued by stakeholders, with each meeting different needs according to their purpose. Thus, a broad range of tools is needed to reflect multiple perspectives. The study also looked at the relationships *between* the different measures, for example between the grades awarded by Ofsted and scores on the ECERS and ITERS. While there was a broad alignment between the two measures, there were also many cases where they did not align with each other, and the study concluded that they largely captured different dimensions of quality. The fact that Ofsted grades do not fully reflect quality as measured by the Environment Rating Scales is important because research has shown that ECERS and ITERS scores are good predictors of children's long-term success (e.g. Sylva et al., 2010), while the evidence for the 'predictive power' of Ofsted grades is less clear (Hopkin et al., 2010). Ofsted inspections provide parents, providers and local authorities with an external measure, help to ensure certain standards are met and provide public accountability. However they are not designed to fulfil all needs for identifying and improving quality.

In summary then, it is important to use multiple tools to provide us with a full and rich picture of quality, and to carefully consider our purpose when selecting the measures we use. Whatever our purpose, we must be critical of our quality measures, using a wide range to meet different needs; matching the tool to the purpose; and asking whether they capture the dimensions of quality which we value, but also which have been shown by research as being related to children's outcomes.

Key points to remember

- Quality in early childhood education is a contested matter.
- Process and structural quality are both related to children's outcomes, but the effects of process quality are stronger.
- There is evidence that structural quality characteristics such as ratios and qualifications can influence process quality.
- Each quality measure has different strengths and limitations. The choice of any measure should depend on the *use* to which it will be put and the *stakeholder* for whom the information is important.
- Multiple tools are needed to capture a rich and full picture of quality.

Points for discussion

- Do you think quality can be defined and measured? Which aspects do you think are universal, and which might vary according to different social or cultural contexts?
- Consider one measure of quality: what is it trying to assess and how successful is it in doing this?
- How might a quality assessment measure developed for research be used to improve practice? Do you know of any examples?

Reflective task

- Reflect on your early years setting, the measures you have in place to ensure and improve quality, and the tools you use to help you identify quality. List the things you think you already do well, and two specific areas you think could be developed further. Note three specific aspects that you plan to develop in your practice.

Notes

1 A meta-analysis is a study that combines the results of several independent studies on the same topic, with the aim of using this larger pool of data to provide firmer evidence than any of the individual studies could do alone.
2 EYPS (Early Years Professional Status) was a graduate level professional accreditation programme for the Early Years sector, launched in 2007. It focused on developing highly skilled practitioners with the ability to lead and support others.
3 The final intake for EYPs was January 2013, and in September 2013 it will be replaced by the Early Years Teacher programme.

Further reading

Mathers, S., Singler, R. and Karemaker, A. (2012) *Improving Quality in the Early Years: A Comparison of Perspectives and Measures*. London: Daycare Trust/ University of Oxford.

Sylva, K., Melhuish, E., Sammons, P., Siraj-Blatchford, I. and Taggart, B. (eds) (2010) *Early Childhood Matters: Evidence from the Effective Pre-School and Primary Education Project*. London: Routledge.

Zaslow, M., Martinez-Beck, I., Tout. K, and Halle, T. (eds) (2011) *Quality Measurement in Early Childhood Settings*. Baltimore, MD: Brookes Publishing.

Useful websites

Useful pages on the Department for Education website:

www.education.gov.uk/childrenandyoungpeople/earlylearningandchildcare/
a0070374/the-importance-of-early-years-education

www.education.gov.uk/childrenandyoungpeople/earlylearningandchildcare/
delivery/education/a0074584/elqualityimprovement

www.education.gov.uk/childrenandyoungpeople/earlylearningandchildcare/
a00199748/review-to-improve-the-training-and-qualifications-for-people-work-
ing-in-the-early-years

www.gov.uk/government/publications/more-great-childcare-raising-quality-and-
giving-parents-more-choice

Links to information/reports from some of the English research studies refer-
enced in the text:

www.education.gov.uk/publications/standard/publicationDetail/Page1/DFE-RR144

www.education.gov.uk/publications/standard/publicationdetail/page1/
DCSF-RR134

http://eppe.ioe.ac.uk/eppe/eppeintro.htm

www.education.gov.uk/publications/RSG/EarlyYearseducationandchildcare/
Page11/SSU/2007/FR/025

www.education.ox.ac.uk/research/fell/research/improving-quality-in-the-early-years/

Useful source for American research relating to early years and to quality:

www.childtrends.org/

To access a variety of additional web resources to accompany this book please
visit: **www.sagepub.co.uk/pughduffy**

References

Arnett, J. (1989) 'Care-givers in day-care centers: Does training matter?', *Journal of Applied Developmental Psychology*, 10, 541–22.

Belsky, J., Vandell, D. L., Burchinal, M., Clarke-Stewart, K. A., McCartney, K., Owen, M. and the NICHD Early Child care Research Network (2007) 'Are there long-term effects of early child care?', *Child Development*, 78, 681–701.

Burchinal, M. R., Cryer, D., Clifford, R. M. and Howes, C. (2002) 'Caregiver training and classroom quality in child care centers', *Applied Developmental Science*, 6 (1), 2–11.

Burchinal, M., Kainz, K. and Cai, Y. (eds) (2011) 'How well do our measures of quality predict child outcomes? A meta-analysis and coordination analysis of data from large-scale studies of early childhood settings', in M. Zaslow, I. Martinez-Beck, K. Tout and T. Halle (eds), *Quality Measurement in Early Childhood Settings*. Baltimore, MD: Brookes Publishing. pp. 11–31.

Burchinal, M. R., Roberts, J. E., Riggins Jr, R., Zeisel, S. A., Neebe, E. and Bryant, D. (2000) 'Relating quality of center-based child care to early cognitive and language development longitudinally', *Child Development*, 71, 339–57.

Cryer, D., Tietze, W., Burchinal, M., Leal, T. and Palacios, J. (1999) 'Predicting process quality from structural quality in preschool programs: a cross-country comparison', *Early Childhood Research Quarterly*, 14, 339–61.

Fukkink, R. and Lont, A. (2007) 'Does training matter? A meta-analysis and review of caregiver training studies', *Early Childhood Research Quarterly*, 22, 294–311.

Harms, T., Clifford, R. M. and Cryer, D. (2005) *Early Childhood Environment Rating Scale-Revised*. New York, NY: Teachers College Press.

Harms, T., Cryer, D. and Clifford, R. M. (2003) *Infant/Toddler Environment Rating Scale-Revised*. New York, NY: Teachers College Press.

Hopkin, R., Stokes, L. and Wilkinson, D. (2010) *Quality, Outcomes and Costs in Early Years Education. Report to the Office for National Statistics*. London: National Institute of Economic and Social Research.

Howes, C. and Brown, J. (2000) 'Improving child care quality: a guide for Proposition 10 commissions', in N. Halfon, E. Shulman, M. Shannon and M. Hochstein (eds), *Building Community Systems for Young Children*. Los Angeles, CA: UCLA Center for Healthier Children, Families and Communities. pp. 1–24.

Howes, C., Mashburn, A., Pianta, R., Hamre, B., Downer, J., Barbarin, O., Bryant, D., Burchinal, M. and Early, D.M. (2008) 'Measures of classroom quality in pre-kindergarten and children's development of academic, language and social skills', *Child Development*, 79, 732–49.

LoCasale-Crouch, J., Konold, T., Pianta, R., Howes, C., Burchinal, M., Bryant, D., Clifford, R., Early, D. and Barbarin, O. (2007) 'Observed classroom quality profiles in state-funded pre-kindergarten programs, and classroom character-istics', *Early Childhood Research Quarterly*, 22, 3–17.

Mashburn, A. J., Pianta, R. C., Hamre, B. K., Downer, J. T., Barbarin, O. A., Bryant, D., Burchinal, M., Early, D. M. and Howes, C. (2008) 'Measures of classroom quality in prekindergarten and children's development of academic, language, and social skills', *Child Development*, 79, 732–49.

Mathers, S., Ranns, H., Karemaker, A. M., Moody, A., Sylva, K., Graham, J. and Siraj-Blatchford, I. (2011) *Evaluation of the Graduate Leader Fund: Final Report*. DFE-RB144. London: Department for Education.

Mathers, S., Singler, R. and Karemaker, A. (2012) *Improving Quality in the Early Years: A Comparison of Perspectives and Measures (Final Report)*. London: Daycare Trust/University of Oxford.

Moss, P. and Dahlberg, G. (2008) 'Beyond quality in early childhood education and care – languages of evaluation', *New Zealand Journal of Teachers' Work*, 5 (1), 3–12.

Munton, T., Mooney, A., Moss, P., Petrie, P., Clark, A., Woolner, J., Barclay, L., Mallardo, M R. and Barreau, S. (2002) *Research on Ratios, Group Size and Staff Qualifications and Training in Early Years and Childcare Settings.* Thomas Coram Research Unit, Institute of Education, University of London: Queen's Printer.

Munton, A. G., Mooney, A. and Rowland, L. (1995) 'Deconstructing quality: A conceptual framework for the new paradigm in daycare provision for the under eights', *Early Childhood Development and Care*, 114, 11–23.

NICHD Early Childcare Research Network (ECCRN) (1996) 'Characteristics of infant child care: Factors contributing to positive caregiving', *Early Childhood Research Quarterly*, 11: 269–306.

NICHD Early Child Care Research Network (ECCRN) (1999) 'Child outcomes when child care center classes meet recommended standards for quality', *American Journal of Public Health*, 89, 1072–7.

NICHD Early Child Care Research Network (ECCRN) (2000a) 'Characteristics and quality of child care for toddlers and preschoolers', *Applied Developmental Science*, 4, 116–35.

NICHD Early Child Care Research Network (ECCRN) (2000b) 'The relation of child care to cognitive and language development', *Child Development*, 71, 960–80.

NICHD Early Child Care Research Network (ECCRN) (2001) 'Child care and Children's Peer Interaction at 24 months: The NICHD Study of Early Child Care', *Child Development*, 72 (5), 1478–500.

NICHD Early Child Care Research Network (ECCRN) (2002) 'Child-care structure, process, outcome: direct and in-direct effects of child-care quality on young children's development', *Psychological Science*, 13, 199–206.

NICHD Early Child Care Research Network (ECCRN) (2003) 'Does quality of child care affect child outcomes at age 4½?', *Developmental Psychology*, 39, 451–69.

NICHD Early Child Care Research Network (ECCRN) (2005) 'Duration and developmental timing of poverty and children's cognitive and social development from birth through third grade', *Child Development*, 76, 795–810.

Nutbrown, C. (2012) *Foundations for Quality: The Independent Review of Early Education and Childcare Qualifications: Final Report* (Nutbrown Review). London: Department for Education.

Peisner-Feinberg, E. S. and Yazejian, N. (2010) 'Research on program quality. The evidence base', in P. W. Wesley and V. Buysse (eds), *The Quest for Quality. Promising Innovations for Early Childhood Programs*. Baltimore, MD: Brookes Publishing.

Pianta, R. C. (2012) *Implementing Observation Protocols Lessons for K-12 Education from the Field of Early Childhood*. Washington, DC: Center for American Progress.

Pianta, R. C., La Paro, K. M. and Hamre, B. K. (2007) *Classroom Assessment Scoring System*. Baltimore, MD: Brookes Publishing.

Scarr, S., Eisenberg, M. and Deater-Deckard, K. (1994) 'Measurement of quality in child care centers', *Early Childhood Research Quarterly*, 9, 131–51.

Siraj-Blatchford, I. and Wong, Y. (1999) *Defining and Evaluating 'Quality' Early Childhood Education in an International Context: Dilemmas and Possibilities*. London: Routledge.

Siraj-Blatchford, I., Milton, E., Sylva, K., Laugharne, J. and Charles, F. (2006) *Monitoring and Evaluation of the Effective Implementation of the Foundation Phase (MEEIFP) Project across Wales.* Cardiff: WAG.

Smith, R., Schneider, V., Purdon, S., La Valle, I., Wollny, Y., Owen, R., Bryson, C., Mathers, S., Sylva, K. and Lloyd, E. (2009) *Early Education Pilot for Two Year Old Children – Evaluation.* Research Report DCSF-RR134. London: Department for Children, Schools and Families.

Soucacou, E. and Sylva, K. (2010) 'Developing observation instruments and arriving at inter-rater reliability for a range of contexts and raters: The early childhood environment rating scales', in G. Walford, E. Tucker, and M. Viswanathan (eds), *The Sage Handbook of Measurement.* London: Sage. pp. 61–85.

Sylva, K. and Roberts, F. (2009) 'Quality in early childhood education: evidence for long-term effects', in G. Pugh and B. Duffy (eds), *Contemporary Issues in the Early Years*, 5th edn. London: Sage. pp. 47–62.

Sylva, K., Melhuish, E., Sammons, P., Siraj-Blatchford, I. and Taggart, B. (2010) *Early Childhood Matters. Evidence from the Effective Pre-School and Primary Education Project.* London: Routledge.

Sylva, K., Siraj-Blatchford, I. and Taggart, B. (2003) *Assessing Quality in the Early Years Early Childhood Environment Rating Scales Extension (ECERS-E). Four Curricular Subscales.* Stoke-on-Trent and Stirling, USA: Trentham Books.

Sylva, K., Siraj Blatchford, I., Taggart, B., Sammons, P., Melhuish, E., Elliot, K. and Totsika, V. (2006) 'Capturing quality in early childhood through Environmental Rating Scales', *Early Childhood Research Quarterly*, 21 (1), 76–92.

Tickell, C. (2011) *The Early Years: Foundations for Life, Health and Learning: An Independent Report on the Early Years Foundation Stage to Her Majesty's Government* (Tickell Review). London: Department for Education.

Vandell, D. L., Belsky, J., Burchinal, M., Steinberg, L., Vandergrift, N. and NICHD Early Child care Research Network (2010) 'Do effects of early child care extend to age 15 years? Results from the NICHD Study of Early Child Care and Youth Development', *Child Development*, 81, 737–56.

Zaslow, M., Tout, K. and Halle, T. (2011) 'Differing purposes for measuring quality in early childhood settings: aligning purpose with procedures', in M. Zaslow, I. Martinez-Beck, K. Tout and T. Halle (eds), Quality *Measurement in Early Childhood Settings.* Baltimore, MD: Brookes Publishing. pp. 389–410.

CHAPTER 5

Inspecting and Evaluating the Quality and Standards of Early Years and Childcare Provision

Brenda Spencer and Jan Dubiel

Chapter contents

- The purpose of inspections
- The types of inspection
- Recent changes in inspection frameworks
- The challenges faced by practitioners and inspectors

Inspection has been a key way governments have attempted to evaluate quality of provision, value for money and compliance to requirements and government policy. Despite tensions and criticism of inspection, it is unlikely to be abandoned. In her review of the Early Years Foundation Stage (EYFS) Tickell remarked 'I believe that we have yet to reach a point where the skills and capacities of the early years workforce have developed far enough for greater self-regulation to become viable' (Tickell, 2011: para 2.5). If the early years workforce does not have the capacity for self-regulation then neither can there be full confidence in its self-evaluation.

The purpose of inspections

In September 2008, as a response to the introduction of the Early Years Foundation Stage (DfES, 2007) in which the learning, development and welfare requirements were brought together as an entitlement of all children from birth to 5 years of age, a common early years evaluation schedule was included in all inspection frameworks. The overriding and common concern was to establish 'How effective is the provision in meeting the needs of children in the Early Years Foundation Stage?' (Ofsted, 2008).

There were different inspection frameworks for different types of provision but these contained a common early years evaluation schedule in which the needs of children were declared to be central to the focus of the inspection. However, the purpose of inspection goes well beyond establishing whether children's needs are met. Broader than the purposes declared by Ofsted, of determining quality, standards and compliance, are the uses to which inspection outcomes are put. From the outcomes of inspection the survival of leaders and institutions are determined, grants given or withheld, the status of settings, be it maintained or academy, decided, and curriculum, staff development and national policies are prioritised. Inspection outcomes feature in the wide-ranging criteria for payment by results being developed for children's centres. They appear in head teachers' performance management targets. The content of frameworks is used to ensure government policy is followed – for example the literacy session in the past, synthetic phonics in the present. 'Fidelity to the programme' is assessed and judgement made. Whatever the original purposes, the uses made of inspection outcomes ensure that the inspection outcome stakes are very high.

The types of inspection

September 2009 was a landmark in the attempt to bring coherence to the entitlements of all children regardless of the provision in which they found themselves. The five outcomes of *Every Child Matters* (DfES, 2003) and common inspection judgements were applied to all settings:

How effective is the provision in meeting the needs of children in the Early Years Foundation Stage?*

How well do children in the EYFS achieve?

How good are the overall personal development and well-being of children in the EYFS?

How effectively are children in the EYFS helped to learn and develop?*

How effectively is the welfare of the children in the EYFS promoted?*

How effectively is provision in the EYFS led and managed?*

(Ofsted, 2008)

The four-judgement scale of Outstanding, Good, Satisfactory, Inadequate applied to all settings, as did the four asterisked judgements. The judgements concerning achievement and personal development were applied in schools, both maintained and independent.

Criticism was levelled that one size cannot fit all because, for example, of differences in opportunities offered by premises, training of staff, ratios, funding and philosophies of education and care. The Tickell Review (Tickell, 2011) surveyed the landscape of early years provision and made recommendations that the government accepted. In its wake came recognition of the differences in provision and acceptance that some aspects of the Early Years Foundation Stage would not apply to all. This in turn has led in 2012 to a fracture in the attempt to provide common evaluation schedules for inspection across the early years sector. The frameworks are different and so too are the evaluation schedules.

Separate inspection frameworks for children from birth to 5 years cover:

- The schools subject to Section 5 inspection:

  o community, foundation and voluntary schools
  o community and foundation special schools
  o maintained nursery schools
  o academics, including sponsor-led academics, academy converter schools, academy special schools, free schools, special free schools, alternative provision free schools, university technical colleges (UTCs), and studio schools (Ofsted, 2012c)

- Independent schools subject to Section 162A inspection
- Early years providers subject to the inspection schedule for registered early years provision
- Children's centres inspections
- Childcare register inspections

Local authority maintained nursery schools, nursery units and reception classes are inspected within the Framework for School Inspection (Ofsted, 2012c) and inspection of early years, in this case nursery and Reception classes, is more or less invisibly subsumed into the 0–19 age range the framework serves. Inspectors must judge the quality of education provided in the school. This is the overarching judgement. In order to make this judgement inspectors must first make four key judgements. These are:

- The achievement of pupils at the school
- The quality of teaching in the school
- The behaviour and safety of pupils at the school
- The quality of leadership in and management of the school

In addition, inspectors must also consider:

- The spiritual, moral, social and cultural development of pupils at the school
- The extent to which the education provided by the school meets the needs of the range of pupils at the school
  (Ofsted, 2012c: 22)

Children attending non-maintained provision are subject to the Evaluation Schedule for inspections of registered early years provision (Ofsted, 2012d). Inspectors will judge the overall quality and standards of the early years provision, taking into account three key judgements:

- How well the early years provision meets the needs of the range of children who attend
- The contribution of the early years provision to children's well-being
- The leadership and management of the early years provision
  (Ofsted, 2012d: 4)

The focus given to children's well-being, welfare and 'meeting children's needs' contrasts with the more academic focus given to 'pupils' in schools.
   The inspection of children's centres differs. Inspectors will judge the effectiveness of the children's centre in meeting the needs of, and improving the outcomes for, families. This judgement takes into account the following:

- The centre's capacity for sustained improvement, including the quality of its leadership and management
- How good are outcomes for families?
- How good is the provision?
- How effective are the leadership and management?
  (Ofsted, 2011: 7–8)

In common with the inspection of maintained schools, inspection of independent schools no longer makes separate judgements about the provision for children in the Early Years Foundation Stage aged between

3 and 5 years. Provision and outcomes for these children are covered in whole school evaluation of:

- Overall effectiveness of the school in meeting its declared aims and whether the school complies with the standards for registration
- Quality of educational provision
- Spiritual, moral, social and cultural development of pupils
- Welfare, health and safety of pupils
- Suitability of staff, supply staff and proprietors
- Premises of and accommodation at the school
- Provision of information

Childcare register inspections do not focus on quality but concern compliance with regulations, and outcomes are judged in terms of meeting or not meeting requirements. As a minimum, inspectors check:

- Suitability of people working with the children
- Documentation and information
- Premises and equipment
- Behaviour management
- Whether ratios are met
  (Ofsted, 2010: 13–14)

The possible outcomes of the compliance check are

- Met
- Not met – actions
- Not met – enforcement action where non-compliance is persistent or significant
  (Ofsted, 2010: 16)

The type of provider critically defines the type of inspection schedule that is followed. The original philosophy of the (Early Years) Foundation Stage strongly asserted the universality of children's experience irrespective of the nature of the provision. However, this does not appear to extend into the current inspection process for children from birth to 5. The different frameworks have different emphases and areas of foci, the judgements follow different patterns, and the nature and scope of the inspection process varies. For example, across all settings, ostensibly the same levels of judgements are made in all inspections concerned with quality: 1 Outstanding, 2 Good, 3 Satisfactory, or 4 Inadequate. However, the actual criteria for attaining the grade differ substantially throughout.

In addition, providers refer to an array of specific documents that, although designed to clarify the different requirements for providers, serve to emphasise the complex range of possibilities that an inspection may include.

Recent changes in inspection frameworks

The inspection frameworks have developed, refined and responded to the changing economic climate and early years context since the beginning of Ofsted's inspection work in September 1994.

Identifying the issues with inspection in the early years is complex. Clarifying where problems lie means deciphering the messages articulated by a very diverse sector and this is not always successful. Since the change of government in May 2010, the commentary on education policy indicates there has been a shift in direction resulting in less guidance and an intention to reduce bureaucracy. The Secretary of State for Education stated that 'We have stopped the weekly bombardment of schools with unnecessary directives and guidance from central Government. We've scrapped the pointless form-filling that was the self-evaluation form and the financial management standard in schools' (Gove, 2011).

Subsequent events indicate that part of the challenge of getting an inspection service fit for purpose is the difficulty in teasing out the exact nature of the criticism being aimed at the service. The Tickell Review (Tickell, 2011), in tune with Gove's comments, reported apparent disgruntlement, expressed not just by teachers but across the diversity of practitioners working in early years, that there was too much bureaucracy. The panel found it difficult to identify where the pressure that led to extensive paperwork originated. The guidance supporting the various types of Ofsted inspections across the early years sector did not require some of the paperwork that was being completed for inspectors conducting the inspections. Nor was it required by QCDA for completion of the EYFS profile.

In an attempt to separate fact from fiction and to reduce unnecessary workload, Tickell wrote:

> to make sure that everyone has the same understanding of requirements, I recommend that Ofsted and local authorities work together to produce clear, consistent information for early years providers and communicate this effectively to all practitioners. This should show how Ofsted will inspect the requirements for what different settings have to do to deliver the EYFS. (Tickell, 2011: para 5.19)

Ofsted is responding by making the procedures yet more transparent. For example, the guidance to inspectors on conducting Section 5 inspections and the evaluation schedule are now to be found in one document, the *School Inspection Handbook*, with effect from September 2012. All the documentation for the different types of inspection is easily found on the Ofsted website.

Despite Tickell's good intentions, fact will not be easily distinguished from fiction. Mixed messages are still evident. Secretary of State Michael Gove has removed the requirement for 'pointless form-filling that was the self-evaluation form'. However, on the first day of a maintained school inspection the lead inspector must make arrangements to have a detailed discussion of the school's self-evaluation (Ofsted, 2012c: 8). In addition, the outcomes of the consultation about the new arrangements for the regulation and inspection of providers on the Early Years Register indicate that the self-evaluation form is desirable. The findings state:

> Respondents were keen for Ofsted to retain the online self-evaluation form with some changes. We will review and revise the online self-evaluation form to make it shorter and less repetitive. In terms of online access and enhanced functionality, we will take the comments made into account as we develop new arrangements for online transactions over the next 12–18 months. (Ofsted, 2012b: 14)

The self-evaluation form is not part of the undesirable bureaucracy. The sector has signalled that it serves as a useful reference point and aide-mémoire for discussion with a range of stakeholders. The response to the review indicates that many settings wish to have some form of recording that draws together its findings on its effectiveness and identifies the ways forward to improved quality of provision and outcomes.

The bureaucracy often arises because settings attempt to keep sufficient evidence for the purposes of accountability and to service inspections. Inspections in the past have invested a large proportion of time in investigating recorded evidence so that first-hand experience of the provision and its impact on children have been sidelined. Ofsted charges itself with the task of making clear and transparent judgements based on sound evidence. However the debate around what is sound evidence is problematic. The Tickell Review observed in its evidence base that practitioners felt inspection was more to do with paperwork than evaluation of provision (DfE, 2011: para 6.4–5). In order to bring clarity to the situation, Tickell made the following recommendation: 'Ofsted and local authorities should not be asking to see overly detailed records, but rather talking directly to practitioners about their methods for checking children's progress' (Tickell, 2011: para 3.39, p. 30)

Ofsted had already moved from some previous inspection practice of spending considerable amounts of time validating settings' own self-assessment and interrogating paperwork to instructing in Section 5 inspections: 'Inspectors must spend as much time as possible in classes, observing lessons, talking to pupils about their work, gauging their understanding and their engagement in learning, and obtaining their perceptions of the school' (Ofsted, 2012c: para 22, p. 10). And while observing, inspectors had to be aware of the following guidance: 'the key objective of lesson observations is to evaluate the quality of teaching and its contribution to learning' (Ofsted, 2012c: para. 25, p. 10).

These key messages from the Section 5 handbook about the importance of first-hand evidence of the quality of provision over paperwork chime well with the evaluation schedule for inspection of registered early years provision implemented September 2012, which states 'the main evidence comes from inspectors' direct observations of the way in which children engage with their environment through play, exploration and active learning, and practitioners' input in facilitating learning' (Ofsted, 2012d: para 14, p. 7).

However, there is much scope still for anxiety-led bureaucracy, as the guidance also states:

> Direct observation should be supplemented by a range of other evidence to enable inspectors to evaluate the impact that practitioners have on the progress children make in their learning. Such additional evidence should include:

> - evidence of assessment that includes the progress of different groups of children:

>   - assessment on entry, including parental contributions
>   - 2-year-old progress checks (where applicable)
>   - ongoing (formative) assessments, including any parental contributions
>   - the Early Years Foundation Stage Profile (where applicable) or any other summative assessment when children leave
>   - evidence of planning for children's next stages of learning based on staff assessment and a secure knowledge of the characteristics of learning and children's development

> - evidence from observations, including:

>   - the inspector's own observations of children's responses to activities
>   - any joint observations with managers or early years professionals
>   - any evidence of practitioners' observations

> - the inspector's tracking of selected children, including children of different ages, funded 2-year-olds and other children whose circumstances may suggest they need particular intervention or support
> - discussions with practitioners, key persons, managers, parents and children. (Ofsted, 2012d: para 15, p. 7)

The latest guidance to inspectors does not clarify what is 'overly detailed' or indeed sufficient evidence and this is in danger of undermining the pre-eminence of direct observation as the most important route to evaluating quality:

> Inspection moving further from interrogation of paperwork towards gaining first hand experience of the provision is not without difficulty, as is identified by a parent. 'Ofsted (or the inspection bodies) need to have clearer guidelines that they all go by as at the moment your inspection totally depends on the inspector's point of view, what one likes another could hate, and we have experienced this a lot.' (Parent quoted in DfE, 2011: 52)

The diversity of provision in early years means there are likely to be lots of differing views of the best way to educate and care for children. Parents are able to choose for their children between, for example, an intimate setting in a childminder's home or the larger provision found in some children's centres or maintained nursery schools and classes. The difficulty of coming to objective judgements on the quality and the suitability of an individual setting for a particular child may be exacerbated by the move away from what are currently deemed to be 'unnecessary directives and guidance from central Government' (Gove, 2011).

In 2009 there was an attempt to bring coherence to the inspection of different kinds of provision in early years by coordinating the criteria and foci of the different inspection frameworks. The frameworks for September 2012 have abandoned this attempt. Children in the early years sector, for example in children's centres and registered early years provision, will have their provision inspected with an early years focus enshrined in the evaluation criteria. While children in community, foundation and voluntary schools, community and foundation special schools, maintained nursery schools, academies, including sponsor-led academies, academy converter schools, academy special schools, free schools, special free schools, alternative provision free schools will not.

A key change in Section 5 inspections and those conducted in independent schools from September 2012 is the removal of evaluation relating exclusively and specifically to early years. The Section 5 framework implemented September 2009 evaluated in common with other frameworks:

- Outcomes for children in the early years foundation stage – the extent to which children enjoy their learning and achieve well, feel safe, learn to lead healthy lifestyles, make a positive contribution, and to develop skills for the future
- The quality of provision – how well children are helped to learn and develop and how effectively children's welfare is promoted
- The effectiveness of leadership and management in the Early Years Foundation Stage
- Overall effectiveness – how well the needs of children are met and the capacity to make improvement or sustain high standards.
  (Ofsted, 2009)

The links with the themes and commitments of EYFS prior to the 2012 inspection frameworks were made clear by italicising all references to them in the inspection evaluation schedule. Descriptors were tailored to reflect the unique character of early years provision such as 'assessment through high quality observation is rigorous', and 'teaching is rooted in expert knowledge of the learning and development requirements'. Inspectors were guided to take account of 'the extent to which there is planned, purposeful *play and exploration*, both in and out of doors, with a balance of adult-led and child-led activities that foster *active learning*' (Ofsted, 2009: 60).

The judgement descriptors in the Section 5 inspection framework 2012 no longer guide inspectors on how to reflect on assessment, for example in ways that acknowledge the specific characteristics of early years practice. For example, in teaching that is Outstanding 'consistently high quality marking and constructive feedback from teachers ensures that pupils make rapid gains'. This descriptor no longer recognises the role of observation in high quality assessment. Inspectors could be encouraged to seek out marked work where such practice would be inappropriate and counter-productive in supporting learning and development of young children (Ofsted, 2012c: 35).

Comparison with part of the descriptor for good provision from the evaluation schedule of registered early years provision shows a difference in the focus:

> The vast majority of practice is based on a secure knowledge and understanding of how to promote the learning and development of young children ... the educational programmes have depth and breadth across the seven areas of learning ... practitioners ... regularly listen perceptively to, carefully observe and skilfully question children during activities ... (Ofsted, 2012d: 8)

The concerns expressed by the parent in the quotation above about differences in points of view of different inspectors may be deepened rather than resolved by less guidance for inspectors and practitioners, and a generalist inspection framework for schools. The language used – pupils in schools and children elsewhere – suggests differences in what might be considered appropriate provision.

The challenges faced by practitioners and inspectors

Ofsted states:

> we inspect and regulate services which care for children and young people, and those providing education and skills for learners of all ages. The aim of all this work is to promote improvement and value for money in the services we inspect and regulate, so that children and young people, parents and carers, adult learners and employers benefit. (www.ofsted.gov.uk/about-us)

The challenge faced by both practitioners and inspectors is to ensure that the declared aim is achieved. An evaluative process is vital in ensuring that provision is 'fit for purpose', of an acceptable quality and provides the entitlement to conditions for successful learning and development. However, the findings of the Tickell Review (Tickell, 2011) gave substance to much-aired anecdotal evidence that the aim of supporting excellence in care, education and skills sometimes does not match the process and effect of inspection.

Inspections are often described as having 'high stakes'. This can lead to an atmosphere of fearfulness surrounding both the inspections and the anticipation of them. The apprehension felt by practitioners regarding the experience and consequences arising from judgements reached by an Ofsted inspection often generates a sense of 'compliance anxiety' that can unduly and disproportionately influence approaches to practice and provision. There appears to be an underlying question of 'What do Ofsted want?' that drives and determines what practitioners do.

Much of this tension revolves around the nature of *what* is being inspected, the necessarily short time frame within which inspectors operate and the nature of the evidence used to form judgements. Provision driven by guessing what Ofsted inspectors want or worse still making that up is the tail wagging the dog. Key to resolving this tension is practitioners ensuring their practice is underpinned by principle and practitioners being confident in articulating these principles. This is particularly important in those inspections where inspection of early years is subsumed within criteria for other key stages and the small inspection team may contain no individual with experience of teaching the early years age group.

The recent changes in inspection frameworks reinforce the importance of inspectors gaining first hand evidence in determining the quality provision. This may rectify practice in the past where judgements have been underpinned by 'convenient' rather than authentic evidence. Judgements have been heavily dependent on what is seen as inappropriately forensic analysis of numerical data (DfE, 2011: para 6.4–6.5). This is regardless of the fact that, apart from EYFS Profile data, no such consistent data are available for children in the EYFS. Attainment and progress data derived from recording stages of development described by *Development Matters* (Early Education, 2012; and see DCSF, 2008) are not subject to a nationally evaluated moderation system. There is no requirement for local authorities or for the Standards and Testing Agency to evaluate the accuracy of judgements made prior to the end of the EYFS, that is, those judgements that are not summarised by the EYFS profile. When this is coupled with the developmental reality that children's progression is unpredictable, idiosyncratic and unlikely to be numerically measurable, doubt is then cast over the effectiveness of any approach that relies on data to determine achievement and quality of provision. The danger is that the inspectors whose experience is not steeped in early years practice will seek confidence from analysing figures and not give due emphasis to the story that is unravelled before their eyes when they observe the provision and its impact on children's well-being, learning and development.

This tension often manifests itself in specific aspects. As practitioners attempt to answer their self-imposed question 'What do Ofsted want?' they can feel compelled to produce reams of 'recorded' evidence: annotated photographs, detailed observations and progress data. This is a compulsion not required by the official inspection guidance. Often, this collection of evidence is far in excess of what practitioners would normally produce for their own information, but is created purely to give authenticity to the stories they can tell about individual children. When questioned, practitioners are aware that it is primarily their knowledge of the child that informs their pedagogy, provision and identification of appropriate steps of development; however, under the duress of 'compliance anxiety', producing a weight of unnecessary paperwork often triumphs. The challenge for practitioners is to be informed both about the essence of good early years practice and about the guidance for inspectors concerning how to evaluate the quality of provision and standards. And be ready to articulate this. Information is power. The inspection handbooks, evaluation schedules and frameworks should be common knowledge. Unless this is the case the practitioner cannot drive the agenda of inspection towards its aim of securing improvement but instead becomes a servicer of what may be a wayward journey.

Equally, the high stakes influence of Ofsted inspections can often blur practitioners' understanding and perception of national documentation and expectations. An obvious and significant example of this is the status of the overlapping age-related stages in *Development Matters* in both the current (Early Education, 2012) and previous (DCSF, 2008) EYFS documentation. In both cases these are clearly labelled as non-statutory guidance. They can be used, if required, in a judicious and flexible manner by practitioners to enable them to support the development of children in their setting to progress towards the statutory Early Learning Goals. However, Ofsted guidance for inspecting the EYFS refers to them alongside the statutory EYFS (Ofsted, 2012d: 4), thus endowing them with a quasi-statutory status, and raising the expectation amongst providers and inspectors that their use is a requirement. Indeed, the advice to inspectors on how to judge progress in maintained settings has rested entirely on their use by practitioners over the two years from the beginning of Nursery to the end of Reception: 'inspectors should make a professional judgement by taking account of the proportions of children meeting expectations in the age-related bands in Development Matters ...' (Ofsted, 2012a: 5–6).

It is a challenge for both inspection providers and early education and care providers to distinguish between statutory requirements and be able to recognise purposeful ways of documenting or demonstrating attainment and progress without demanding one way for all. This requires a confident and knowledgeable workforce on both sides of the inspection fence.

The most frequently aired perception of Ofsted inspections by EYFS practitioners is that the experience and outcomes rely heavily on the calibre and understanding of the individual inspectors involved. This lack of consistency and variability of some inspectors' knowledge and expertise in early years (it is widely believed that very few have a birth to 5 specialism, particularly those inspecting maintained settings), weighs heavily against the high stakes outcomes and the consequences that an inspection involves. In her review Tickell recommended 'that Ofsted reviews the training, capacity and capability of the current early years inspectorate and existing guidance to inspectors, with a view to setting clear minimum requirements for all early years inspectors in terms of experience, skills and qualifications' (Tickell, 2011: para 5.20). Given that inspection of early years in maintained and independent schools is no longer separately reported it is unlikely that every inspection team reporting on these schools will have an early years specialist. Capable inspectors of early years should be an entitlement of all children in EYFS whose provision is inspected. The loss of an early years section in Section 5 inspections and also shortened guidance for all inspectors mean it is more likely that there may be the diversity of view on quality rather than a resolution of the problem.

The issue that underpins this, and one that is reflected across early years settings in other areas too, is the need for practitioners, managers and head teachers to view Ofsted inspections proportionately and be aware of the information and inconsistencies that surround them. All educators have a primary duty to care for and facilitate the learning and development of the children in their settings. All early years personnel, at whatever level they work, need to empower themselves to be proactive advocates of the appropriate pedagogy and provision for children aged birth to 5, and be prepared to take ownership of the agenda during inspection, rather than have it dictated to them. In practice this means practitioners in settings must have an agreed clear, coherent approach to

- how appropriate progress and development are demonstrated,
- what is relevant and useful evidence of this, and have
- agreed approaches to issues such as recording assessments and the use – or not – of the non-statutory materials.

However, as the Tickell Review reported, practitioners regard inspection as imposing an extra bureaucratic burden and they remain unclear about what is required. Although the documentation surrounding inspection is readily available on the Ofsted website, myths still abound about what is appropriate and sufficient evidence. This is a matter of confidence and knowledge. Given the renewed emphasis on gaining first-hand evidence of quality rather than analysis of paperwork, inspectors must be able to make the leap from observing the involvement of children in their activities and their interactions with adults to what this reveals about achievement and attainment. The challenges within the current inspection process largely mirror wider challenges within the early years community, that is the quality and training of the workforce – inspectors and practitioners.

Key points to remember

- The aim of inspection is to bring about improvement.
- Practitioners must be able to articulate the principles underpinning their practice and need to be familiar with the protocols and purpose of inspection so that they can guide inspectors who may well not be or may never have been knowledgeable early years practitioners.
- Inspectors must be able to interpret what children do and say and their interactions with practitioners so that first-hand observation of the provision becomes the prime way of understanding the quality of what is on offer and of identifying the attainment and achievement of the children in the setting. Inspection should not be a paperwork exercise.

 Points for discussion

- What kinds of evidence will be helpful to keep which would have the primary purpose of understanding the nature of children's learning and planning next steps?
- How far is our understanding of what is required for inspection driven by anecdotal stories and how far by reading the guidance and frameworks available on the Ofsted website?
- When inspecting, what balance should inspection give in time and in making judgements to what is seen to be actually going on and what weight should be given to recorded evidence?

Reflective tasks

- Reflect on the ways you capture the attainment and progress of children in your setting.
- Are you able to articulate the purpose of what you do in terms of supporting learning and development?
- Does the evidence, including practitioner knowledge, give a useful picture of each individual's journey in learning?

Further reading

Ofsted (Office for Standards in Education, Children's Services and Skills) (2011) *The Impact of the Early Years Foundation Stage*. London: Ofsted.

Tickell, C. (2011) *The Early Years: Foundations for Life, Health and Learning. An Independent Report on the Early Years Foundation Stage to Her Majesty's Government* (Tickell Review). London: Department for Education.

Useful websites

www.education.gov.uk/a0068102/early-years-foundation-stage-eyfs
www.foundationyears.org.uk
www.ofsted.gov.uk

To access a variety of additional web resources to accompany this book please visit: **www.sagepub.co.uk/pughduffy**

References

Department for Children, Schools and Families (DCSF) (2008) *Practice Guidance for the Early Years Foundation Stage*. Nottingham: DCSF Publications.

Department for Education (DfE) (2011) *The Early Years Foundation Stage Review: Report on the Evidence*. London: DfE.

Department for Education and Skills (DfES) (2003) *Every Child Matters*. Green Paper. Cm 5860. Norwich: TSO.

Department for Education and Skills (DfES) (2007) *The Early Years Foundation Stage*. Nottingham: DfES Publications.

Early Education (2012) *Development Matters in the Early Years Foundation Stage (EYFS)*. London: British Association for Early Childhood Education. www.early-education.org.uk/sites/default/files/Development%20Matters%20FINAL%20PRINT%20AMENDED.pdf (accessed April 2013).

Gove, M. (2011) Statement in *Times Education Supplement*, 13 May 2011. www.education.gov.uk/inthenews/articles/a0077295/michael-gove-article-in-times-education-supplement (accessed 18 July 2012).

Ofsted (Office for Standards in Education, Children's Services and Skills) (2008) *Inspecting the Early Years Foundation Stage: Guidance for Inspectors, September 2008*. London: Ofsted.

Ofsted (Office for Standards in Education, Children's Services and Skills) (2009) *The Evaluation Schedule for Schools*. Ref. 090098. London: Ofsted.

Ofsted (Office for Standards in Education, Children's Services and Skills) (2010) *Conducting Childcare Register Inspections: Guidance for Inspectors Inspecting those Registered on the Compulsory and Voluntary Parts of the Childcare Register*. Ref. 080174. London: Ofsted.

Ofsted (Office for Standards in Education, Children's Services and Skills) (2011) *Inspection of Children's Centres: Evaluation Schedule and Grade Descriptors*. Ref. 100005. London: Ofsted.

Ofsted (Office for Standards in Education, Children's Services and Skills) (2012a) *Subsidiary Guidance: Supporting the Inspection of Maintained Schools and Academies from January 2012*. Ref 110166. London: Ofsted.

Ofsted (Office for Standards in Education, Children's Services and Skills) (2012b) *Regulation of Providers on the Early Years Register: A Report on the Responses to the Consultation.* Ref. 120037. London: Ofsted.

Ofsted (Office for Standards in Education, Children's Services and Skills) (2012c) *School Inspection Handbook.* Ref. 120101. London: Ofsted.

Ofsted (Office for Standards in Education, Children's Services and Skills) (2012d) *Evaluation Schedule for Inspections of Registered Early Years Provision.* Ref. 120086. London: Ofsted.

Tickell, C. (2011) *The Early Years: Foundations for Life, Health and Learning. An Independent Report on the Early Years Foundation Stage to Her Majesty's Government* (Tickell Review). London: Department for Education.

PART 2

Practice

'Seen and Heard': Exploring Assumptions, Beliefs and Values Underpinning Young Children's Participation

Y. Penny Lancaster and Perpetua Kirby

Chapter contents

- Defining listening to young children within the context of the United Nations Convention on the Rights of the Child, Every Child Matters and the revised Early Years Foundation Stage
- Our view of childhood: a tapestry of assumptions
- Exploring the strands of a 'seen and heard' view of childhood
- Imagined boundaries
- Ethical relationships with children

Introduction

Recent years have been an exciting era in which the emphasis on listening to young children's views in matters that affect them has wrought a dramatic shift in thinking and practice within early years. The assumptions, values, and beliefs that underpin the United Nations Convention on the Rights of the Child (UNCRC), Every Child Matters (ECM) and the Early Years Foundation Stage (EYFS) have played a central role in constructing this emphasis. They have signposted young children's entitlement to expressing their perspectives of their experiences, facilitated an increased understanding of what it means to work with children respectfully and have countered the stance that children are passive recipients in their daily lives. They have largely quashed the adage that children should be seen and not heard and have brought an end to the practice of 'paying lip service' to children's perspectives. As a result, children are increasingly being recognised as active participants in their daily lives, whose perspectives of service provision are valuable within their everyday care, as well as the planning and delivery of children's services. The themes and principles that are embedded in the revised EYFS endorse children's status as stakeholders of early years settings and the importance for practitioners to embark on effective practice that is respectful of children's views as well as their well-being. The guidance acknowledges that effective practice involves:

- understanding that children have an entitlement to be listened to and have their views valued
- respecting what children express, whether communicating visually or verbally
- encouraging children to be involved in choices and decisions, including their own learning journey
- creating opportunities for children to design practical physical environments
- collaborating with children (in creating explicit rules for the care of the environment).

In this chapter, within the context of the UNCRC, as well as ECM (which was in place under the previous Labour government), we will explore the assumptions and values that underpin the practice of listening to young children within early years contexts. We will also consider how current thinking about the notions of 'being' and 'becoming' has implications for listening to young children. We will explore how listening requires a commitment to learning with children and how adults 'become' skilled practitioners in and through their caring relationships with children. Throughout this chapter, we will also include examples of how practitioners are already listening to young children. First, however, it is important to explain what we mean by listening to young children.

Defining listening to young children

Listening to young children is defined here as opportunities in which children are participating in making decisions about matters that affect them in their daily lives. Time, space, caring relationships and genuine choices are key features of listening: time for children to formulate their views and in spaces where children feel comfortable to express their perspectives in ways that they prefer; within positive relationships where together with staff and peers they can explore answers that are not already known; where the opportunities to express preferences, make choices and inform decisions are genuine (including the choice not to participate) (Lancaster and Kirby, 2010). Listening to young children includes taking seriously children's perspectives, whether articulated through visual representations, body language, or talk and ensuring that children receive feedback as to how their perspectives have influenced, or not, outcomes. The responsibility for any outcomes rests, however, with the adult, who is accountable for decisions ultimately made. When children are supported to express a view about their nursery setting, for example, it is the responsibility of staff to decide how to act on this feedback, whilst working closely with children to inform them of changes, and to carry these out together where possible.

Listening to children within the context of the UN Convention on the Rights of the Child

Article 12 of the UN Convention of the Rights of the Child (UNCRC) provides all children with a legal entitlement to express their perspective on matters that concern them. However, this is not an unqualified right. This entitlement includes the condition that adults will give 'due weight' to children's views. Adults are obligated to consider seriously children's capability and perspectives in light of their age and maturity, although it has been made clear that children can have a view even if they do not have 'comprehensive knowledge of all aspects of the matter', if they have 'sufficient understanding to be capable of appropriately forming her or his own views on the matter' (UN Committee on the Rights of the Child, 2009: para. 21). There is an expectation that the role adults play in assessing children's understanding will forge a protective shield around outcomes affecting children. Children's entitlement to have a say in matters that affect them is in effect a space with boundaries. How adults understand the 'due weight' they should afford children's contributions determines the extent to which children's perspectives influence decision-making. Children have an entitlement to participate in decision-making, but it is adults who decide the extent of children's understanding and therefore are by implication ultimately responsible for any decisions made.

Article 5 of the UNCRC also obligates the significant adults in children's lives to take into account the evolving nature of children's cognitive, physical, social, emotional and moral development within decision-making. This is not a passive obligation or a one-off commitment, but rather an active and recurrent responsibility to ensure that the direction and guidance given to children within decision-making is continually adjusted to match children's evolving yet varying social, emotional, cognitive and moral capacities. Article 5 provides children with two significant entitlements: to have increasing autonomy in decision-making according to their evolving capacities *and* to be protected from being responsible for outcomes because of their unevolved capacities (Lansdown, 2005). This, again, is an article which balances children's entitlement to participate in matters that affect them, and protecting them from the responsibility of decisions that are ultimately made. Children are entitled to be encouraged to participate increasingly in decision-making, but within an adult-led supportive framework that protects them from being exposed prematurely to responsibilities beyond their capacities. The boundaries that determine children's participation are not fixed. The boundaries are expected to move, to progressively broaden, so that children gain increasing independence in matters that concern them. How adults make sense of their obligation to judge the extent to which children understand their experiences is likely, however, to be underpinned with their particular belief system. The particular values and assumptions that they hold about what children understand socially, cognitively and emotionally within childhood will mediate what they ultimately understand to be the appropriate 'due weight' they need to place on children's perspectives.

But together Article 12 and Article 5 provide all children with a legal entitlement to engage in decision-making, within a space that ebbs and flows according to their understanding of the particular issue at hand – even the youngest children. By observing babies' facial expressions, body language, noises and time spent engaged with different objects or activities, for example, we can identify and respond to their preferences.

Listening to children within the context of Every Child Matters

Every Child Matters (ECM) was a hugely influential policy initiative that implemented radical reform across social, health and educational services for children. Whilst no longer current government policy, it was under the ECM agenda that the expansion of listening to young children began in earnest and that this chapter was originally written. Its legacy and inclusion for discussion within this updated chapter remains because the language and influence of ECM is still so clearly evident within early years settings, and because ECM highlights a tension in how children's contribution can be viewed.

ECM was underpinned by an explicit assumption that 'children and young people learn and thrive when they are healthy, safeguarded from harm, and engaged' (DfES, 2004). The five interdependent outcome indicators of the ECM Outcomes Framework steered an emphasis towards understanding effective service provision as one that reflects the needs and interests of children, in particular the outcome of 'making a positive contribution'. Underpinning

ECM was an aspiration that children are involved in the designing and planning of service provision and this led to an increase in practice, such as the following example:

Young children planning learning experiences

Two childminders in Kirklees wanted to enable the young children in their care to inform planning, so developed a pictorial system to remember available toys and resources for children to choose what they want to play with. Together children and childminders photographed all the resources, which were then laminated. The cards are kept where the children can easily access them, and they choose from the cards to indicate what activities they want to do. Their engagement in activities they have chosen for themselves is increased and the children build negotiation skills as adults cannot always provide what they want straight away (due to insufficient time or if another child is using the activity). (see Lancaster and Kirby, 2010: 36)

Despite this, the notion of children 'making a positive contribution' highlights a tension. The values and assumptions embedded in the particular aims for this outcome gave rise to a set of mixed messages. 'Making a positive contribution' was defined as children engaging in decision-making and supporting the community and environment, but also, for example, engaging in law-abiding and positive behaviour in and out of school; developing positive relationships and choosing not to bully and discriminate; and developing enterprising behaviour.

On one hand the emphasis on children engaging in decision-making implies that children's perspectives of service delivery are integral to developing effective service provision. This raises children's status. Whilst the other objectives emphasise that if children's contributions to their communities are to be positive, they need support and direction on how to develop particular personal and social skills that promote their well-being, encourage them to be involved in good works, and reduce the behaviour that puts them at risk. While all this is well intended and in children's best interests, 'making a positive contribution' in this sense is about normalising children's behaviour according to pre-determined indicators because they are not yet the appropriate social beings they need to be (Prout, 2005). These objectives focus on shaping children towards becoming appropriate members of society.

The competing aims highlight a potential tension for practitioners in both listening and working towards specified targets and expected outcomes for children. It also raises questions about how children may experience their engagement in decisions within a context that has pre-defined their appropriate engagement and development goals.

Our view of childhood: a tapestry of assumptions

The UNCRC and EYFS continue to offer potential mechanisms for listening to young children in matters that affect them. They provide a platform from which children's status as active participants of their communities can be realised. However, as Prout (2001) has argued the starting point for listening to young children is not the policy initiative, or intention to involve children in decision-making, but rather the belief system that individual practitioners bring to their practice. The assumptions we hold about children and childhood shape children's experiences of decision-making. Children's experiences of early years provision is determined by how practitioners are making sense of the policies they are encouraged to implement (Borko, 2004). ECM's 'making a positive contribution' had the potential to be understood as nothing more than an exercise in learning what is already determined as 'appropriate' decision-making behaviour and skills rather than supporting children to increasingly participate in decision-making that genuinely includes their perspectives of what it means to deliver effective early years provision.

Claire Tickell's (2011) recent review of the EYFS introduced 'characteristics of effective learning' which put a clearer emphasis on children's own views and agendas, by encouraging children, for example, to 'have and develop their own ideas, make links between ideas, and develop strategies for doing things' (DfE, 2012: 7). The review was informed by research emphasising the need for children to feel a level of control over what and how they learn (e.g. Deci and Ryan, 1985). There is limited mention within the EYFS, however, of children informing the design of their setting beyond their personal learning (an exception being the rules for the care of their environment).

Each one of us has in our possession a unique social and cultural lens through which we attempt to make sense of the world and our experiences. This lens is made up of a particular set of assumptions, values, and beliefs that we have acquired from our families, social networks, our experiences of education and the workplace and from our faith community. The particular set that we develop over time helps us to make sense of our experiences and the experiences of others (Vygotsky, 1962; Rogoff, 1990; Prout, 2001; Borko, 2004). These different strands of assumptions and values weave together, so to speak, a tapestry that ultimately informs our practice. They determine the expectations we have of children. For instance, whether children can participate in staff recruitment?

Young children involved in recruitment

At Little Jacks Daycare in Kirklees, children aged 3 to 5 years devised their own questions for candidates interviewed for the new centre manager post. Children were then supported to observe, meet and ask questions of applicants when they came to spend time with them. Afterwards the children were invited to discuss their thoughts and feelings about the candidates with staff, which were fed back to the recruitment panel together with staff observations of the children's body language and verbal comments when meeting the candidates. (see Lancaster and Kirby, 2010: 79)

Our values and assumptions help us think about what children should and should not do and say in different socio-cultural contexts and at different stages within their journey through childhood to adulthood. They also inform the role we believe we should play in children's development; the responsibilities we should shoulder in supporting children to reach their potential, cognitively, socially, emotionally and socially, and the particular relationship we should build with children to achieve this.

We are aware of some of these assumptions, but we also have a set of implicit assumptions. These tend to be deeply entrenched in 'taken for granted' and 'common-sense' language that others may be aware of, but we ourselves are not (Vygotsky, 1962; Foucault, 1984; Fairclough, 1989; Rogoff, 1990; Prout, 2001). Subsequently we may not, at any point in time, ever understand fully the diverse set of assumptions that informs our practice, but what we do have is the option to be committed to pursue awareness and understanding. This involves subscribing to a reflective practice (Lancaster and Kirby, 2010), continually examining our view of childhood and our preferred way of working with children. It is a reflective and dialogical space within which to think and discuss critically our view of childhood: to what extent do we understand children as socially active participants whose perspectives of their experiences are integral in developing effective service provision?

Exploring the strands of a 'seen and heard' view of childhood

Listening to young children is underpinned by the standpoint that children from birth are people in their own right and as such should be recognised as socially active participants of their families, communities, and societies. This assumption fits with the emerging sociology of childhood in which children are ascribed the status of social actors (James and Prout, 1997). Children are active in the construction and determination of their own social lives and the lives of those around them. This locates children as active participants of their lives rather than passive recipients, who have an inherent desire and competency to actively engage with other human beings from birth. Childhood in this view is understood as a social construction and as such makes a distinction between biological and social maturity. Empirical evidence from educationalists, psychologists, anthropologists and sociologists has for some time demonstrated how different children are already accomplishing in a range of childhood contexts (e.g. David, 1986; Malaguzzi, 1993; Ennew, 1994; Mayall, 1996; James and Prout, 1997; Christensen and James, 2000; Clark and Moss, 2001; Brooker, 2002; Jenks, 2005; James, 2007). This understanding has led to a vanguard of advocacy to move beyond understanding children as people who are simply learning and practising for the future. Understanding children as incomplete and in need of childhood to prepare for membership of society, as social *becomings*, is recognised as no longer reflecting children's childhoods.

Work on brain maturation (see for instance Shonkoff and Phillips, 2000; Woodhead, 2005) has shown that children's cognitive, emotional and social development is inextricably linked to the physical and social context in which children are living. This has implications for how we view children's development. Children raised in environments that stimulate their capacities are developing enhanced cognitive, emotional and social skills and moral capabilities. Children are not acquiring competencies merely as a consequence of age, but rather through experiences, the culture they are a member of and the levels of adult support and expectation that are proffered (Lansdown, 2005). This has given rise to re-conceptualising children's development as a combination of social and cultural practices and processes of maturation (Woodhead, 2005) which ultimately leads to children developing their capacities in diverse ways, as recognised within revised EYFS guidance: 'children develop at their own rates, and in their own ways' (Early Education, 2012: 6). This nature and nurture framework understands that the various encounters children experience in different socio-cultural contexts in combination with their individual brain maturation will give rise to differing capacities evolving. As Woodhead (2005) and others (see James and Prout, 1997; Prout, 2005; Qvortrup, 1997) argue, the nature and nurture framework assumes that children's participation in decision-making will facilitate the development of their social, cognitive, and emotional capacities.

A 'seen and heard' view of childhood draws on the understanding that children are socially active participants, who are already contributing to their daily lives, yet who are dependent upon adults to provide stimulating environments that continually facilitate their participation in decision-making, consistent with their evolving understanding, interests and preferred ways of communicating (Lansdown, 2005; Woodhead, 2005).

Imagined boundaries

The empirical evidence of children that has been gathered illustrating children as social actors has helped to shift thinking about how we understand children and childhood. Children are now being understood as socially prepared, adequate, and capable of actively contributing to their social lives and environment, just like adults. This has led to a call to move away from the thinking that children are social becomings and instead acknowledge children as social beings. Subsequently, the binary of 'adults are social beings and children are social becomings' is for the most part discarded as no longer relevant. But is the notion of 'social becomings' obsolete? Recent thinking about how we understand evolving capacities within adulthood has implications for rethinking the notions of social beings and social becomings.

Lee (2001) claims that adulthood can no longer be understood as a state of completeness and competency. The recent emphasis for instance on lifelong learning, with its opportunities to re-skill so as to make employment changes during the life course, has given rise to an understanding that adulthood is a site in which adults are continually evolving their capacities. This is ascribing adulthood as a period within the life course that is not complete; it has an evolving and by implication an unfinished nature. Jenks (2005) suggests that since the process of individuals evolving their capacities is contingent on the presence and communication of 'others' (see Vygotsky, 1962, 1978; Rogoff, 1990) this gives rise to a state of 'becoming'. The other can include children (Lee, 2001; Uprichard, 2008), who have been found, for example, to support their parents to develop technological competencies.

We need to re-conceptualise children and adults therefore as both 'social beings *and* social becomings' (Lee, 2001). We need to understand that adults and children alike are active social beings who are competently contributing to their daily lives and environments, and in the process of evolving their capacities. This reinstates the notion of children as 'social becomings' without compromising their status as 'social beings' and within an account of childhood and adulthood that is interdependent in nature (Prout, 2005). The thinking that understands children as both 'social beings *and* social becomings' helps us to see children in processes of evolving their capacities whilst they are likewise competently contributing to their daily lives, as the following example illustrates.

Young children planning healthy snacks

Children aged birth to 5 were consulted on their preferences for the food available for snacks. The older ones were given a basket with a selection of fruits and encouraged to use their five senses to explore and self-select the contents at their own pace and preference. They had equipment to peel/cut as they explored. A pictorial tally chart of the preferred fruits was used to visually represent the data. Adults and peers gave verbal descriptions and language around

(Continued)

> *(Continued)*
>
> preferences and differences of food, building vocabulary and classification. Key questions put to the children included:
>
> - Which fruit/vegetable would you like to try?
> - Which is your favourite fruit?
> - Which shall we ask Mandy [the cook] to give us for snack?
>
> For the youngest children the key person placed the basket on the floor so the contents could be easily accessed and the children could self-select. Adults observed and took photos to indicate the preferences. The nursery cook was given the results and adapted the menu accordingly. Preferences are reviewed regularly.
>
> (Kirklees Early Years Service, 2008)[1]

Developing ethical relationships with children

Listening is about deepening relationships between adults and children. The EYFS sets out a framework for 'education and care' with guidance emphasising relationships that are 'warm and loving', 'sensitive and responsive to the child's needs, feelings and interests', 'supportive of the child's own efforts and independence' and with clear boundaries (Early Education, 2012: 2). Fielding and Moss (2011) offer a detailed discussion of the importance of an ethic of care in which we are open to what others are saying and might be experiencing, able to reflect and respond, and also the ethics of an encounter in which we recognise and respect the Other's absolute otherness and do not attempt to categorise or make them the Same. They stress that whilst we are each 'irredeemably Other' (p. 49) we are also intrinsically bound to each other and it is through our relationships that together we develop. Noddings (2002), known for her work on the ethics of care (including within education), similarly emphasised this interdependence:

> Without the other's gaze, touch and smile, how would we live? Both carer and cared-for develop as human selves through interactions in which the response is treasured. The young child learns that she is valued and has some control over her own fate ... The caregiver learns to appreciate a full range of human response. (Noddings, 2002: 134)

We as adults therefore 'become' carers, parents and educators in and through our relationships with children (as well as other adults). Mannion (2007) suggests the term 'intergenerational becoming' to capture an understanding of child–adult relations. In this way listening is more relational and less individualistic than simply ensuring children's rights or fulfilling other policy requirements; as Peter Moss and his colleagues described it, 'more "I want to be part of this", less "I know my rights"' (Moss et al., 2005: 9).

Listening to young children offers them opportunities to participate in decision-making while at the same time learning a range of skills and fostering positive relationships, including how to listen respectfully to the views of others, taking into account the needs of others and to negotiate. If listening is viewed simply as an exercise in developing the child, it remains inauthentic and tokenistic, or at worse manipulative. In the following example staff were committed to creating opportunities for children to have a say about the purchase of resources for younger children, but they viewed it as an exercise for children to learn by doing and had decided the desired outcomes in advance.

Listening to children for educational purposes

In an early years setting, 5-year-old children were involved in a consultation to help decide on outside garden toys for another group of younger children in the nursery. They were supported to observe the younger children playing, to see what they liked and disliked, and to decide on new equipment. When asked to reflect on this exercise staff felt their professional training meant they already knew what was best for the younger children, and they felt those aged 5 would not. They saw this exercise primarily as an opportunity for the older children to develop their communication and problem solving skills: 'We had to get children to make the decisions but we worked with them and talked with them to come round to the right decision.' Staff were keen to ensure children choose 'appropriate' equipment for the other children: 'Where there were inappropriate suggestions we would talk through them; work out a way of how the children would reach an appropriate conclusion.'

(Personal correspondence)

The learning above was deterministic without an attempt by staff to understand the younger children's needs *together with* the 5-year-olds (or indeed with the younger children). Drawing on the work of Reggio Emilia (the early years approach in northern Italy), Fielding and Moss (2011) detail how the process of learning more helpfully involves co-construction which includes a process of together creating and re-creating theories:

> This requires listening to thought – the ideas and theories, questions and answers of children and adults alike; treating thought seriously and with respect; and struggling to make meaning from what is said, without preconceived ideas of what is correct or appropriate. (p. 5)

The skilled listening practitioner does, by necessity, guide children towards certain desired norms but where this is done, Noddings (2002) advised, it is through a process of engagement in which children are supported to understand, reflect upon and question those norms together with adults.

As discussed earlier, reflective practice is important for questioning our assumptions about children. By listening we learn about the children in our care, learn to re-see children, and to discover more about how we care and 'become' experienced practitioners in relation to children. Noddings explored what it means to be 'caring' by reflecting on the experience of being in a caring encounter: 'Perhaps the first thing we discover about ourselves as carers is that we are receptive; we are attentive in a special way' (2002: 13), for 'attentive love listens, it is moved, it responds, and it monitors its own action in light of the response of the cared for' (pp. 136–7). This focus on reflective practice is particularly important given how easy it is for adults, within the unequal relationship, to influence, distort or limit how much we hear; to ensure the adults' interests are met above the children's. This includes the role our talk plays, including our body language, in enabling or hindering communication. In the following extract a worker reflects on how she inadvertently creates barriers to encourage young children to talk:

> Where I really failed was to get children responding to each other's talk. ... The first [strategy] has to be to say less and explicitly leave more time for children to comment. The second is resisting commenting on what the children say and to smile, or nod as if in appreciation and then wait in silence. My third strategy will be to look at other children when someone has said something. All these three sound incredibly simple, but I have to ask myself why I did not do it in the first activity. I think the answer is that I have some deep-rooted, unconscious behaviour that makes me use language to be in charge. (Sure Start, 2007: 44–45)

Noddings (2002) stressed the need for dialogue and search for mutual understanding, including solutions to problems, with children; in particular when there is a discrepancy between a child's expressed need and those inferred by the carer. She looked to caring within domestic life to help explore what it might mean for professional practice and so, following her lead, we use below an example of a mother and child undertaking the joint business of buying shoes. Here the mother prioritises the child's inferred physical well-being plus her own concern with affordability and limiting shopping time, whilst giving little space for the child's expressed concern for aesthetics; after reflecting on how the child experienced this dynamic, together they managed to accommodate different priorities.

Competing priorities

A mother and 4-year-old daughter, Rosa, went to buy a pair of shoes. They agreed that Rosa could choose which shoes she wanted as long as they fitted properly. In the shop just two pairs fitted well; Rosa was disappointed as she had wanted another pair with flowers, but reluctantly chose a pair of sandals. She wore these once, but then decided she did not like them and refused to wear them. The mother explained she could not afford to buy another pair and that Rosa had to wear them. She became increasingly frustrated at her daughter's refusal and tears.

The mother then reflected on how important clothes are to Rosa; she had been choosing what to wear each day since she was 2 years old. She accepted she had only gone to one shop because she disliked shopping herself, and had insisted Rosa choose from shoes she was not keen on. The mother recognised that she would never herself buy shoes she did not like.

So the mother talked with Rosa, acknowledged her daughter's disappointment and how clearly getting the right shoes was important; she suggested that when they next buy shoes they set aside more time to go to different shops. But in the mean time they needed together to find a way for Rosa to wear the sandals; they discussed options and Rosa came up with the idea of putting flower stickers on the shoes. They shopped for stickers and Rosa wore the shoes, although they were never her favourite.

(Personal correspondence)

When thinking about the many activities that happen within a typical day in an early years setting, both children and adults are busy making choices about what to do, who to engage with (or not), and how. Children can and do have a degree of relative independence in their day and make decisions alone or with peers (e.g. choosing activities; negotiation with peers); and there are decisions that adults must make (e.g. financial planning; broad curriculum goals), but also many areas where there is room for greater dialogue and collaboration (e.g. planning activities; designing spaces; purchasing resources; recruiting staff). When coming together adults and children may have similar, overlapping or conflicting perspectives; reflecting on these helps to ensure both are heard and responded to, whilst recognising that not everyone's expressed needs can always be met. At the same time as supporting children to achieve the skills and knowledge to achieve greater independence, our caring role demands we both model and promote sensitivity to the views and needs of others, in recognition of our continuing interdependence (Noddings, 2002).

Conclusion

The UNCRC, former ECM and EYFS provide a context in which children's status as active participants of their communities can be realised. However, practices ultimately rely on the assumptions, beliefs and values that we bring to the workplace. Understanding which assumptions and values are mediating our practice requires a commitment to an ongoing reflexivity. Being self-critical of how we understand children and childhood will help us to understand how we are making sense of children engaging in decision-making, of informing and shaping the services we provide.

However, this is not a static process but a journey. Listening to young children involves continually facing challenging nudges, step changes, and shifts of thinking. The thinking that is leading to the call to reinstate understanding children as 'social becomings', without the loss of status of being understood as active social 'beings', is one of these nudges. This dual-natured reconceptualisation takes into account the reality that both adults and children are together in processes of evolving their capacities while they are competently contributing to their daily lives. This helps to make visible the learning that occurs between adults and children without the 'other' being understood as not yet grown up, or incomplete or incompetent. Understanding the life course as 'social beings and social becomings', and one in which adults and children are interdependent, helps us to re-see adult caring roles as those in which we must listen to young children to ensure effective services. Spaces for listening can be inclusive and stimulating spaces in which children feel able to express themselves, where adults and children engage in conversation and joint problem-solving, and learn from one another, but where adults retain ultimate responsibility for outcomes.

Key points to remember

- Listening to young children requires time, spaces where they feel able to express themselves, positive caring relationships and genuine choices. The responsibility for outcomes rests with the adult.
- Adults judge the boundaries to children's involvement according to their particular belief system. Ongoing reflective practice is essential for examining our view of childhood and ways of engaging with children.
- Adults and children are both 'social beings' and 'social becomings'; we 'become' carers in and through our relationships with children.
- Caring roles depend on listening, dialogue and the search for mutual understanding with children. Skilled practitioners guide children towards certain desired norms through a process in which children are supported to understand, reflect upon and question these norms with adults.

Points for discussion

- What values and assumptions mediate your practice of listening to young children?
- What role does your talk and body language play when children are engaging in decision-making?
- In what ways has listening to children helped you 'become' a more ex-perienced practitioner?

Reflective tasks

- Firstly, list all the decisions adults made yesterday within your setting that had some impact on the children in your care. Identify which decisions were made by adults only or together with children. Now consider where there might have been scope to collaborate and hear the children's perspectives within decisions made only by adults.
- How might the children's perspective have influenced the outcomes of these decisions?
- What prevented children from being involved in these decisions?
- What next step could be taken to enable children to influence, understand, reflect upon and question decisions within your setting?

Note

1 Thanks to Gillian Butterfield from Kirklees Early Years Service (KEYS) for her kind permission to include this example in this chapter.

Further reading

Clark, A., Kjørholt, A. T. and Moss, P. (2005) *Beyond Listening: Children's Perspectives on Early Childhood Services*. Bristol: Policy Press.
Lancaster, P. Y. and Kirby, P. (2010) *Listening to Young Children*. Maidenhead: Open University Press and Coram.
Noddings, N. (2002) *Starting at Home: Caring and Social Policy*. London: University of California Press.

Useful websites

Early Years Foundation Stage: www.education.gov.uk/schools/teachingandlearning/curriculum/a0068102/early-years-foundation-stage-eyfs
The work of Nell Noddings: http://www.infed.org/thinkers/noddings.htm

For information and resources on ongoing changes to policy and practice in listening to young children see: www.ncb.org.uk/ecu

To access a variety of additional web resources to accompany this book please visit: **www.sagepub.co.uk/pughduffy**

References

Borko, H. (2004) 'Professional development and teacher learning: mapping the terrain', *Educational Researcher*, 33 (8), 3–15.

Brooker, L. (2002) *Starting School: Young Children Learning Cultures*. London: Open University Press.

Christensen, P. H. and James, A. (2000) *Research with Children*, London: Falmer Press.

Clark, A. and Moss, P. (2001) *Listening to Young Children: The Mosaic Approach*. London: National Children's Bureau.

David, T. (1986) 'One picture is worth a thousand words', *Education 3–13*, 14 (2), 23–27.

Deci, E. L. and Ryan, R. M. (1985) *Intrinsic Motivation and Self-Determination in Human Behavior*. New York: Plenum Publishing.

Department for Education (DfE) (2012) *Statutory Framework for the Early Years Foundation Stage 2012: Setting the Standards for Learning, Development and Care for Children from Birth to Five*. Runcorn: DfE Publications.

Department for Education and Skills (DfES) (2004) *Every Child Matters: Change for Children*. Nottingham: DfES Publications.

Early Education (2012) *Development Matters in the Early Years Foundation Stage (EYFS)*. London: British Association for Early Childhood Education. www.early-education.org.uk/sites/default/files/Development%20Matters%20FINAL%20PRINT%20AMENDED.pdf (accessed August 2012).

Ennew, J. (1994) 'Time for children or time for adults?', in Jens Qvortrup, Marjatta Bardy, Giovanni Sgritta and Helmut Wintersberger (eds), *Childhood Matters: Social Theory, Practice and Politics*. Aldershot: Avebury.

Fairclough, N. (1989) *Language and Power*. Harlow: Longman.

Fielding, M. and Moss, P. (2011) *Radical Education and the Common School: A Democratic Alternative*. London: Routledge.

Foucault, M. (1984) 'Space, knowledge and power', in P. Rabinow (ed.), *The Foucault Reader*. London: Penguin. pp. 239–56.

James, A. (2007) 'Ethnography in the study of children and childhood', in Paul Atkinson, Amanda Coffey, Sara Delamont, John Lofland and Lyn Lofland (eds), *Handbook of Ethnography*. London: SAGE.

James, A. and Prout, A. (eds) (1997) *Constructing and Reconstructing Childhood: Contemporary Issues in the Sociological Study of Childhood*. London: Routledge.

Jenks, C. (2005) *Childhood*. London: Routledge.

Kirklees Early Years Service (2008) *The Listening Book*. Kirklees Council.

Lancaster, P. Y. and Kirby, P. (2010) *Listening to Young Children.* Maidenhead: Open University Press and Coram.

Lansdown, G. (2005) *The Evolving Capacities of the Child.* Innocenti Insight. Florence: UNICEF Innocenti Research Centre.

Lee, N. (2001) *Childhood and Society: Growing Up in an Age of Uncertainty.* Buckingham: Open University Press.

Malaguzzi, L. (1993) 'History, ideas and basic philosophy', in C. Edwards, L. Gandini and G. Forman (eds), *The Hundred Languages of Children.* Norwood, NJ: Ablex.

Mannion, G. (2007) 'Going spatial, going relational: why "listening to children" and children's participation needs reframing', *Discourse,* 28 (3), Special Issue on Pupil Voice in Educational Research, pp. 405–20.

Mayall, B. (1996) *Children, Health and the Social Order.* Buckingham: Open University Press.

Moss, P., Clark, A. and Kjørholt, A. T. (2005) 'Introduction', in Alison Clark, Anne Trine Kjørholt and Peter Moss (eds), *Beyond Listening.* Bristol: Policy Press.

Noddings, N. (2002) *Starting at Home: Caring and Social Care.* London: University of California Press.

Prout, A. (2001) 'Representing children: reflections on the Children 5–16 programme', *Children & Society,* 15 (3), 193–201.

Prout, A. (2005) *The Future of Childhood: Towards the Interdisciplinary Study of Children.* London: RoutledgeFalmer.

Qvortrup, J. (1997) 'A voice for children in statistical and social accounting: a plea for children's right to be heard', in A. James and A. Prout (eds), *Constructing and Reconstructing Childhood: Contemporary Issues in the Sociological Study of Childhood.* London: Routledge.

Rogoff, B. (1990) *Apprenticeship in Thinking: Cognitive Development in Social Context.* New York: Oxford University Press.

Shonkoff, J. P. and Phillips, D. A. (eds) (2000) *From Neurons to Neighbourhoods. The Science of Early Childhood Development.* Washington, DC: National Academy Press.

Sure Start (2007) *Communication Matters Trainer's Pack.* London: Department for Children, Schools and Families.

Tickell, C. (2011) *The Early Years: Foundations for Life, Health and Learning. An Independent Report on the Early Years Foundation Stage to Her Majesty's Government* (Tickell Review). London: Department for Education.

UN Committee on the Rights of the Child (2009) The Right of the Child to be Heard. Fifty-first session, Geneva, 25 May to 12 June. www2.ohchr.org/english/bodies/crc (accessed July 2013).

Uprichard, E. (2008) 'Children as "beings and becomings": children, childhood and temporality', *Children & Society,* 22 (4), 303–13.

Vygotsky, L. S. (1962) *Thought and Language.* Cambridge, MA: MIT Press and Wiley.

Vygotsky, L. S. (1978) *Mind in Society.* Cambridge, MA: Harvard University Press.

Woodhead, M. (2005) 'Early childhood development: a question of rights', *International Journal of Early Childhood,* 37 (3): 79–98.

CHAPTER 7

The Early Years Curriculum

Bernadette Duffy

Introduction

Since Owen and Froebel opened their school and kindergartens in the nineteenth century people have had strong views on what young children need in their early years settings and how this should be organised. Today all 5-year-olds attend schools along with most 4-year-olds. The majority of 3-year-olds now attend an early years setting and more children under 3 attend some form of provision outside the home then ever before (Tickell, 2011). The national rollout out of free places to 40% of 2-year-olds by September 2014 means that numbers will continue to grow significantly. As more and more young children experience provision outside the home, supported by significant public investment, the debate about what they need has involved an ever-widening group of people, some with differing views.

At home parents are supporting babies and young children they know extremely well and are in tune with. However adults outside the home may not share this level of understanding, indeed they are unlikely to when we consider the diverse backgrounds that children entering our provision come from. The Tickell Review of the Early Years Foundation Stage (Tickell, 2011) found that the majority of early years practitioners believe it is important to have an agreed framework to help them fulfil their role, to understand what is important for children at different ages and how best to support children from a range of backgrounds.

But do we have the right framework? This chapter starts with a brief explanation of how the early years curriculum in England has developed and the current framework before going on to look at this key question.

Part One: The current framework and how it has developed

The development of the early years curriculum

The *Curriculum Guidance for the Foundation Stage* (CGFS) (QCA, 2000) was published in 2000, following the launch of the Desirable Learning Outcomes (SCAA 1996), introduced in response to the start of national funding for first 4-year-olds then 3-year-olds. In 2002 the Foundation Stage was made a statutory part of the National Curriculum to ensure that it had the same status as the curriculum for older children. The guidance was warmly welcomed by most practitioners and the Foundation Stage as a distinct phase in education was seen as a success (HM Treasury, 2004). *Birth to Three Matters* (DfES, 2002) (BTTM) signalled an understanding that practitioners also needed guidance for their work with children before the age of 3 and was also well received (Abbott and Langston, 2005). Both documents helped to show that working with young children requires knowledge, skills, insights and commitment and that those who work with this age group play a valuable role.

While each document was appreciated by practitioners it was clear that there was a lack of continuity between their status, principles, aims, pedagogy and content. This lack of continuity and the increasing recognition of the importance of high quality early education led to the decision to create a single framework as part of the 10-year childcare strategy *Choice for Parents, the Best Start for Children* (HM Treasury, 2004). The Early Years Foundation Stage framework (EYFS) became statutory in September 2008 and brought together BTTM and the CGFS; it also incorporated the national standards for daycare and childminding. All providers were required to use the EYFS to ensure that whatever setting parents chose, they could be confident that their child would receive a quality experience that would support their development and learning (DCSF, 2008).

The Coalition government's policy for England

A review of the EYFS had been planned by the Labour administration but with a change of government in 2010 the review was conducted in the context of the changed agenda described in Chapter 1.

Tickell was asked to conduct the review, drawing on evidence from a review of research (Evangelou et al., 2009) and with support from an advisory group. Following widespread consultation, Tickell published her findings in March 2011 (Tickell, 2011). The feedback received demonstrated strong support for the EYFS. Respondents thought the EYFS had had a positive overall impact on children in early years settings. Parents/carers and professionals liked the approach and felt that it encouraged good reflective practice but that there were instances of repetition and opportunities to enhance the framework. Forty-six recommendations were made, including:

- A greater emphasis on the role of parents as partners in their children's learning.
- Introducing a statutory short summary of the child's communication and language, personal, social and emotional, and physical development between the ages of 24 and 36 months.
- A move to prime and specific areas of learning and the recommendation that those working with the youngest children should focus on the prime areas, but that the foundations of all areas are from birth.
- A reduction in Early Learning Goals from 69 to 17 and a slimmed down Early Years Foundations Stage Profile for the end of the foundation years.

The government responded in July 2011 in *Supporting Families in the Foundation Years* (DfE/DH, 2011). The key messages included:

- The first years of life are fundamentally important and children should be able to enjoy their childhood.
- Early intervention is key to improved outcomes for children.
- Parents and families are at the heart of services.

- The primary aim of the foundation years is promoting children's development and while, like school, universal early education may help parents with childcare costs and work commitments, that is not its principal purpose.
- As well as 15 hours per week for 3- and 4-year-olds, 40% of 2-year-olds would be entitled to 15 hours per week free education.
- There is a strong focus on school readiness, so that by 5 years old children are ready to take full advantage of the next stage of learning.

The Department for Education consultation on the revised EYFS statutory framework demonstrated broad support for the changes recommended by the Tickell Review. However, practitioners wanted supplementary information and guidance to help them implement them, and the phrase 'school readiness' was a concern for a significant minority. The final framework was published in March 2012 ready for implementation from September 2012.

The revised EYFS framework

In response to feedback from the early years sector much remains the same in the revised EYFS. The statutory framework continues to consist of *Learning and Development requirements* and *Safeguarding and Welfare requirements*, the only change being the introduction of safeguarding to the title. It sets out the legal requirements relating to learning and development (the early learning goals, the educational programmes and the assessment arrangements) and the requirements relating to safeguarding welfare (safeguarding and promoting children's welfare; suitable people; suitable premises, environment and equipment; organisation; and documentation) (DfE, 2012).

The framework still contains the principles at the heart of the previous EYFS and these underpin practitioners' work with young children whichever setting they attend:

- every child is a **unique child**, who is constantly learning and can be resilient, capable, confident and self-assured;
- children learn to be strong and independent through **positive relationships**;
- children learn and develop well in **enabling environments**, in which their experiences respond to their individual needs and there is a strong partnership between practitioners and parents and/or carers; and
- **children develop and learn in different ways and at different rates**. (DfE, 2012: 3)

There are some changes that reflect the research review and practitioners' feedback on their experience of using the previous EYFS framework. The revised framework includes seven areas of learning, rather than the previous six. While all the areas of learning and development are seen as important and inter-connected three are seen as particularly important as they stimulate curiosity and enthusiasm for learning, and the capacity to learn, form relationships and thrive (DfE, 2012: 4). For those practitioners who remember *Birth to Three Matters* there are clear links with the past. These three areas, the *prime areas of learning*, are the essential foundations for children's life, learning and success and develop through the interaction of children's innate developmental patterns with experiences (Tickell, 2011: 95).

The prime areas are:

- **Communication and Language** – Listening and Attention, and Understanding and Speaking
- **Physical Development** – Moving and Handling, and Health and Self-care
- **Personal, Social and Emotional Development** – Self-confidence and Self-awareness, Managing Feelings and Behaviour, and Making Relationships

The other four areas are called the *specific areas of learning*, and are the areas in which learning developed through the prime areas are applied. They are influenced by the times we live in and society's beliefs about what is important for children to learn (Tickell, 2011: 96).

The specific areas are:

- **Literacy** – Reading and Writing
- **Mathematics** – Numbers and Shape, Space, and Measures
- **Understanding of the World** – People and Communities, The World and Technology
- **Expressive Arts and Design** – Exploring and Using Media and Materials, and Being Imaginative

The areas of learning are about what children learn, but another change to the revised framework is a greater emphasis on how children learn, referred to as the characteristics of effective teaching and learning. These highlight the importance of the child's disposition and attitude to learning and ability to engage in exploration, play and creativity across all areas of learning. The three characteristics are:

- **Playing and Exploring** – children investigate and experience things, and 'have a go'
- **Active Learning** – children concentrate and keep on trying if they encounter difficulties, and enjoy achievements
- **Creating and Thinking Critically** – children have and develop their own ideas, make links between ideas, and develop strategies for doing things. (DfE, 2012: 7)

The EYFS requires early years practitioners to review children's progress and share a summary with parents at two points: between children's second and third birthdays and at the end of the academic year in which they become 5. These are explored in Chapter 8, which looks at assessment, and the possibility of integrating the 2-year-old progress review with the current health review is discussed in Chapter 10.

Guidance on the progress report at 2 years and a refreshed *Development Matters* have been made available in response to practitioners' requests for supplementary guidance. They have been produced by the British Association for Early Childhood Education and the National Children's Bureau and are not part of the statutory framework nor are they statutory guidance. *Development Matters* is similar to the previous materials but has been slimmed down, overlaps removed, and reflects the characteristics and prime and specific areas (Early Education, 2012).

Much remains the same in the Safeguarding and Welfare requirements. There has been no alteration to ratios, despite concerns regarding Reception class ratios of one teacher to 30 children; or to qualifications, despite concerns that only one member of staff needs to have a full and relevant level 3 qualification and only half of all other staff need to hold a full and relevant level 2 qualification; to space or to key persons requirements. There is a new requirement for providers to have appropriate arrangements for the supervision of staff who have contact with children and families (DfE, 2012: 17). Chapter 14 examines safeguarding issues in depth.

How do the frameworks used across the United Kingdom compare?

In recent years all four countries of the United Kingdom have reviewed their curriculum frameworks for young children. It is not possible in this small section to do justice to the work and thought that has gone on in each country but it is illuminating to see some of the similarities and differences.

In Wales the *The Foundation Phase* applies to all 3–7-year-olds in both maintained and non-maintained settings. At its centre is a belief in the importance of the holistic development of children and their skills across the curriculum, building on their previous learning (DCELLS, 2008: 4). The curriculum and outcomes are described in seven areas of learning, most the same as EYFS, and educational programmes for each set out what children should be taught and the outcomes or expected standards of children's performance.

In Scotland for children from birth to 3 there is *Pre-Birth to Three: Positive Outcomes for Scotland's Children and Families* (Learning and Teaching Scotland, 2010). This sets out the four principles – rights of the child, relationships, responsive care and respect – that should underpin work with this age group and highlights the importance of attachments; transitions; observation assessment and planning; partnership working; health and well-being; literacy and numeracy; environments and play.

A Curriculum for Excellence (Scottish Executive, 2004) outlines Scotland's curriculum guidance for children and young people from 3 to 18 and there is specific guidance for children in pre-school settings and Primary 1. Its aim is to develop four capacities – successful learners, confident individuals, responsible citizens and effective contributors. The curriculum includes all the experiences that are planned for the children in eight areas that reflect the wider age range covered.

In Northern Ireland there is curricular guidance for those working with Pre-School 3–4-year-olds in the year prior to compulsory education. It is set out under six areas, similar to the EYFS, with the expectation that children will experience the curriculum in a holistic way through play and other relevant experiences (DENI, 2006a). The *Foundation Stage* (DENI, 2006b) sets out the curriculum requirements for compulsory education in Years 1 (4–5-year-olds) and 2 (5–6-year-olds) in the primary school. The aim is to promote children's development of positive attitudes and dispositions to learning; thinking skills and personal capabilities; creativity and imagination; physical confidence and competence; curiosity and interest in the world around them; communication in a variety of ways; literacy and numeracy skills in meaningful contexts. The curriculum is set out under the same six areas of learning as pre-school education.

The age range included in the early years frameworks varies between countries reflecting historical decisions as well as current policies. For England it is from birth to the end of the school year in which the child becomes 5, for Wales, from 3 to 7 years, and for Northern Ireland from 4 to 6 years. Scotland's curriculum guidance has the widest age range, including early years with primary and secondary, which suggests that Scotland sees the education system as an ongoing journey, with each year building on the previous one.

Interestingly all the documents except the English one use the term *curriculum* to describe their framework for children from 3–5 years. This may reflect an English concern about over formalising provision for the youngest children; alternatively this could reflect a lack of confidence about the role of education and teaching for this age group. However, only England has a statutory framework for children from birth to 3. It could be argued that this is over-regulation in what should be a less formal stage in children's lives, but on the other hand it could be seen as giving children in this age group the same status, legal protection and entitlement as older children.

All four countries include language and literacy, mathematics, the arts (in Wales creative development) and the world (in Scotland divided into sciences, social studies and technologies) in their areas of learning. Wales and England have physical development as an area while the other two countries refer to health. Scotland does not contain personal, social and emotional development as an area, though it does include well-being. But while there are similarities in the areas of learning included there are differences that reflect the history and context for each country. Northern Ireland's framework places great emphasis on mutual understanding between communities and, with Scotland, draws out religious education as a distinct area. In Wales the Welsh language is highlighted, and England is the only country to have literacy as a separate area, though strongly linked to communication and language in the documentation. Like the English EYFS, the recent Welsh document *How is my child doing in the Foundation phase? A guide for parents and carers* places a strong emphasis on literacy and future learning: 'The Foundation Phase has been designed to give your child the best possible skills for future learning with a strong emphasis on developing reading and writing skills' (DCELLS, 2012: 2).

Part Two: Does the Early Years Foundation Stage framework provide what children need?

What is the curriculum and is it the right concept for the early years?

There has always been much debate about how the curriculum should be defined. Does it include the 'hidden curriculum', that is the things children learn through the way in which the setting or school is planned and organised and the materials that are provided, for example such things as identity? Does it include the 'planned' and 'received' curriculum, that is the experiences the practitioner intends to offer and what the child actually understands and learns, which are not always the same. Does it include the 'formal' and 'informal', that is the elements that are seen as part of the 'school' day and those that are seen as extra curricular (Kelly, 2009)? Does it only include 'school' aged children and those in receipt of public funding, or does it also include the youngest children, the babies and young children up to 3 who are increasingly part of early years settings?

The curriculum is much more than a body of knowledge to be transmitted, subjects to be delivered, formal learning contexts or schooling. The *Curriculum Guidance for the Foundation Stage* described the curriculum as 'everything children do, see, hear or feel in their setting, both planned and unplanned' (QCA, 2000: 2), a view reflected by Kelly, for whom the curriculum is 'the totality of the experiences the pupil has as a result of the provision made' (Kelly, 2009: 8).

While most practitioners agree that there is a need for guidance, for many the use of the term *curriculum* for young children, especially those from birth to 3, raises particular questions. Practitioners and the wider public have been concerned that the use of the term will lead to formalised learning and introduce pressure for children to confirm too early to targets for their development (Abbot and Langston, 2005). There are concerns about the 'schoolification' of the early years, and in the EYFS framework while the term 'educational programmes' is used, 'curriculum' is not.

The term curriculum will be used by many to describe any framework to support young children learning and the EYFS is often described in the press as the 'Nappy Curriculum' (Paton, 2012). I would argue that we need to make the term our own and define curriculum in ways that stress the particular needs of children in the early years, applying it as confidently as the other countries of the United Kingdom. Using the term curriculum for this age group is about giving the youngest children the same status as older children. It is showing that the learning and development of a 1-year-old is as important as that of a 15-year-old.

Each curriculum reflects 'a set of beliefs and values about what is considered to be worthwhile in terms of children's immediate needs, their future needs and the wider society' (Wood and Attfield, 2005: 138). As a society we need to agree what is important for children based on evidence from research and experience, the role of any national curriculum framework is to support practitioners in ensuring that children get what they need.

The EYFS and theories of children's learning and development

The revised EYFS states that 'A secure, safe and happy childhood is important in its own right ... all early years providers must ... ensure that children learn and develop well' (DfE, 2012: 2). While there is usually broad agreement about sequences of development in social, physical and linguistic areas of learning, views on pace of development, the nature of childhood and how best to support children do vary, as we can see from the example of toilet training in Chapter 8.

Some practitioners draw on particular theories to inform their practice, for example Steiner and Montessori. Many draw on a range of theories of learning and development, some based on the work of researchers and thinkers and others based on their own experience of children and childhood. This section describes some of these theories very briefly; they all repay much closer study, and an eye to their links to EYFS.

Children's development is dependent on a number of components: their genetically pre-programmed inheritance; the experiences and opportunities they have to develop understanding and skills and the culture, ethnic group and social class of individual families and communities and their expectations for the child (Duffy, 2006: 50). Bronfenbrenner (2005) described three ecological domains – the family, the settings attended and the community in which the child lives – which influence each child's learning and development. This model is reflected in the principles of the EYFS, which place the unique child at the centre, enabled by positive relationships and environments.

Froebel (1826) believed that children had innate qualities that were best developed in natural settings, which he called kindergartens, that emphasised play, creativity, social interaction, physical activity and learning. Isaacs continued the emphasis on play, seeing it as essential for development and promoting mental well-being as well as providing the opportunity to take risks and find out through trial and error (Isaacs, 1971). Isaacs, who was strongly influenced by Freud's ideas, stressed the importance of understanding the child's point of view through observation and reflecting on this to inform practice. These writers' ideas can be seen in the EYFS characteristics of effective learning, and the importance placed on outside play and observation.

The idea of stages and sequential steps in learning can be seen in the *Development Matters* bands of learning and reflects the work of Piaget, who identified distinct phases and steps in children's learning. For him there were four universal and consecutive stages in children's cognitive development: sensorimotor, preoperational, concrete operations, and formal operations (Piaget, 1926). Progression from one stage to the next was the result of children's efforts to assimilate and accommodate new experiences. Development was largely unaffected by adult's interventions in the process, learning followed development and development was dependent on the child's pace.

Vygotsky (1978) offered an alternative model. Unlike Piaget, he stressed the importance of the social context – what children can do with other people rather than what children can do unaided. For Vygotsky, children develop through their learning and while learning should be matched to the child's level of development it should also take them beyond it. He identified a period in which children need assistance to complete a task that fell between two levels of development: the actual and the potential. He described the distance between these as the 'zone of proximal development'. Once children have internalised a concept, skill or idea and were able to use it by themselves, without the assistance of a competent learner, it became their actual level of development.

Bruner (1975) built on Vygotsky's ideas and introduced the concept of 'scaffolding' children's learning from his observations of the way in which parents interact with their children, and especially their role in language development. The EPPE project (Sylva et al., 2004) identified the importance of a form of interaction between children and adults they called 'sustained shared thinking'. This occurred when practitioners and children worked together in an intellectual way to solve a problem, clarify a concept, evaluate an activity or extend a narrative. Sustained shared thinking contributed to thinking and developed and extended the child's understanding. The EYFS emphasis on the importance of the practitioner responding to each child's emerging needs and interests and guiding their development through warm, positive interaction (DfE, 2012: 6) draws on Vygotsky's and Bruner's ideas and EPPE research.

Bowlby (1953) and Goldschmied and Jackson (2004) stressed the importance of relationships and secure attachments, and Rutter (1979) explained that while the child's main attachment is important children can successfully form other attachments. He also focused on the importance of resilience and helping children to develop strategies to cope successfully with the challenges that are part of life (Rutter, 1985), an approach that is reflected in the characteristics of effective learning. Gerhardt (2004) points out that love is essential to brain development in the early years of life while Gopnik et al. (2001) describe how babies' brains are designed to enable them to make sense of the world around them. This understanding of the importance of the period from birth to 3 has led to the inclusion of this age group in the EYFS, the emphasis on key persons and attachment, and the prime areas of learning.

The literature review that informed the revised EYFS summarised the research and provided new insights on the importance of:

- adults' responding to the child's initiation
- different kinds of play, and how it can be enriched by guiding, planning and resourcing by practitioners
- two broad types of conversation: one confirms a child's understanding or feelings, the other elaborates and extends that understanding
- narrative that enables children to create a meaningful personal and social world and is a 'tool for thinking': it is most effective when children are encouraged to form their own accounts, rather than passively accepting those of adults
- depth and not breadth when developing children's thinking; deep understanding is more important than superficial coverage
- opportunities for problem solving to develop logico-mathematical thinking rather than focusing only on context-specific elements
- vocabulary: phonological skills at age 5 are better predictors of reading at age 7 than at age 11; vocabulary at age 5 is a better predictor of the more complex tasks of reading at age 11
- new theories that see development as a web of multiple strands, with different children following different pathways rather than all following similar linear pathways
- research from neuroscience that is starting to show the infant's capacity to recognise similarity between their own actions and actions they see others do, and the tendency of the child's brain to generate rules based on small datasets that are resistant to change subsequently
- self-regulation, which requires the development of effortful control that facilitates the internalisation of social rules

- cultural niches and repertoires in shaping the context of children's learning. (Evangelou et al., 2009: 5)

The EYFS draws on the theories described in this section but there are contradictions in the way the framework views the child. The EYFS refers to each child as a unique individual and *Development Matters* states 'Children develop at their own rates, and in their own ways' (Early Education, 2012: 6–46). However, there is also an expectation that by the June of the academic year in which they become 5 all children will reach the early learning goals, despite some being 5 years 10 months and others not yet having reached their fifth birthday. Does this expectation reflect evidence of the actual achievements of children from a wide range of backgrounds and if it does not may the unintended consequence be that some children are viewed as failing before they have even started statutory schooling?

The role of play

'Children learn through play' is a much-repeated phrase in early years circles and the EYFS describes it as 'essential for children's development, building their confidence as they learn to explore, to think about problems, and relate to others' (DfE, 2012: 6).

Vygotsky (1978) emphasised the importance of play, believing that in play the child behaves beyond their age. Through play children realise in their imagination the things that cannot be realised in reality and the projection into an imaginary world stretches their conceptual abilities and develops their abstract thought. For Issacs play had the greatest value for the young child when it was freely chosen by the child and controlled by them (Isaacs, 1971). Cecil et al. (1985) described play as part of the creative process and characterised by spontaneity, often without clear final objectives. As there is little or no focus on a predetermined product children are free to examine all kinds of detail during this period that they may have missed if they had been concentrating on the end product. Play is an opportunity to practise and consolidate the skills and knowledge children have acquired. It is also an opportunity for the imagination to come into play and ideas from the unconscious to bubble up. As they play children become aware of patterns and start to see possible connections (Duffy, 2006: 32).

The use of phrases such as *well planned and challenging play* and *planned, purposeful play* in the Northern Ireland and English curriculum documents suggests that all play is not viewed as equally valuable. It also suggests that children's play needs to be structured by adults in a way that risks losing the benefits of play identified by Vygotsky and others. This may be due to an overuse of the word 'play' and a tendency to use it to describe a very wide range of experiences. If we label everything children do as play we undermine the particular value of experiences that are initiated and controlled by the child and also undervalue the importance of other experiences that promote learning. While the EYFS states that children learn by leading their own play it also refers to the importance of activities led or guided by adults.

Learning, Playing and Interacting (DCSF, 2009) examines the relationship between child-initiated and adult-led experiences, seeing them as part of a continuum. Play without adults is valuable but without any support it may become chaotic or repetitive. On the other hand, too much adult direction and control leaves few opportunities for play and its benefits. There is a role for carefully planned, adult-led experiences which enable children to learn specific skills and knowledge and it is often through their play that we gain an understanding of what children have actually learnt and understood through these experiences.

The relationship of EYFS and Key Stage 1: 'school readiness'

The EYFS states that as children grow older the expectation is that the balance will gradually shift towards more activities led by adults, to help children prepare for more formal learning, ready for Year 1 (DfE, 2012: 6). This has led to concerns that despite the comments about children enjoying their childhoods and an emphasis on the characteristics of effective learning there is a danger that the Foundation Stage may be hijacked by a narrow 'school readiness' agenda.

Tickell took the view that the skills a child needs for school are part of the skills they need for life (Tickell, 2011: 19). Personal, social and emotional development, communication and language, and physical development, the prime areas of learning, were seen as the essential foundations and linked to progress in key skills such as reading and writing. The Secretary of State for Education recognised that there have been different views about how children become ready for school. For him it was important to recognise that when children are playing, they are learning; and that creativity is essential. However, it was also critical that children were introduced to formal knowledge in a way and at a time appropriate for their own development (Gove, 2011). The question is, who decides when is the appropriate time for each child?

The introduction of the phonics test early in Year 1 has not reassured practitioners. There is a concern that it risks narrowing school readiness to phonological awareness rather than the wider range of skill and understanding described by Tickell above. The desire to improve outcomes for all children, especially those already disadvantaged, is to be commended and phonological awareness is important. But it can be argued that by concentrating on a narrow definition of school readiness and ignoring evidence about the range of skills and knowledge other than phonological awareness that is key to success we are in danger of further disadvantaging the very children we seek to help.

The Cambridge Primary Review recommended that the foundation years should be extended into primary schools until at least age 6 (Alexander, 2010). However, the revised National Curriculum does not reflect this view (DfE, 2011). It does seek to give schools more freedom over the curriculum by specifying only the essential knowledge that all children should acquire, freeing schools to design a wider school curriculum that best meets the needs of their pupils and to decide how to teach this most effectively. However, there is still a requirement to teach the foundation subjects art, design, technology, geography, history, ICT, music and physical education alongside the core subjects mathematics, science and English. It is hoped that schools will be creative in using the revised National Curriculum to design a curriculum that ensures increased continuity with the EYFS.

Conclusion

The curriculum is only as good as the people who offer it to the children; practitioners are the key element and what each child experiences will depend on them. It is not possible to 'practitioner proof' the curriculum or provide schemes of work or support materials that all practitioners will use the way the planner intended (Kelly, 2009). Children and settings are different and the curriculum needs to reflect this. This requires practitioners to be reflective, to be able to use theory, research and evidence from practice to develop a curriculum that works best for the children in their setting. This is a highly skilled role: practitioners need to differentiate, to understand each child as an individual as well as part of a family, community, society and culture and personalise the curriculum content to reflect and build on their needs and interests.

One of the key strengths of the revised EYFS is the way it has built on what we have learnt from the implementation of past frameworks and new research. We need a curriculum that can grow and evolve in response to changes in society and our understanding about how children learn – neither stands still and nor should the curriculum.

Key points to remember

- Any curriculum framework will reflect the values and beliefs of those who devise it.
- How well children learn and develop is related to the experiences and opportunities we give them.
- It is important to understand the value of play and ensure an appropriate balance with adult-led experiences.
- The curriculum children experience is only as good as the practitioners who offer it to them.

Points for discussion

- Do you think there should be a statutory curriculum for the early years?
- What are the key experiences children should have in their earliest years?
- Why are there differences between the curriculum frameworks of the four United Kingdom countries?

Reflective task

- Choose three of the writers on child learning and development referred to in this chapter and find out more about how their work has influenced our practice today.

Further reading

Department for Education (DfE) (2012) *Statutory Framework for the Early Years Foundation Stage 2012: Setting the Standards for Learning, Development and Care for Children from Birth to Five.* Runcorn: DfE Publications.

Duffy, B. (2006) *Supporting Creativity and Imagination in the Early Years.* Maidenhead: Open University Press.

Evangelou, M., Sylva, K., Kyriacou, M., Wild, M. and Glenny, G. (2009) *Early Years Learning and Development Literature Review.* London: DCSF.

Tickell, C. (2011) *The Early Years: Foundations for Life, Health and Learning. An Independent Report on the Early Years Foundation Stage to Her Majesty's Government* (Tickell Review). London: Department for Education.

Web material

www.educationscotland.gov.uk/earlyyears – resources related to Scottish early years practice

www.foundationyears.org.uk – resources related to English early years practice

www.nicurriculum.org.uk/docs/foundation_stage – resources related to Northern Ireland's early years practice

http://wales.gov.uk/topics/educationandskills/earlyyearshome/foundation_phase – resources related to Welsh early years practice

To access a variety of additional web resources to accompany this book please visit: **www.sagepub.co.uk/pughduffy**

References

Abbott, L. and Langston, A. (2005) *Birth to Three Matters – Supporting the Framework of Effective Practice*. Maidenhead: Open University Press.

Alexander, R. (ed.) (2010) *Children, their World, their Education. Final Report and Recommendations of the Cambridge Primary Review*. London: Routledge.

Bowlby, J. (1953) *Child Care and the Growth of Love*. London: Penguin Books.

Bronfenbrenner, U. (ed.) (2005) *Making Human Being Human: Bioecological Perspectives on Human Development*. Thousand Oaks, CA: Sage.

Bruner, J. (1975) 'The ontogenesis of speech acts', *Journal of Child Language*, 2, 1–9.

Cecil, L. M., Gray, M. M., Thornburg, K. R. and Ispa, J. (1985) 'Curiosity-exploration-play: the early childhood mosaic', *Early Child Development and Care*, 19, 199–217.

Department for Children, Education, Lifelong Learning and Skills (DCELLS) (2008) *Framework for Children's Learning for 3 to 7-year-olds in Wales*. Cardiff: Welsh Assembly Government.

Department for Children, Education, Lifelong Learning and Skills (DCELLS) (2012) *How Is My Child Doing in the Foundation Phase? A Guide for Parents and Carers*. Cardiff: Welsh Assembly Government.

Department for Children, Schools and Families (DCSF) (2008) *Statutory Framework for the Early Years Foundation Stage: Setting the Standards for Learning, Development and Care for Children from Birth to Five*. Nottingham: DCSF Publications.

Department for Children, Schools and Families (DCSF) (2009) *Learning, Playing and Interacting*. London: DCSF.

Department for Education (DfE) (2011) *The Framework for the National Curriculum. A Report by the Expert Panel for the National Curriculum Review*. London: DfE.

Department for Education (DfE) (2012) *Statutory Framework for the Early Years Foundation Stage 2012: Setting the Standards for Learning, Development and Care for Children from Birth to Five*. Runcorn: DfE Publications.

Department for Education and Department for Health (DfE/DH) (2011) *Supporting Families in the Foundation Years*. London: DfE/DH.

Department for Education – Northern Ireland (DENI) (2006a) *Understanding the Foundation Stage Early Years*. Belfast: DENI.

Department for Education – Northern Ireland (DENI) (2006b) *Curricular Guidance for Pre-School Education*. Belfast: DENI.

Department for Education and Skills (DfES) (2002) *Birth to Three Matters: A Framework to Support Children in Their Earliest Years*. London: DfES.

Duffy, B. (2006) *Supporting Creativity and Imagination in the Early Years*. Maidenhead: Open University Press.

Early Education (2012) *Development Matters in the Early Years Foundation Stage (EYFS)*. London: British Association for Early Childhood Education. www.

early-education.org.uk/sites/default/files/Development%20Matters%20 FINAL%20PRINT%20AMENDED.pdf (accessed July 2013)

Evangelou, M., Sylva, K., Kyriacou, M.,Wild, M. and Glenny, G. (2009) *Early Years Learning and Development Literature Review*. London: DCSF.

Froebel, F. (1826) *The Education of Man*. New York: Appleton.

Gerhardt, S. (2004) *Why Love Matters*. Hove: Brunner–Routledge.

Goldschmied, E. and Jackson, S. (2004) *People under Three: Young Children in Daycare*. London: Routledge.

Gopnik, A., Metfzoff, A. and Kuhl, P. (2001) *How Babies Think*. London: Phoenix.

Gove, M. (2011) *Michael Gove Speaks to the London Early Years Foundation about the Importance of the Early Years*. Speech 28 October 2011. www.education.gov. uk/inthenews/speeches/a00199946/michael-gove-speaks-to-the-london-early-years-foundation-about-the-importance-of-early-years (accessed July 2013)

HM Treasury (2004) *Choice for Parents, the Best Start for Children: a Ten Year Strategy for Child Care*. London: Stationary Office.

Isaacs, S. (1971) *The Nursery Years: The Mind of the Child from Birth to Six Years*. London: Routledge.

Kelly, A. V. (2009) *The Curriculum Theory and Practice*. London: Sage.

Learning and Teaching Scotland (2010) *Pre-Birth to Three: Positive Outcomes for Scotland's Children and Families*. Edinburgh: Scottish Government.

Paton, G (2012) 'Private schools to axe the "nappy curriculum" for toddlers', *Daily Telegraph*, 2 October.

Piaget, J. (1926) *The Language and Thought of the Child*. London: Routledge and Kegan Paul.

Qualification and Curriculum Authority (QCA) (2000) *Curriculum Guidance for the Foundation Stage*. London: QCA.

Rutter, M. (1979) 'Maternal deprivation, 1972–1978: New findings, new concepts, new approaches', *Child Development*, 50 (2), 283–305.

Rutter, M. (1985) 'Resilience in the face of adversity: protective factors and resistance to psychiatric disorder', *British Journal of Psychiatry*, 147, 598–611.

School Curriculum Assessment Authority (SCAA) (1996) *Nursery Education: Desirable Outcomes for Children's Learning on Entering Compulsory Education*. London: SCAA and Department for Education and Employment.

Scottish Executive (2004) *A Curriculum for Excellence*. Edinburgh: Scottish Executive.

Sylva, K., Melhuish, E. C., Sammons, P., Siraj-Blatchford, I. and Taggart, B. (2004) The Effective Provision of Pre-School Education (EPPE) Project: *Technical Paper 12 – The Final Report: Effective Pre-School Education*. London: Department for Education and Skills/Institute of Education, University of London.

Tickell, C. (2011) *The Early Years: Foundations for Life, Health and Learning. An Independent Report on the Early Years Foundation Stage to Her Majesty's Government* (Tickell Review). London: Department for Education.

Vygotsky, L. (1978) *Mind in Society*. Cambridge, MA: Harvard University Press.

Wood, E. and Attfield, J. (2005) *Play, Learning and the Early Childhood Curriculum*. London: Paul Chapman Publishing.

CHAPTER 8

The Tools of Assessment: Watching and Learning

Caron Carter and Cathy Nutbrown

Chapter contents

- What is assessment?
- Why assess young children's learning and development?
- Values and vision underpinning assessment
- National policy on assessment of early learning
- Assessment for the purposes of teaching and learning

What is assessment?

The word 'assessment' is used in different contexts to mean different things. Nutbrown (2011a) has suggested three different purposes for assessment, arguing that different tools are needed for different purposes. *Assessment for teaching and learning* involves identifying the details of children's knowledge, skills and understanding in order to build a detailed picture of their individual development and subsequent learning needs. *Assessment for management and accountability* prefers scores over narrative accounts of children's learning. Such assessments included the *baseline assessment* system which measured children's progress in predetermined objectives (SCAA, 1997) and allowed the 'value added' by the school to be calculated. *Assessment for research* includes (often numerical) assessments which are used specifically in research projects where quickly administered measures are needed and where uniformity of approach is necessary. Table 8.1 summarises the characteristics of these three purposes of assessment.

Table 8.1 Some characteristics of the three purposes of assessment

Assessment for teaching and learning	Assessment for management and accountability	Assessment for research
Focus on individuals	Focus on age cohort	Focus on samples
Concerned with details about each individual learner	Concerned with a sample of group performance	Concerned with performance of the sample
Is ongoing	Occurs within specific time frame	Takes place at planned points in a study
'Takes as long as it takes'	Is briefly administered or completed from previous assessment for teaching	Can be brief, depends on assessment and ages
Needs no numerical outcome to be meaningful	Numerical outcome provides meaning	Numerical outcomes often essential
Is open-ended	Often consists of closed list of items	Often consists of closed items
Informs next teaching steps	Informs management strategy and policy	Informs research decisions, and findings – measures outcomes
Information relates primarily to individuals	Information relates primarily to classes, groups, settings or areas	Information relates to the sample, not to individuals or schools
Assessments required for each child	Some missing cases permissible	Some missing cases permissible
Main purpose is teaching	Main purpose is accountability	Purpose is to add to knowledge
Only useful if information is used to guide teaching	Only useful when compared to other outcomes (of other measures of cohorts)	Only useful as evidence of effectiveness of research study
Requires professional insight into children's learning	Requires competence in administration of the test	Requires competence in administration of the test
Depends on established relationship with individual children to be effective	Can draw on information derived through interaction with individual children, but not dependent on relationship	Often requires no previous relationship, but the ability to establish a rapport with the child at the time of the assessment
Requires on going professional development and experience	Requires short training session/ learning the test and practice	Requires short training session. Learning the test and practice

Source: Nutbrown, 2011b: 6

Assessment of young children, whatever the purpose, raises a number of concerns in relation to their well-being and self-esteem and how children come to see themselves as learners (Roberts, 2006).

Why assess young children's learning and development?

Children's learning is so complex, so rich, so fascinating, so varied, so surprising and so full of enthusiasm that to see it taking place every day, before one's very eyes is one of the greatest privileges. Watching young children can open our eyes to their astonishing capacity to learn, and make us marvel at their powers to think, to do, to communicate and to create. As well as being in awe at young children's capacities, early childhood practitioners must understand, really understand, what they see when they observe.

Several pioneers (Froebel, Piaget, Vygotsky and Isaacs) and more recent researchers and commentators (Donaldson, 1978; Athey, 2006; Elfer, Goldschmied and Selleck, 2003; Nutbrown, 2011a) have illuminated children's learning and development and provided practitioners with strategies for reflecting upon and interpreting their observations of children. This rich resource illuminates the meanings of children's words, representations and actions. For example, those who work with babies and toddlers can draw on recent work to embellish their own understanding of the children (Elfer et al., 2003; Goldschmied and Jackson, 2004; Abbott and Moylett, 1997; Page et al., 2012). When early childhood educators use the work of others as a mirror to their own, they can see the essentials of their own practice reflected more clearly and so better understand the learning and development of the children with whom they work.

The observations of Susan Isaacs (1929) can be useful to present-day educators as tools for reflection on children's processes of learning and as a means of moving from the specifics of personal experiences to general understandings about children's thinking. Isaacs' Malting House School in Cambridge was the setting (from 1924 to 1927) for her compelling accounts of the day-to-day doings of the children which show clearly how children's intellectual development can result from reflecting on detailed anecdotal insights. Isaacs described the development of the basic concepts of biology (change, growth, life, and death), illustrating the process with a rich body of observational evidence:

18th June 1925

The children let the rabbit out to run about the garden for the first time, to their great delight. They followed him about, stroked him and talked about his fur, his shape and his ways.

13th July 1925

Some of the children called out that the rabbit was dying. They found it in the summerhouse, hardly able to move. They were very sorry and talked much about it. They shut it up in the hutch and gave it warm milk.

14th July 1925

The rabbit had died in the night. Dan found it and said: 'It's dead – it's tummy does not move up and down now.' Paul said, 'My daddy says that if we put it in water it will get alive again.' Mrs I said, 'Shall we do so and see?' They put it into a bath of water. Some of them said. 'It's alive, because it's moving.' This was a circular motion, due to the currents in the water. Mrs I therefore put a small stick which also moved round and round, and they agreed that the stick was not alive. They then suggested that they should bury the rabbit, and all helped to dig a hole and bury it.

15th July 1925

Frank and Duncan talked of digging the rabbit up – but Frank said, 'It's not there – it's gone up to the sky.' They began to dig, but tired of it and ran off to something else. Later they came back and dug again. Duncan, however, said, 'Don't bother – it's gone – it's up in the sky' and gave up digging. Mrs I therefore said, 'Shall we see if it's there?' and also dug. They found the rabbit, and were very interested to see it still there.

Isaacs' diary entries about the play and questioning of young children formed the basis of her analysis of children's scientific thinking and understanding and offer rich evidence of the development of children's theories about the world and what they find in it. Isaacs learned about children's learning through diligent and meticulous reflection on observations of their play. Practitioners need continued opportunity to practise their skills of observation as well as time to reflect with colleagues on those observations. Many researchers and practitioners have followed Isaacs' observational practices (Rinaldi, 1999; Clark, 2001; Jenkinson, 2001; Athey, 2006; Nutbrown, 2011a). The pioneering practice of Reggio Emilia in northern Italy is developed largely through careful documentation which includes observations, notes, photographs and reflections upon the children's work as it unfolds in their learning communities (Filippini and Vecchi, 1996; Abbott and Nutbrown, 2001).

Goldschmied (1989) illustrates the importance of close observation of babies. Watching babies playing with the Treasure Basket can give the adult valuable insights into their learning and development. The following extract from an observation of Matthew shows the fine detail of this 9-month-old's persistent interests:

Kate places Matthew close enough for him to reach right into the basket. He immediately reaches in with his right hand and selects a long wooden handled spatula. 'oohh, ahh,' he says and looks directly at his mother. She smiles at him in approval. Still holding the spatula he proceeds to kneel up and lean across the basket in order to reach a long brown silk scarf. He pulls at the scarf and squeals in delight as he pulls the fabric through his fingers, 'oohh, ahh,' he repeats. He lets go of the spatula and abandons the scarf to his side, his eyes rest on a large blue stone, he picks up the large stone with his right hand and turns it over on his lap using both hands. Still using both hands he picks the stone up and begins to bite it, making a noise as his teeth grind against the hard surface. He smiles; looking at his mother as he repeatedly bites the stone over and over again.

(Nutbrown, 2011b)

Other reasons for observing and assessing young children centre around adults' role as provider of care and education. Young children's awesome capacity for learning imposes a potentially overwhelming responsibility on early years practitioners to support, enrich and extend that learning. When educators understand more about children's learning they must then assume an even greater obligation to take steps to foster and develop that learning further. The extent to which educators can create a high quality learning environment of care and education is a measure of the extent to which they succeed in developing positive learning interactions between themselves and the children such that the children's learning is nurtured and developed.

'Quality' is often culturally defined and community-specific (Woodhead, 1996) but whatever their setting and wherever they are located, where educators watch children and use those observations to generate their own under-standings of children's learning and their needs, they are contributing to the development of a quality environment in which those children might thrive. When educators observe young children they are working to provide high quality learning experiences. The evaluative purpose of assessment is central for early childhood educators, for they cannot know if the environments they create and the support they provide for children are effective unless they watch and unless they learn from what they see. *Observation can provide starting points* for reviewing the effectiveness of provision and observational assessments of children's learning can be used daily to identify strengths, weaknesses, gaps, and inconsistencies in the curriculum provided for all children. *Assessment can be used to plan and review* the provision, adult involve-ment and teaching as well as to identify those significant moments in each child's learning which educators can build upon to shape a curriculum that matches each child's pressing cognitive and affective concerns. *Observation and assessment can provide a basis for high quality provision.* Curriculum, pedagogy, interactions and relationships can all be illuminated and their effec-tiveness reviewed through adults' close observation of children. Despite the introduction of the EYFS and the EYFS Profile, formal assessments continue to be used routinely to diagnose children's abilities and there is a danger that over-formalised assessment at the age of 4 can limit the opportunities children are offered rather than opening up a broad canvas of opportunity for learning. It is important, however, to use the active process of assessment to identify for

each child the next teaching steps so that learning opportunities in the immediate future are well matched to the children for whom they are offered.

This focus on the *next steps* in teaching and learning takes us into the 'zone
of proximal development' – a concept developed by Vygotsky (1978), who
argued that assessment does not end with a description of a pupil's present
state of knowing, but rather begins there. Vygotsky (1978: 85) wrote: 'I do
not terminate my study at this point, but only begin it.' Effective assessment
is dynamic, not static, and can be used by educators as a way of identifying
what she/he might do next in order to support children's learning. Assessment
reveals learning potential as well as learning achievements.

Observation and assessment are the essential tools of watching and learning with which practitioners can both establish the progress that has already
taken place and explore the future – the learning that is embryonic. The role
of the adult in paying careful and informed attention to children's learning
and reflecting upon that learning is crucial to the enhancement of children's
future learning.

Values and vision

Against the backdrop, in England, of the EYFS Profile, and an emphasis on
the acquisition of some identified elements of knowledge, skills and understanding, practitioners can assess children in ways that are appropriate to
their age and learning stage. As devolution gathers pace around the United
Kingdom, different policies are being developed to allow, to varying degrees,
a freedom of practitioners to decide how and what to assess. Whatever the
national policy, practitioners' bring to assessment their personal and professional values and their beliefs about children. Whatever the framework for
national assessment, wherever in the world that might be, how children are
assessed depends upon adults' views on the nature of childhood, children's
behaviour, children's feelings, and their personal approaches to living and
learning. Whenever, wherever educators observe, assess and interpret young
children's learning, they are influenced by personal beliefs and values.

Policy since the early 1990s shows a shift in the language about children
and childhood and the purposes of early education and care which perhaps
indicate a change in the dominant political view of childhood. The language
in policy documents of the 1990s suggested that 'childhood' had been recon-
structed for policy (or perhaps *through* policy), with very young children
becoming 'pupils' and early 'experiences' designed to promote learning giving way to 'outcomes' (Nutbrown, 1998). In 2000, a more appropriate language re-emerged, with talk of 'foundations', 'play' and 'children'. However,
target-driven assessment remained until 2002, when the Foundation Stage
Profile heralded a more flexible approach to ongoing assessment of young
children's learning and needs through observation. It is crucial that early

childhood educators are supported in articulating their own personal vision of early experiences for children (how things might be), because such vision derives from the values they hold, and their own constructions of childhood. Practitioners must challenge the language of policy when it is at odds with a holistic and developmental view of children's early learning.

National policy on assessment of early learning – up to August 2012

The first Early Years Foundation Stage became statutory in September 2008. Education and care, brought together in a single framework, focus on the holistic development of each child (DfES, 2007a). Echoes of baseline assessment of the early 1990s rang in the ears of many who raised concerns about the new framework and its potential for misuse. The statutory framework for the Early Years Foundation Stage (DfES, 2007a) was paralleled by the Early Years Foundation Stage Profile – a summative assessment at the end of Foundation Stage 2 – just before children enter Key Stage 1. The intention is that evidence collected over two years is used to compile the Profile, using observation, analysis and planning. The language used is formal and on a par with that used in Key Stage 1 and Key Stage 2 summative assessments. Additionally, there is an element of reporting and accountability not dissimilar to that of KS1 and KS2; local authorities are permitted access to the outcomes of children's end of EYFS assessments, which is across 13 scales. This means that the potential for 'league tables', 'value-added' judgements and versions of baseline assessment remains. Even with the EYFS Profile young children may, yet again, be invisible as individuals if settings, local authorities and government resort to generalised statistics to demonstrate their overall success in 'raising standards'.

Despite changes in policy that emphasise observation and ongoing assessment of young children's learning and development, the tendency to use assessment for purposes of *management and accountability* remains. Though official league tables of performance for the youngest children no longer apply and despite the long awaited abolition of SATS for pupils up to the age of 14, assessment is still used as a way of showing how well (or poorly) a setting has done. *Assessment for management and accountability* often involves numerical assessment of young children's progress and fear has been expressed that the EYFS Profile will result in 'checklist' type assessments of babies, toddlers and young children which are given a percentage score. Settings and local authorities are often tempted to demonstrate their success in achievements by producing tables that list high achieving institutions (and of course those who do not achieve high assessment scores are also identified). If such assessments are used it is important to remember that such assessments are not useful in teaching young children and for that, the different tools of observation and reflection are needed in order to identify next learning steps for each child. However, the underpinning philosophy of *personalised learning* in the EYFS will succeed if practitioners experience effective professional development, and receive appropriate support and leadership which accentuate *all* children's learning and lead to high quality inclusive provision.

Statutory Framework for the Early Years Foundation Stage – from September 2012

The new Statutory Framework for the Early Years Foundation Stage (DfE, 2012) incorporates both formative and summative assessment formats. The formative or ongoing assessment is at the core of learning and development during the Foundation Phase. It encourages practitioners to tune into children using a cyclical format with observation being key. Figure 8.1 illustrates this.

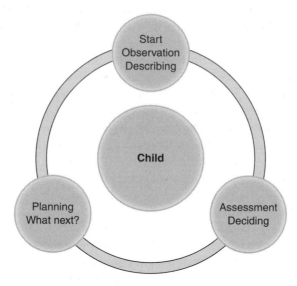

Figure 8.1   Formative Assessment Cycle (*Adapted from EYFS Statutory Framework, DfE, 2012*)

Formative assessment

The purpose of formative assessment requires practitioners to get to know children really well, over time and using observation to build a clearer picture of the child, including their needs, interests and learning styles. Moylett and Stewart (2012: 43) articulate this process:

> Practitioners tune into individual children's signals and communication (observation), consider what this means (assessment), and decide how to respond in the next moment (planning).

To get to know children well necessitates regular and extended periods of time interacting with children. The Statutory Framework (DfE, 2012) suggests using a key person approach to achieve this. In fact, there is a legal requirement for every setting to implement such a system (Moylett and Stewart, 2012). This echoes the work of Elfer et al. (2012) and it would be beneficial for leaders and managers to read this work to consider how to implement a key person approach that will be workable in practice. An approach needs to be beneficial to children, parents and practitioners and to achieve this will require some creative thinking. For instance, if a child does not see the same familiar face each morning this could make a smooth transition more challenging. Staff shifts, leave, absence and turnover make this more challenging to achieve in reality.

The call for limited paperwork when recording children's formative assessment is welcoming. The focus here is upon interaction with children, ensuring that paperwork does not detract from this. This is important, but maintaining a good balance will also be vital. Moylett and Stewart (2012: 44) suggest 'Write down only the "wow moments" instead of wasting time on routine matters'. However, some everyday and taken-for-granted happenings could tell a great deal about a child and be overlooked. It calls for practitioners to be well trained, knowledgeable and know children well in order to be confident about what is relevant to record about individual children.

Summative assessment

The summative assessment within the new framework comes in the form of a Progress Check at Age Two and the Early Years Foundation Stage Profile at the end of the Foundation Stage.

The EYFS Progress Check at Age Two
The National Children's Bureau and Department for Education guide to the Progress Check states that parents should be 'supplied with a short written summary of their child's development in the three prime learning and development areas of the EYFS ... when the child is aged between 24–36 months' (NCB/DfE, 2012: 2). The purpose of this progress check is primarily about early identification of any additional needs that a child may have so that appropriate support can be put in place from an early age. Where there are concerns about a child's progress practitioners are asked to share the progress check summary with other agencies such as health visitors and inclusion coordinators, with the consent of parents. Part of this process requires practitioners to be reflective, in terms of considering possible reasons as to why a child may not be reaching expected levels of progress, such as the birth of a sibling (NCB/DfE, 2012: 18). If the progress check is used appropriately, it will be important for identifying children who indeed require significant support and who might ordinarily slip through the net. Children's attendance at a setting would also be key to the success of this progress

check. Additional details of the aims and principles of this check can be found in *A Know How Guide ...* (NCB/DfE, 2012: 3).

There is no prescriptive way of doing this so practitioners can be creative; however, this may also leave room for vast variations in terms of quality. The progress check calls for the identification of children's strengths and any areas where it is deemed that a child is not progressing at a typical rate. The prime areas have to be reported upon and beyond this will be for practitioners to decide upon in relation to individual children. Early Education (2012) suggests commenting on the three characteristics of effective learning, if this is relevant. Again this needs practitioners to be well trained, sensitive and knowledgeable about how children learn and develop. This will ensure that decisions are made that are appropriate for individual children.

Practitioners undertaking this check should hold on to the fact that children are individual and progress at different levels and rates. Early Education (2012: 45) notes this fact:

> Research shows that children's learning is not linear, progressing smoothly from one step to the next, but occurs in overlapping waves, with stops and starts, reverses, plateaus and spurts.

Acknowledging that individual rates of learning go in peaks and troughs is a philosophy that should be shared with parents to avoid potential anxiety or additional pressure being placed upon a very young child. Parents may also feel that they have in some way failed to support their child if they are not at the same stage as their peers. Children may also pick up on a negative overtone being related to their learning and this could impact upon their confidence and identity as learners, when some children will 'move forward more quickly with no special attention' and just require some additional time to develop at their own rate (Moylett and Stewart, 2012: 46).

An example of this nowadays can be related to the usual impatience to get children toilet trained. The following case study discusses this.

Case Study 8.1

Isla was 2 years and 8 months and the staff at her setting kept asking her mum if she was ready to be toilet trained. Claire, Isla's mum, knew that all her friends' children were already toilet trained or going through the process of becoming toilet trained. She felt a pressure to move on with this despite Isla showing no signs of being ready for this. She discussed this with one of her friends who talked about the fact that both her children were toilet trained by their second birthday. She also said that some children were now starting school without being toilet trained because modern nappies meant that toddlers did not know they were wet, suggesting an element of laziness or apathy. Claire felt she must move forward with this so bought Isla some pants and explained that she would wear the pants and use the potty. The first day Isla wet herself 12 times. Each day Claire was sending her to her setting with several sets of clothes to change into after each accident. After a week, with no signs of improvement, accidents all over the house and a mountain of washing with Isla's baby sibling to consider too Claire decided not to bow to this pressure any longer. She put Isla back into pull-ups and decided to wait for the right time. When Isla was 3 years and 2 months she asked to wear pants. After just a couple of accidents Isla was dry within a few days. Claire reflected on this experience and felt she should have stood firm on this one and waited just a while longer to meet Isla's needs rather than go with the typical expectation.

We need to guard against pushing children too early. The *Development Matters* guidance provides 'a typical range of development' and suggests 'a best-fit approach' acknowledging that there will be individual variations (Early Education, 2012). One of the principles of the Progress Check is to allow children to contribute and to listen to them through their learning experiences. This needs to be evident in practice, showing respect for individual children rather than pushing before they are ready. This is important for children's personal and emotional development and ultimately to nurture their motivation and disposition to learn and develop.

The EYFS Profile
The second form of summative assessment in the Early Years Foundation Stage is the Profile. This is completed for all children during the final term of the academic year in which the child becomes 5 (see the Statutory Framework [DfE, 2012] for additional details). This assessment is informed by formative ongoing observation and assessment. Children's levels of development are assessed using the early learning goals in both the prime and specific areas. The profile must also report on whether children are:

- meeting expected levels of development
- exceeding expected levels
- not yet reaching expected levels (emerging)

Having to state whether children are meeting typical levels of development is slightly at odds with the fact that children develop at different rates. Using the *Development Matters* guidance (Early Education, 2012) and the Statutory Framework for the Early Years Foundation Stage (DfE, 2012) alongside each other needs to maintain a focus on what children can do. Again, like the Progress Check, we should avoid pushing children too early or dwelling on what they cannot do. Reporting to parents at the end of the Foundation Stage could potentially be a negative experience if children are classed as 'emerging'. This echoes the baseline assessment in the 1990s. For children who did not score highly on some or all of the desirable outcomes this provided a negative start to school life. The new summative assessment (DfE, 2012) needs careful management to avoid potential negative identity being impinged upon children.

All children are assessed using the early learning goals on the profile, including children with special educational needs. The Statutory Framework (DfE, 2012) does state that 'Reasonable adjustments to the assessment process for children with SENs and disabilities must be made as appropriate'. The framework also says that specialist assistance may need to be sought for help in such instances. How this is interpreted will vary greatly. This will need to be considered sensitively and respectfully in order to make sure that some children are not disadvantaged by the use of a one size fits all assessment model. Similarly, settings will have to think about how English as an Additional Language (EAL) learners can be accurately assessed across all areas of the profile. Assumptions based on their levels of English language should not mask their true ability.

The EYFS encourages 'snap shot' observations of children – both spontaneous and planned to create individual portfolios, which document children's learning journeys. Table 8.2 summarises four ways to document children's learning which can be used for formative and summative assessment.

Practitioners may need time to try different observation techniques for different purposes and to analyse or interpret observations and question how they inform practice or individualised children's learning. When it comes to learning – it is not the case that 'one size fits all' and settings need to focus on individuals in order to remain distinctive in their ethos and pedagogy.

Table 8.2 Some types of observation and their main purposes

Observation	Purpose
Time sampling/Target child	To capture detail relating to the behaviour and language of a child (Hobart and Frankel, 2004)
Learning stories	To look for behaviours that link in with the strands of the curriculum. Observation is woven into the curriculum with a focus upon strengthening learning dispositions (Clark, 2001; Palaiologou, 2008)
Snap shot	To record spontaneous or planned observations focusing on a short episode on any area of the curriculum
Observation without a note book	A narrative observation that usually lasts about 10 minutes. The observer watches the child with no fixed agenda but a concern for overall holistic development. Significant events in the observation episode are recorded after the observer has stopped watching. Some things, such as the detail of dialogue could be lost but advocates of this approach say that essential details are remembered and recorded (Elfer, 2005)

Elfer (2005) suggests that practitioners are better able to focus on the child if they observe *without* taking notes, spending 5–10 minutes watching a child then moving to a different space to write up their observation. The following is an example:

Example: Without a notebook

Sophie has been in the setting for 30 minutes. She snuggles up on the lap of her key worker. She is sucking her thumb and strokes her face with her square of comfort blanket. They are sitting at a table with Lego boards and bricks laid out ready for the children. Three other children are standing around the children. They have selected their boards and are busy building and chatting about their creations. Sophie is watching the Lego building from the safety of her key worker's lap. She does not speak but her eyes watch the creation of the boy by her side. This continues for several minutes. Sophie's key worker then takes a board and starts to build. Sophie's attention is now diverted to her key worker. She watches for a couple of minutes and then she picks up a brick and offers it to her key worker. This is repeated several times until the design is complete and her key worker announces in a sing-songy style, 'Da-Dah!!' A smile forms from behind Sophie's thumb.

Elfer's point is that what has been learned remains in the mind of the observer with key events, information and emotions being written down later. Such observations can result in fewer words but a higher quality of observation and insight. Children's words and conversations are less likely to be recorded but, as part of a range of observational strategies the '*without a notebook*' approach has an important place.

Using observations to inform planning

It is important to personalise learning, and many practitioners use PLOD planning (Possible Lines of Direction; Whalley, 2007) to achieve this. This tool can be used to plan individual or small group learning across six areas of learning. All practitioners and parents can contribute suggestions to such planning tools. This form of personalised learning planning can be effective if based on observation and practitioners should feel confident in experimenting with different planning formats and tools that are flexible and allow for spontaneous experiences to be developed (DfES, 2007b).

Observation is crucial to understanding and assessing young children's learning. Effective and meaningful work with young children that supports their learning must be based on appropriate assessment strategies to identify their needs and capabilities. The *fine mesh* of learning requires detailed, ongoing and sensitive observations of children as they play. Importantly, aspects of respectful assessment can include the development of inclusive practices which seek to allow children to 'have their say' in the assessment of their own learning (Critchley, 2002).

Key aspects in assessing young children

If assessment is to work for children it is important to consider the following questions:

- *Clarity of purpose* – why are children being assessed?
- *Fitness for purpose* – is the assessment instrument or process appropriate?
- *Authenticity* – do the assessment tasks reflect processes of children's learning and their interests?
- *Informed practitioners* – are practitioners appropriately trained and supported?
- *Child involvement* – how can children be fittingly involved in assessment of their learning?
- *Respectful assessment* – are assessments fair and honest with appropriate concern for children's well-being and involvement and do they inform planning of next learning steps?
- *Parental involvement* – do parents contribute to their child's assessment? (adapted from Nutbrown, 2011a)

With due respect ...

This chapter has considered *why* early childhood educators should observe and assess young children in the context of assessment policy in England. Answers to remaining questions depend upon the principles on which early education and assessment are based; the principle of *respect* is crucial. Assessment must be carried out with proper respect for the children, their parents, carers and their educators. Respectful assessment governs what is *done*, what is *said*, how *relationships* are conducted and the *attitudes* that practitioners bring to their work. Those who watch young children – really watch and listen and reflect on their learning – will know that time to watch and reflect is essential to really understanding what young children are doing. Observations that are not reflected upon are wasted effort. It is only when practitioners seek to understand the *meanings* behind what they have seen that the real worth of observational practices is realised.

Whatever the implications of the EYFS Profile in England, and policies and practices around the world, two things are essential: the involvement of parents and practitioners in generating respectful understandings of children's learning, and professional development for educators which is worthy of children's amazing capacity to learn.

Time for teaching and assessment, *confidence* in educators' capabilities, *recognition* of the judgements practitioners make can create the important climate of *respectful early assessment*. The concept of *respect* can underpin and inform the way adults make judgements about young children's learning and how curriculum and assessment policies are developed and implemented:

> Respect is not about 'being nice' – it is about being clear, honest, courteous, diligent and consistent. (Nutbrown, 1996)

Teaching young children requires clarity, honesty, courtesy, diligence and consistency. It means identifying what children *can* do, what they *might* do and what their educators need next to do to support and challenge them in their learning. Despite repeated policy attempts to 'keep it simple' supporting young children as they learn can never be other than complex. Watching young children as they learn and understanding their learning moments is complex and difficult work, and places the highest of demands upon their educators. There are no short cuts, instead there are long, interesting and unique journeys.

Key points to remember

- Assessment can be for a range of different purposes.
- Observation and assessment are important for supporting and scaffolding children's learning and development.
- The EYFS guidance should be used to nurture children's development and learning at their own rate.

 Points for discussion

- How do individual children and their needs underpin practice?
- Thinking about the EYFS, what steps might be taken in your setting to further develop children's involvement in their assessment?
- Table 8.2 shows examples of observation types. Is there a place for each type of observation? Have you used any of these in your setting? Could you try to evaluate a method you have not used before?
- How can parents be involved in the assessment of their children's learning?

Reflective task

- Consider the case study of Isla and her mum, Claire (p. 136–7). Discuss how various approaches to toilet training could impact on children's development. Consider how pushing children too early could be related to other situations in early years practice.

Further reading

Moylett, H. and Stewart, N. (2012) *Understanding the Revised Early Years Foundation Stage*. London: Early Education.

Nutbrown, C. (2011) *Key Concepts in Early Childhood Education and Care*, 2nd edn. London: Sage.

 To access a variety of additional web resources to accompany this book please visit: **www.sagepub.co.uk/pughduffy**

References

Abbott, L. and Moylett, H. (eds) (1997) *Working with the Under-Threes: Training and Professional Development*. Buckingham: Open University Press.

Abbott, L. and Nutbrown, C. (eds.) (2001) *Experiencing Reggio Emilia: Implications for Preschool Provision*. Milton Keynes: Open University Press.

Athey, C. (2006) *Extending Thought in Young Children, a Parent–Teacher Partnership*. London: Paul Chapman.

Clark, M. (2001) *Assessment in Early Childhood Settings: Learning Stories*. London: Paul Chapman.

Critchley, D. (2002) 'Children's assessment of their own learning', in C. Nutbrown (ed.), *Research Studies in Early Childhood Education*. Stoke-on-Trent: Trentham Books.

Department for Education (DfE) (2012) *Statutory Framework for the Early Years Foundation Stage 2012: Setting the Standards for Learning and Development and Care for Children from Birth to Five*. Runcorn: DfE. www.education.gov. uk/publications/eOrderingDownload/EYFS%20Statutory%20Framework.pdf (accessed 10 December 2012).

Department for Education and Skills (DfES) (2007a) *The Early Years Foundation Stage*. Nottingham: DfES Publications.

DfES (2007b) *The Children's Plan: Building Brighter Futures* Norwich: TSO.

Donaldson, M. (1978) *Children's Minds*. London: HarperCollins.

Early Education (2012) *Development Matters in the Early Years Foundation Stage*. London: British Association for Early Childhood Education. www.early-education. org.uk/sites/default/files/Development%20Matters%20FINAL%20PRINT%20 AMENDED.pdf (accessed 10 December 2012).

Elfer, P. (2005) 'Observation matters', in L. Abbott and A. Langston (eds), *Birth to Three Matters: Supporting the Framework of Effective Practice*. Maidenhead: Open University Press.

Elfer, P., Goldschmied, E. and Selleck, D. (2003) *Key Persons in the Nursery: Building Relationships for Quality Provision*. London: David Fulton.

Elfer, P., Goldschmied, E. and Selleck, D. Y. (2012) *Key Persons in the Early Years: Building Relationships for Quality Provision in Early Years Settings and Primary Schools*, 2nd edn. London: Routledge.

Filippini, T. and Vecchi, V. (eds) (1996) *The Hundred Languages of Children: The Exhibit*. Reggio Emilia: Reggio Children.

Goldschmied, E. (1989) *Infants at Work. The Treasure Basket Explained*. London: National Children's Bureau.

Goldschmied, E. and Jackson, S. (2004) *People Under Three: Young Children in Daycare*. London: Routledge.

Hobart, C. and Frankel, J. (2004) *A Practical Guide to Child Observation and Assessments*, 3rd edn. Cheltenham: Stanley Thornes.

Isaacs, S. (1929) *The Nursery Years*. London: Routledge and Kegan Paul.

Jenkinson, S. (2001) *The Genius of Play: Celebrating the Spirit of Childhood*. Stroud: Hawthorne Press.

Moylett, H. and Stewart, N. (2012) *Understanding the Revised Early Years Foundation Stage*. London: Early Education.

National Children's Bureau and Department for Education (NCB/DfE) (2012) *A Know How Guide: The EYFS Progress Check at Age Two*. London: NCB/DFE. www.education.gov.uk/publications/eOrderingDownload/EYFS%20-%20know%20how%20materials.pdf (accessed 10 December 2012).

Nutbrown, C. (ed.) (1996) *Respectful Educators, Capable Learners: Children's Rights and Early Education*. London: Paul Chapman Publishing.

Nutbrown, C. (1998) 'Early assessment – examining the baselines', *Early Years*, 19 (1), 50–61.

Nutbrown, C. (2011a) *Key Concepts in Early Childhood Education and Care*. London: Sage.

Nutbrown, C. (2011b) *Threads of Thinking: Young Children Learning and the Role of Early Education*, 4th edn. London: Sage.

Page, J., Clare, A. and Nutbrown, C. (2012) *Working with Babies and Children: From Birth to Three*, 2nd edn. London: Sage.

Palaiologou, I. (2008) *Childhood Observation*. Exeter: Learning Matters.

Rinaldi, C. (1999) 'The pedagogy of listening', Paper given at the Reggio Emilia Conference, Reggio Emilia, Italy, 28 April.

Roberts, R. (2006) *Self-Esteem and Successful Early Learning*, 3rd edn. London: Hodder and Stoughton.

SCAA (1997) *National Framework for Baseline Assessment: Criteria and Procedures for the Accreditation of Baseline Assessment Schemes*. London: Department for Education and Employment/School Curriculum and Assessment Authority.

Vygotsky, L. S. (1978) *Mind in Society*. Cambridge, MA: Harvard University Press.

Whalley, M. (2007) *Involving Parents in their Children's Learning*, 2nd edn. London: Paul Chapman Publishing.

Woodhead, M. (1996) *In Search of the Rainbow: Pathways to Quality in Large-Scale Programmes for Young Disadvantaged Children*. Early Childhood Development: Practice and Reflections Number 10. Bernard van Leer Foundation: The Hague, Netherlands.

CHAPTER 9

Sure Start Children's Centres

Ann Crichton

The aim of children's centres

Children's centres have a major role to play in helping families provide their children with the love, care and stimulation they need to play, learn, be healthy and happy and have the best possible start in life. Children's centres aim to improve outcomes for young children and their families by offering a range of high quality integrated services, usually under one roof. Because centres respond to local needs, they may not offer exactly the same services but they will either directly provide, or signpost families to:

- early education and daycare;
- health services from pregnancy, through birth to the early years;

- family learning and support with parenting;
- support for parents to access education, training and employment.

Centres have a defined reach area, usually with around 1,000 children under 5.

The development of children's centres

The origins of integrated services for young children can be traced back to the late nineteenth and early twentieth century, with the establishment of health visiting and the pioneering nursery schools developed by Margaret McMillan and Susan Isaacs, who stated that:

> By the time children go to school, some of the most important things that ever happen to them are already in the past. (Isaacs, 1929: 3)

Individual professionals and settings continued to develop integrated care and education but this was not underpinned by national policy until the late 1990s, at which time an international survey of early childhood education and care described provision in the UK as: 'fragmented as to auspices and programs, diversified regarding philosophy, curriculum, and program focus, inadequate as to supply, and of mixed quality at best' (Kamerman, 2000: 25).

The belief that integrating services would contribute to improving outcomes for children was fundamental to the development first of Early Excellence Centres (EECs) in 1997, then of Sure Start Local Programmes (SSLPs) from 1999 and, most recently, of Sure Start Children's Centres (SSCCs). EECs were nursery schools that provided integrated care and education and brought multi-agency partners together to deliver a range of services, whilst disseminating good practice across the sector. By 2003 they were offering an impressive range of services, including family learning, adult training and health (Pascal et al., 2001).

SSLPs were new initiatives, established in areas of high deprivation. They shared many of the aims of EECs but had a responsibility towards every child in their reach area. They were required to undertake outreach and home visiting and were clearly identified as part of the government's policy for reducing child poverty and social exclusion (Glass, 1999). SSLPs were intended to be parent-led, with Management Boards that included multi-agency partners and parent representatives, but there was an inherent tension between national targets and the stated aim of giving control to local people (Eisenstadt, 2011). The final national evaluation of SSLPs found positive effects, with mothers in SSLP areas:

- engaging in less harsh discipline;
- providing a more stimulating home learning environment;
- providing a less chaotic home environment for boys;
- having better life satisfaction (lone parent and workless households only) (NESS, 2012: 25–7)

A warmer relationship between parents and children, with an authoritative, rather than harshly authoritarian, approach has been shown to reduce the risk of offending behaviour and psychological distress in adolescents (Chambers et al., 2001). Parental well-being can have a significant effect on parenting (Bowers et al., 2012).

Sure Start children's centres were launched in 2004, with the aim of establishing a centre in every community in England. In 2007 the Children's Plan identified children's centres as the key delivery mechanism for improving outcomes for children and families (DCSF, 2007). In 2009 children's centres gained legal status and local authorities were given a statutory duty to provide sufficient children's centres. By 2010 there were 3,631 designated children's centres; by April 2012 this had gone down to 3,350 with 16 centres closing and others merging (Hansard, 2012).

In 2011, the DfE published the 'core purpose' for children's centres. This requires centres to improve 'outcomes for young children and their families, with a particular focus on the most disadvantaged families, in order to reduce inequalities in child development and school readiness'. It also requires centres to provide 'targeted evidence based early interventions for families in greatest need, in the context of integrated services' and identifies the core principles of 'respecting and engaging parents' and 'working in partnership across professional/agency boundaries' (DfE, 2011c).

Case studies

Children's centres have expanded rapidly from EECs and SSLPs to include centres based on schools and community organisations. I will describe three very different centres and explore the common threads that help us understand how diverse children's centres fulfil the core purpose and provide high quality services.

Case Study 9.1

St Werburgh's Park Nursery School and Children's Centre in Bristol was founded in 1931 in the tradition of Margaret McMillan and Susan Isaacs. One hundred and sixty children attend the nursery school, which also provides 19 places for under 3s, a breakfast club, after school club and holiday scheme. St Werburgh's started working as a children's centre in 2007, using the additional funding to build on the work they were already doing to support families. Sixty-two per cent of the local community are of black and minority ethnic heritage (BME) with 29 languages spoken by children attending the centre. The centre

(Continued)

(Continued)

has built a diverse team through thoughtful recruitment processes that are fair to all candidates, regardless of culture or first language, and through a commitment to helping staff gain skills and qualifications. Practitioners understand the barriers faced by families with English as an additional language (EAL), so they will help them to complete forms, for example for entry to school.

Liz Jenkins, the headteacher, believes that the first impression families receive is vitally important; families feel more confident about using services when they receive a warm welcome. The centre's approach is rooted in the belief that parents want what is best for their children and that they can connect with the parents through their shared interest in the child. The centre works with families in complex and challenging circumstances. The family support team works closely with partners such as a counsellor, speech and language therapist, link social worker and an Asian Community Police Officer; cultural mediators help the centre understand the complexities within communities. When families with additional support needs make the transition to school, the headteacher and social worker will, if necessary, go with the parents to meet the school head and the centre will continue supporting families after their child starts school.

The nursery school and children's centre are fully integrated. The board of governors leads both the nursery school and the children's centre and Liz is clear about the importance of having parent representation within a strong governance structure: 'An advisory body gives advice, a governing body makes decisions'. Liz is a Local Leader of Education and is part of an active network of school heads. The centre is also a part of the Pen Green Early Years Teaching Centres programme (see below). Liz believes that one key to success is a strong leadership team that sets high standards, gives staff clear expectations and supports their learning and development. This provides a solid foundation for supporting practitioners undertaking challenging and emotionally demanding work.

Case Study 9.2

*In **West Northumberland** a cluster of five children's centres covers an area of 975 square miles using 13 outreach bases and three play vans. The cluster started with a Mini Sure Start, set up in 2002 in Haltwhistle, partly in response to the devastating effects of foot and mouth disease on rural communities. A second centre in Prudhoe was established, followed by North Tyne, Hexham and Ponteland. The super output areas range from the 22% most deprived to the 2% least deprived with significant hidden poverty. Families who live in tied accommodation may experience fuel poverty, cold and damp. Many parents get seasonal work in tourism or at lambing time, which makes claiming benefits difficult and there is a stigma attached to claiming benefits in these small close-knit communities. The use* *of benefits to means test entitlement to other services, such as free nursery places for 2-year-olds, can mean that vulnerable children and families miss out on essential support.*

Isolation can impact on mental health and emotional well-being, play a part in domestic abuse and adversely affect children's speech and language development; it is a major issue in rural areas and for military families at Albemarle Barracks, who are often a long way from home and can feel unsupported when their husbands are posted overseas. A multi-agency steering group, led by the children's centre and including health, local authority, voluntary sector, the Ministry of Defence, schools and parents, has created the 'Mini Mess', which offers children's centre services at the barracks.

Transport, mileage and travelling time place a strain on the centre's resources. It can be hard to create viable groups so the centre has to undertake a lot of 1:1 work. As Jackie McCormick, the Locality Manager, says: 'We've got to always think of innovative ways to overcome the barriers.' One successful initiative was to negotiate for the use of rural fire stations, which open for just a few hours per week, and which now house pre-school groups, baby clinics and breastfeeding support.

The mixed demographics can be an asset; parents from different backgrounds mix socially and offer each other support, generating a strong sense of equality and helping raise aspirations across the community. Jackie believes that children's centres should respond flexibly to individual families' needs with family support continuing beyond the age of 5 where needed. She also emphasises the importance of knowing and listening to the community: 'Each children's centre is unique because each children's centre delivers to the needs of its community.'

Case Study 9.3

*Coin Street Community Builders in London was established in the late 1970s and early 1980s by local people, who successfully campaigned to acquire 13 acres of South Bank land for good quality, affordable housing, leisure facilities and childcare. A small nursery was set up in a temporary building and later joined by a breakfast club, after school provision and holiday playscheme. In 2007 the organisation moved into a purpose-built neighbourhood centre, and **Coin Street Family and Children's Centre** was born. The local community is both ethnically and financially diverse; it has affluent households balanced by a very large number of households on low wages or benefits and relatively few middle income residents. Coin Street's main focus is child poverty, both material poverty and the lack of opportunities for learning and play. Jenny Deeks, the centre leader, says: 'Daily we are addressing poor housing, parental debt, mental health,*

(Continued)

(Continued)

domestic violence, neglect, child protection, "no recourse to public funds", newly arrived families with no GP or knowledge of their entitlements to education and associated isolation and stress. There will always be a number of open access, universal sessions run at Coin Street – often a good way to initially engage with families and identify needs early – but targeted groups or, as we call them "invited" children and parents, will always take up 70–80% of our time and resources.'

Having a social enterprise as the 'parent organisation' places the needs and aspirations of the local community at the core of the centre. Parents' groups are a vital part of the governance structure, supporting the various boards with their knowledge of the community, assisting the centre team to review services and playing an integral part in decisions and overall vision and strategy.

A training and employment manager offers 1:1 advice and coordinates a range of basic skills, EAL, IT and vocational training courses. The barriers to accessing training and employment are addressed by offering childcare and advice on benefits, welfare and debts. Parents generally achieve pass rates of 95–100% and the drop-out rate is very low; family support will chase up non-attendees and offer help.

Jenny says: 'Our real successes are the outcomes that have been achieved by our children and their families; the number of children who have shown that, despite many challenges in their young lives, they can achieve when they start school; parents and carers who have achieved qualifications and found employment; the integration of the three strands of our team – early education and daycare, family support and training and employment.'

High quality integrated services

Although the three centres described above have developed along very different paths and serve very different communities, there are common threads, which help in understanding how centres can achieve the best possible outcomes for children and families:

- services informed by a deep understanding of the local community;
- a culture that promotes learning, reflection and challenging of practice;
- a clear focus on outcomes for children, combined with support for parents.

All three leaders have a deep understanding of the communities they serve and a commitment to working with parents and the wider community in equal partnership to develop services that meet local needs. Parents have a strong voice in decision-making despite different governance structures. Centre leaders and practitioners act as advocates, for example by challenging local authorities and other stakeholders to recognise the barriers faced by BME families, by people with no recourse to public funding, or by families who are excluded from essential services because they choose not to claim benefits.

None of the leaders is complacent. Their commitment to children and families drives them to keep improving services. They all believe in the importance of learning for children, parents and practitioners to keep building skills, knowledge and community capacity. All three centres support families facing complex challenges and have recognised the need for a broad set of skills within the team. They have developed partnerships that meet this range of needs and understand that building and sustaining relationships is at the heart of successful multi-agency working. The varying professional heritages of the three leaders, from teaching to community development, might suggest that they would prioritise parents' and children's needs differently but this is not the case. All the centres keep a clear focus on improving outcomes for children. They never lose sight of the child but they know that it is in children's interests to help parents address the issues that make it harder for them to give their children a secure and stimulating home life.

Challenges for children's centres

The core purpose poses some significant challenges for children's centres:

- demonstrating improved outcomes;
- balancing universal and targeted services;
- engaging parents in service planning, delivery, evaluation and leadership;
- developing effective partnerships.

Demonstrating improved outcomes

Across the country the gap in Foundation Stage Profile scores is narrowing (DfE, 2011a), children's centres are improving parent–child interactions and helping parents provide a more stimulating home environment (NESS, 2012) and obesity rates in Reception are falling (National Obesity Observatory, 2012).

Centres need robust information for planning and evaluating outcomes. Some regularly receive names and addresses of new babies from NHS Trusts so they can start offering support but some cannot get this basic information (DfE, 2011b). Centres need data for their reach area, such as breastfeeding or obesity rates, but many can access information only for their borough or locality. At the time of writing, a joint DfE and DH working party is developing recommendations to improve information sharing between health services and children's centres.

The Allen Report (2011) on early intervention placed heavy emphasis on the use of evidence-based programmes. The rationale for this is clear: what happens to children in the early years has a critical impact on their life chances so we must provide the most effective support possible. However, the emphasis on randomised controlled trials, which are beyond the reach of individual centres, could reduce innovation and prevent the use of locally developed programmes unless centres seek external validation for their programmes through C4EO (2012). This provides an evidence base whilst supporting fresh approaches. A recent report by the UCL Institute for Health Equity (Bowers et al., 2012) proposes a well-considered framework for measuring outcomes across the three vital strands of children's centre work: child development, parenting skills and a family context that enables good parenting.

Payment by results for children's centres has been piloted by a number of local authorities with the aim of developing national and local outcome measures for children's centres. The pilot programme is currently being evaluated but there is no longer any intention to generate a national PbR scheme. Local authorities may still choose to pay children's centres additional funding for meeting locally agreed targets. This approach has potential benefits but:

- PbR should not over-emphasise outcomes that are easily measurable, such as increases in breastfeeding rates, at the expense of outcomes that are harder to measure, such as supporting mothers with post-natal depression to bond with their babies. Long-term outcomes, which may be demonstrated only over the course of a generation, are vitally important.
- PbR should reward centres for targeting work effectively but not for delivering services to a checklist of marginalised groups. Targeting should reflect the challenges individual families face. There is evidence that the most significant factors for poor outcomes for children are persistent experience of maternal depression, poor general maternal health, living in poverty and living in a workless household and, when assessing support needs, 'there is no substitute for good professional judgement' (Chimat, 2011: 24).
- PbR needs to reward distance travelled. Foundation Stage Profile (FSP) scores are higher in more affluent areas. This is a reflection of a range of socio-economic factors; to assess the impact of the local children's centre, we need to look at how the FSP scores change from year to year.
- PbR needs to be an additional payment, rather than part of the core funding of a centre. Centres that do not have the financial backing of large organisations will not be sustainable without predictable funding.
- PbR should reward effective collaboration, rather than competition, between centres, by incentivising some locality targets.

Centres have been subject to Ofsted inspection since 2010. A new framework was introduced in autumn 2011 and a third framework introduced in 2013 (Ofsted, 2013). The revisions of the framework reflect the complexity of inspecting children's centres; unlike schools and other settings, children's centres do not have a defined cohort of children attending regularly. They provide multi-disciplinary services and may operate as clusters. The revised frameworks have undoubtedly been instrumental in driving a stronger focus on outcomes and a more determined effort to collect the necessary data. The inspection process could be strengthened further by using experienced centre leaders and health professionals within the inspection team to provide a multi-disciplinary perspective.

Universal and targeted services

The core purpose makes it clear that children's centres should be for everyone but that they should be doing more for families that need additional support. Universal services promote community cohesion by bringing families together, they reduce any stigma attached to attending a children's centre and they provide a means of identifying and engaging with vulnerable families. There is no clear cut-off between parents who need additional support and those who do not; there is a gradient and each family will move up and down this gradient as their circumstances change, so we need an approach of 'proportionate universalism' (Marmot, 2010: 15). This means careful assessment of individual needs, followed by referral to specialist services or an invitation to attend centre-based groups, working on issues such as parents' involvement in their children's learning, speech and language development or domestic abuse. There is also a need for 1:1 work in the family home to build relationships and trust and to engage with families who may be reluctant to come to the centre.

Family support and outreach are used, often interchangeably, to describe much of the work that is undertaken by children's centres with families, rather than directly with children. Outreach aims to facilitate access to services for all families, particularly those who are less likely to engage with children's centre services, whilst family support aims to improve outcomes for children by providing personalised support to individual families to manage the challenges of everyday life. Difficulties with housing, relationships, finance or health can cause stress, which is likely to have a negative impact on parenting (Katz et al., 2007), depression is associated with problems with bonding and attachment and can affect children's development (Cooper and Murray, 1998) and domestic violence, which was identified as a significant issue by all three of the centre leaders, is damaging to both mothers and children (Hill et al., 2007). Family support has to be differentiated to address the multiple needs of the family (Bull et al., 2004; Barlow, 2006). For support to be effective, workers must first engage with the parents and establish trust, they must recognise that parents may need emotional as well as practical support and ensure that the process of support is a partnership between parents and professionals (Campbell, 2000; Quinton, 2004; Browne et al., 2006).

Family support is challenging and emotionally demanding. The centre leaders in this chapter all talked about the complexity of the work and, increasingly, children's centres appear to be taking on work that would once have been the province of children's social care. If they are to do this safely and effectively, they need qualified, skilled practitioners, receiving regular professional supervision. Larger centres, such as St Werburgh's and Coin Street, have the scope to employ practitioners from a range of disciplines and have dedicated family support teams. Smaller centres may have to rely on effective partnerships or pool resources with other centres.

Engaging parents

Respecting and engaging with parents is an underpinning principle of the core purpose. Pen Green's PICL (Parents Involved in their Children's Learning) approach is one example of practice:

> ... underpinned by a strong ethos which respects parents as co-educators of their children, redressing the imbalance of power between parents and professionals ... parents are acknowledged as knowing their children best and wanting the best for them. (C4EO, 2012)

It is impossible to engage fully with parents without first taking the time to see the world through their eyes. Parents' needs may go unnoticed because too few professionals ask how they are coping in a way that suggests they really want to hear the answer. Services must meet parents' needs, be accessible, well organised, professional, flexible, welcoming and responsive, and provide both practical and emotional support (Quinton, 2004). Even when all these criteria are met, children's centres need to undertake effective outreach to find and engage with families that do not access services. We also need to recognise that change is a gradual process and that some families will need long term support.

Respecting and listening to parents is a good start. Involving parents in planning, delivery and evaluation of services is the next step. Many centres use creative methods for consultation, such as parent forums, participatory appraisal, talking postcards, peer researchers, practitioner research and case studies. Volunteering gives parents insight into services and an opportunity to ask questions and make suggestions, as well as a possible route into employment; the use of volunteers is increasing (4Children, 2012). Actively involving parents in decision-making is less well embedded. Advisory groups and governing bodies can be daunting for parents who are new to committees, so training can help. Some centres set up task groups for projects, including parents and practitioners; task groups are likely to be less formal and participants can see that they are making a difference. They may then go on to become advisory group members. Involving parents throughout the organisation and ensuring that every parent can have a voice makes a real difference to the quality of services.

Effective partnerships

Children's centres need to work closely with partners from schools, health, social care, housing, debt advice agencies, domestic abuse support services, Home Start, and other third sector organisations to ensure that families receive skilled, multi-agency support. Partnership working depends on successfully negotiating a shared vision, ethos and language, an understanding of professional roles and responsibilities, and mutual respect. This takes time, commitment and a willingness to give in order to get. Co-location of services is the ideal, together with shared records, although this is not always logistically possible.

Health inequalities are inextricably linked with educational and socio-economic outcomes. In his major review of health inequalities, Marmot (2010: 3) offers a powerful illustration of what this means: 'For people aged 30 and above, if everyone without a degree had their death rate reduced to that of people with degrees there would be 202,000 fewer premature deaths each year.' Marmot concludes that: 'Action on health inequalities requires action on all the social determinants of health', especially poverty, housing, domestic abuse, mental health problems and substance misuse (Marmot, 2010: 16). Children's centres, working in partnerships, are well placed to make a real difference to children's health.

Over the last few years there has been a growing tendency to move midwifery and health visitor clinics into children's centres. In a memorandum submitted to the Parliamentary Select Committee on Sure Start Children's Centres, the Royal College of Midwives (RCM, 2009) strongly supported this move, saying that children's centres 'are able to deliver improved quality of care, particularly for those less likely to access mainstream services'. Locating clinics in children's centres allows health professionals to draw on the additional support centres can offer children and families, helps families get to know their children's centre, lets children play in a stimulating environment while their parents wait for appointments, and improves communication, which can be vitally important in safeguarding children.

The future of children's centres

Funding

Writing on the lessons that can be learned from the US Head Start programme, Gray and Francis (2007: 657) warn:

> Expansion without adequate funding threatens quality. Moreover, where priorities compete, broader objectives of fostering children's development and maximizing community involvement risk subordination to more pressing concerns about providing childcare and promoting school readiness.

The rapid roll-out of children's centres to every community was intended to ensure universal provision but it has stretched scarce resources and given rise to criticism of children's centres being taken over by what David Cameron called the 'sharp-elbowed middle classes' (*Guardian*, 2010). This is seldom an issue for centres in areas of high deprivation but it does highlight the need to get the right balance between targeted and universal services in more affluent areas, remembering that affluent areas may contain pockets of deprivation and that issues such as isolation, health problems and domestic abuse are not confined to any income group or social class. Centres are being asked to take on more responsibility – working with older children, providing family support at higher levels of need, supporting other settings – whilst funding is being cut year on year. A children's centre census (4Children, 2012: 4) found a 'picture of resilience and creativity', with service provision being sustained despite cuts. However, 10% of centres said they were struggling and most were concerned about long-term sustainability. Some centres were reducing, or charging for, universal services, such as Stay and Play. Some childcare provision has closed and many centres were considering reducing qualified teachers. This suggests that children's centres are managing well at present but that further cuts in funding could threaten quality.

Models of provision

Children's centres are commissioned by local authorities with service delivery managed by a range of organisations, including local authorities, school governing bodies, health trusts, national voluntary organisations and a small number of local community groups. There is little research into the relative merits of different providers and models but the case studies in this chapter suggest that effective centres start with what they already do well and build on that to develop the areas of work that are newer to them; the journey may be different, but the destination is the same.

The voluntary sector has a history of innovation and community engagement but a report on its potential within early years services highlighted the barriers faced by voluntary sector organisations competing for tenders (ACEVO, 2011). Smaller community-based organisations are less likely to have the skills and resources for writing bids. Local authorities may decide to commission a cluster of centres; a community organisation that currently runs one centre may not feel able to take on others and may therefore be excluded from the process.

There is an increasing tendency for children's centres to operate as clusters. This may provide scope for recruiting a multi-disciplinary team and may reduce overall expenditure on management and administration. However, if clustering is used simply as a means of paying centre leaders less, quality will be diluted. It is vital to ensure that every centre has a committed, accessible leader with the vision and skills to drive quality; service development must be based on in-depth knowledge of the community and the amount of time needed to build and sustain relationships with community and professional partners should not be under-estimated.

In some areas, children's centres are part of the 0–19 agenda and there appears to be a growing consensus that centres should continue to support families after their children start school. Lancashire is developing a Children's Centre

Plus model. One or two centres in a locality will act as a hub, coordinating some services across the area and working with older children as well as under 5s. This model is likely to include integration with children's social care family support teams.

Governance and leadership

To continue to flourish, children's centres need to be underpinned by strong leadership and governance. Children's centres are required to have an advisory group, which should include partner agencies and parents. The key word here is 'advisory'. Most centres are led by public sector bodies or by national organisations; these organisations employ centre staff and are financially and legally accountable for the centres. Although they may delegate day-to-day decision-making to the advisory groups, they retain the right to make final decisions. A smaller number of centres are led by school governing bodies, charitable trusts or social enterprises. These boards are usually close enough to the centre to have a deep understanding of the community and its needs and, as they are directly accountable, they have the power to make decisions. At the time of writing, the DfE has invited expressions of interest from groups of parents who want to develop their own community models of governance for children's centres, which would be an exciting development.

Children's centre leaders need vision, stamina and determination as well as knowledge, skills and experience. Since it is unlikely that a centre leader will be expert at pedagogy, health promotion, social care and community development, it is important that the centre can draw on the collective wisdom of the senior leadership team, practitioners, partner agencies, parents and the community. The National Professional Qualification in Integrated Centre Leadership (NPQICL) aims to equip centre leaders to work in this way, developing centres as reflective learning communities and empowering practitioners and parents to play a part in centre leadership. There is also an onus on centre leaders to play a part in the development of system leadership through supporting other settings and through offering specialist peer support to leaders from different disciplines. Pen Green is piloting a Teaching Centres approach, which supports outstanding children's centres to share their expertise with other centres, through training and mentoring. The Teaching Schools approach, led by the National College for School Leadership, also supports groups of schools, including nursery schools, to pool expertise. Children's centres can have a voice in the development of national policy through the Children's Centre Leaders' Network, which arranges regional seminars to share good practice and debate current issues and the Children's Centre Leaders Reference Group, which acts as a sounding board for the DfE, giving feedback on, and input to, policymaking.

Early years strategy

The government's pledge to increase the health visitor workforce by 2015 (DfE, 2011b) has enormous potential but if we want to capitalise on this opportunity we need to develop effective integrated working that avoids duplication, reduces the risk of some families being left without support, makes the best use of professional skills, ensures that work with families is undertaken by the most appropriate practitioner and shares information to promote safeguarding. Despite the development of strong partnerships in some areas, integrated working with health services is patchy, although targets, such as reducing childhood obesity, cannot be achieved by any agency working alone. There is also a need for much stronger working with JobCentre Plus to support parents into employment. Commissioners of services should consider shared targets to incentivise joint working and should include the requirement to work in partnership in service contracts.

The introduction of free nursery places for disadvantaged 2-year-olds is a welcome move but finding sufficient high quality places will be challenging. This will be made harder by the fact that some children's centres in areas of high deprivation are considering closing or reducing daycare provision because of budget reductions. Providing high quality early education for 2-year-olds will have maximum impact if it is complemented by children's centre family support and if the new progress check for 2-year-olds is used as an opportunity for health visitors, children's centres and daycare settings to plan, train and work together.

The potential synergy between services can be driven by:

- effective national policy which ensures sustained funding for children's centres;
- local policy and commissioning which puts integrated preventive work at the heart of early intervention and holds all agencies to account for their performance;
- leadership which builds and sustains robust partnerships.

Key points to remember

- The core purpose of children's centres is to improve outcomes for children and families by supporting child development, parenting skills and a family context that promotes good parenting.
- Quality services are underpinned by knowledge of the local community and by respecting and involving parents as partners.
- Children's centres are open to all but should do progressively more for families in need of additional support.
- Developing and sustaining partnerships is fundamental to effective provision.

Points for discussion

- How can children's centres identify and engage with the families who would most benefit from services?
- How can centres work with partners to ensure that policies, procedures and practices are aligned, resources are pooled and professional skills are shared in the best interests of children and families?

Reflective task

- Think about recent examples of your practice with parents and partners and note down what went well and what was less successful. Do you always think of parents as equal partners with a unique understanding of their child? Do you genuinely welcome the opportunity to work with other agencies and professionals and to learn from them? Identify three things you could do to strengthen partnerships with parents or other agencies.

Further reading

Department for Education (DfE) (2011) *Families in the Foundation Years: Evidence Pack*. www.education.gov.uk/publications/standard/publicationDetail/Page1/ DFE-00214-2011 This brings together a wide range of research to use as an evidence base for practice.

Joseph Rowntree Foundation: www.jrf.org.uk/publications. This website contains a wealth of publications on social policy and children and families.

Quinton, D. (2004) *Supporting Parents: Messages from Research*. London: Jessica Kingsley Publishers. This draws together the lessons from research on support for parents and children.

To access a variety of additional web resources to accompany this book please visit: **www.sagepub.co.uk/pughduffy**

References

ACEVO (2011) *One Million Reasons for Reform: Unleashing the Potential for the Voluntary Sector in Early Years Services*. London: Association of Chief Executives of Voluntary Organisations.

Allen, G. (2011) *Early Intervention: The Next Steps*. An Independent Report to Her Majesty's Government. London: Cabinet Office.

Barlow, J. (2006) 'Home visiting for parents of pre-school children in the UK', in *Enhancing the Well-being of Children and Families through Effective Interventions*. London: Jessica Kingsley Publishers.

Bowers, A. P., Strelitz, J., Allen, J. and Donkin, A. (2012) *An Equal Start: Improving Outcomes in Children's Centres: An Evidence Review*. London: UCL Institute of Health Equity.

Browne, K., Douglas, J., Hamilton-Giachritsis, C. and Hegarty, J. (2006) *A Community Health Approach to the Assessment of Infants and Their Parents*. Chichester: John Wiley.

Bull, J., McCormick, G., Swann, C. and Mulvihill, C. (2004) *Ante- and Post-natal Home-visiting Programmes: A Review of Reviews*. London: Health Development Agency.

C4EO (2012) *Validated Local Practice*. www.c4eo.org.uk/themes/earlyyears/localpractice.aspx?themeid=1 (accessed 16 July 2012).

Campbell, C. (2000) 'Social capital and health: Contextualizing health promotion within local community networks', in S. Baron, J. Field and T. Schuller (eds), *Social Capital: Critical Perspectives*. Oxford: Oxford University Press.

Chambers, J., Powers, K., Loucks, N. and Swanson, V. (2001) 'The interaction of perceived maternal and paternal parenting styles and their relation with the psychological distress and offending characterisitics of incarcerated young offenders', *Journal of Adolescence*, 24 (2), 209–27.

Chimat (2011) *PreView Resources for Professionals*. http://atlas.chimat.org.uk/IAS/resource/view?resourceId=54 (accessed 29 October 2011).

Cooper, P. and Murray, L. (1998) 'Postnatal depression', *BMJ*, 316, 1884–6.

Department for Children, Schools and Families (DCSF) (2007) *The Children's Plan: Building Brighter Futures*. Norwich: TSO.

Department for Education (DfE) (2011a) *Early Years Foundation Stage Profile Results in England 2010/2011*. www.education.gov.uk/rsgateway/DB/SFR/s001033/index.shtml (accessed 6 August 2012).

Department for Education (DfE) (2011b) *Supporting Families in the Foundation Years*. London: DfE.

Department for Education (DfE) (2011c) *The Core Purpose of Sure Start Children's Centres*. www.education.gov.uk/childrenandyoungpeople/earlylearning andchildcare/a00191780/core-purpose-of-sure-start-childrens-centres (accessed 19 May 2012).

Eisenstadt, N. (2011) *Providing a Sure Start: How Government Discovered Early Childhood*. Bristol: Policy Press.

4Children (2012) Sure Start Children's Centres Census 2012. www.4children.org.uk/Resources/Detail/Sure-Start-Childrens-Centres-Census-2012 (accessed 6 August 2012).

Glass, N. (1999) 'Sure Start: the development of an early intervention programme for young children in the United Kingdom', *Children & Society*, 13 (4), 257–64.

Gray, R. and Francis, E. (2007) 'The implications of US experiences with early childhood interventions for the UK Sure Start programme', *Child: Care, Health and Development*, 33 (6), 655–63.

Guardian (2010) David Cameron Q & A live in Manchester. www.guardian.co. uk/politics/blog/2010/aug/10/davidcameron (accessed 2 August 2012).

Hansard (2012) House of Commons Written Answers for 10 July 2012: Sarah Teather – Column 173W. www.publications.parliament.uk/pa/cm201213/ cmhansrd/cm120710/text/120710w0003.htm#1207111001493 (accessed 2 August 2012).

Hill, M., Stafford, A., Seaman, P., Ross, N., and Daniel, B. (2007) *Parenting and Resilience.* York: Joseph Rowntree Foundation.

Isaacs, S. (1929) *The Nursery Years.* London: Routledge and Kegan Paul.

Kamerman, S. (2000) 'Early childhood education and care: an overview of developments in the OECD countries', *International Journal of Educational Research,* 33 (1), 7–29.

Katz, I., Corlyon, J.; La Placa, V. and Hunter, S. (2007) *The Relationship between Parenting and Poverty.* York: Joseph Rowntree Foundation.

Marmot, M. (2010) *Fair Society, Healthy Lives. Strategic Review of Health Inequalities in England Post 2010* (Marmot Review). London: Department of Health.

National Obesity Observatory (2012) *National Child Measurement Programme.* www.noo.org.uk/uploads/doc/vid_15180_NCMP_Changes%20in%20 children's%20BMI%20between%202006-07%20and%202010-11.pdf (accessed 31 July 2012).

NESS (2012) *The Impact of Sure Start Local Programmes on Seven Year Olds and Their Families.* London: Institute for the Study of Children, Families and Social Issues, Birkbeck, University of London.

Ofsted (2013) *The framework for children's centre inspections from April 2013.* Online: www.ofsted.gov.uk/resources/frameworkfor-childrens-centre-inspections-april2013 (accessed 7 June 2013).

Pascal, C., Bertram, T., Gasper, M., Mould, C., Ramsden, F. and Saunders, M. (2001) *Research to Inform the Evaluation of the Early Excellence Centres Pilot Programme.* http://dera.ioe.ac.uk/4567/1/RR259.pdf (accessed 12 July 2012).

Quinton, D. (2004) *Supporting Parents: Messages from Research.* London: Jessica Kingsley Publishers.

RCM (2009) *Memorandum Submitted by the Royal College of Midwives to the Sure Start Children's Centres – Children, Schools and Families Committee.* www. publications.parliament.uk/pa/cm200910/cmselect/cmchilsch/130/ 10011303. html (accessed 16 July 2012).

CHAPTER 10

The Role of Health in Early Years Services

Kate Billingham and Jacqueline Barnes

Chapter contents

- The role of health in early years services
- Understanding children's health
- Health services in the early years
- Sure Start: working together with health in the early years

Introduction

Early years services (EYS) offer children and parents a range of programmes that will help children to achieve their potential and, for some, to overcome the impact of early disadvantage. Health plays a key part in children's early development; it is therefore a core function and responsibility of everyone who works in EYS. The fact that health is a core element of children's well-being can be seen in both practice and policy in the early years. The current Coalition government is continuing previous governments' moves to greater integration through its policy document *Supporting Families in the Foundation Years* (DfE/DH, 2011), in which health is seen as integral to wider services for young children. In England this is further supported through new structures to integrate children's public health with education and social care by giving local authorities responsibility for children's public health through Health and Wellbeing Boards (HWBs) from 2015 (HM Government, 2010).

This chapter provides an overview of health in EYS, exploring the potential role of health services as part of the range of services available for families with young children. We draw on our experience in England of Sure Start, the Child Health Promotion Programme (CHPP), now the Healthy Child Programme (HCP), and the Family Nurse Partnership (FNP) programme to suggest how EYS can most effectively protect and promote the health of children. Scotland and Northern Ireland have different organisational and policy context for their early years services. However, both provide universal programmes (called the Child Health Surveillance programme in Scotland) and both are implementing the Family Nurse Partnership programme.

The health roles of early years services

As the universal first point of contact for parents, the services provided by midwives, health visitors and general practitioners make up a core part of EYS and, in conjunction with community health services and hospitals, they are also responsible for providing children and families with care and treatment for acute and long term conditions. However, because health is a broad concept that is influenced by many different factors, responsibility for health goes beyond the health service and EYS have a number of key health roles.

Protecting and promoting the health of children

All practitioners working with young children and their families, whether or not they have a health title or role, have a responsibility to proactively protect and promote children's health and to know what to do when a child is unwell. The 'health work' of EYS ranges from deciding what snacks and drinks will help meet each of a child's 'five a day' and prevent dental decay, to making sure children are safe and protected against accidents, that toileting and hand washing habits prevent the spread of communicable diseases, knowing what first aid to give and what good health advice to offer parents. Because of the influence of wider social factors on child health the work of EYS will also extend to giving advice on benefits, housing and employment or supporting a parent with relationship problems or difficult life events.

Integrating health-led services within early years services

As well as promoting and protecting the health of children in their care and supporting parents to do likewise, EYS are increasingly the location for the delivery of health services including maternity care and support. Sure Start children's centres provided the setting for greater integration as part of the policy as described in *Every Child Matters* (DfES, 2003) and reinforced more recently in *Supporting Families in the Foundation Years* (DfE/DH, 2011). *Every Child Matters* (DfES, 2003, 2004) made the integration of children's services a priority for front line services supported by joint working at a strategic level. Integration is a mechanism for improving outcomes for children by increasing access, reducing duplication and enhancing the skills of the children's workforce. This goes beyond co-location of services to multi-professional teams, joint management, shared outcomes and combined assessments and programmes, such as bringing together the Early Years Foundation Stage Assessment with the Healthy Child Programme 2½ year review and *Preparation for Birth and Beyond* (DH/NHS, 2011, updated 2012). As the recession puts pressure on public funding the momentum for integration grows on a rationale of greater cost effectiveness. However, this is a claim based more on anecdote and aspiration than quantitative research evidence (O'Brien et al., 2009).

Contributing to health services provided outside early years settings

Most children's and families' contacts with health services take place outside early years setting in general medical practices, accident and emergency departments, walk-in-centres and community health services. Nonetheless, EYS staff have much to offer to these health services. Their expertise in working with young children and their knowledge of individual children and their families can provide useful information to support decision-making by health professionals. In addition they play a role in supporting parents to access health services and contribute to a treatment or care plan that may be in place for a child with health or behaviour problems or developmental delay. As a result EYS staff need to be familiar with wider health services beyond those co-located in their early years' setting.

Understanding children's health

Definition of health

Throughout this chapter we define health in its broadest sense to include physical, social and emotional well-being, each of which is interdependent and overlapping. Considering the child holistically provides the rationale for integrating services and working together as the many factors that influence children's health are the responsibility of many services, including housing, income, education as well as the NHS and early years services

Children's health today

The patterns of child health and the causes of ill health change over time as societies develop and science advances (Blair et al., 2010). The health of children has improved dramatically in the last 100 years but the history of child health shows that these improvements were more to do with improvements in the social and physical environment (e.g. better housing, nutrition, education, water and sewage treatment) than health care interventions. It is only recently that public health programmes and medical treatments have played a role in improving health of children through immunisations, antibiotics and advances in medical care and treatment (Blair et al., 2010).

Today in the United Kingdom the public health priorities for children are:

- Obesity: rates for 2–10-year-olds rose by more than 50% from 1995 to 2006. In 2010 30.3% of children were overweight or obese (NHS Information Centre, 2012).
- Inequalities in infant mortality: the overall rate has fallen but inequalities remain. For example, there was a 16% difference in infant mortality rates between babies with fathers in routine or manual occupations and the population as a whole between 2006 and 2008 (ONS, 2010).
- Psychological health: the prevalence of child mental health problems has increased since the 1970s. In 2004 it was estimated that 10% of children between 5 and 15 in the UK had a clinically diagnosed mental health disorder (ONS, 2004).
- Accidental injury is one of the major causes of death in childhood; and injuries disproportionately affect some children more than others. Great variations occur which reflect a child's age, gender, socio-economic group, ethnic group, and where they live (NHS Health Development Agency 2005).
- Chronic illnesses are increasing amongst children, particularly in asthma and diabetes (Blair et al., 2010).

Inequalities in health

Good health is not evenly distributed and inequalities in child health persist in the UK (Blair et al., 2010). Child well-being in the UK is lower than in 20 other industrialised countries (UNICEF, 2008). Some groups are more vulnerable than others, in particular children born to teenage mothers and to women born in some developing countries. For example, the mortality rate for infants of mothers born in Pakistan is double the rate of UK-born mothers. The mortality rate for babies born to mothers under 20 is 60% greater than for babies born to older mothers (DH, 2007). Government policies have brought about reductions in child poverty and investment in early years education, but there is concern that the recession will reverse that trend with reductions in welfare benefits and public funding (Joseph Rowntree Foundation, 2011).

Factors influencing child health and well-being

Pregnancy and the first years of life are when humans are most vulnerable. Bronfenbrenner's (1979) ecological system of direct and indirect factors is a helpful model to understand health issues because it recognises the importance of the wide range of services, relationships and societal influences and the relatively minor role that health services play in the health and well-being of children. It enables factors such as poverty, poor housing and unemployment to be incorporated when planning child health services.

Inequalities in health are the result of social and economic inequalities in society and begin in childhood. Professor Sir Michael Marmot concluded that 'Giving every child the best start in life is crucial to reducing health inequalities across the life course' (Marmot Review, 2010). In addition to the impact of income, other factors linked with child health outcomes include the age of the mother, her level of education and mental health as well as quality of parenting and parental relationships. Some children growing up in poverty do well and the quality of parenting is a mediating factor building resilience in children (Kienan and Mensah, 2009).

Neurological development and genetics

Our expanding knowledge of brain development (Tierney and Nelson, 2009) and genetics (National Scientific Council on the Developing Child, 2010) are having a profound influence on the understanding of child development and parenting (Center on the Developing Child, 2010). This knowledge highlights pregnancy and early childhood and is shaping policy and practice in relation to early years settings (Center on the Developing Child, 2007). We now know how and why early relationships and interactions matter so much for the young child and their impact on how the neural pathways of the brain are pruned and shaped (Cozolino, 2006). It is well established that pregnancy is a key time for the developing child. New knowledge on the impact during pregnancy of toxic substances, such as nicotine and toxic chemicals from tobacco, alcohol and stress on the development of the brain and long term cognitive and psychological well-being has made this time more important than ever for health professionals and families (Glover and O'Connor, 2002).

Whilst there are genetic differences between children, research suggests that genes are not necessarily a fixed blueprint determining who we are and how we behave. Gene expression may be influenced by the environment in which the unborn child is growing and is born (Graham, 2007; Rutter, 2007). We must be cautious about how we interpret the research but it is clear that this area of scientific discovery will change how we understand the development of children and what services should be offered and when.

Relationship between child and adult health

Health in childhood matters not only for the child but in terms of their future adult life (Center on the Developing Child, 2010). From conception onwards, experiences leave 'lasting memories on children's body system and therefore on their future health' (Graham, 2007). It is thought that adult health is influenced by what happens in the womb. The hypothesis that poor maternal nutrition and fetal health puts the child at greater risk of long term ill health in adult life, such as heart disease and diabetes (Barker, 1998) is gaining greater legitimacy as the evidence strengthens (Marmot Review, 2010). Thus ensuring the health and well-being of the mother-to-be is as, if not more, important that maintaining a range of services for infants and young children.

Summary

The health of children is shaped from conception by the complex interrelationship of biological, social and psychological factors. This means that EYS need to think broadly in their health work with children and families to include both social factors such as income, jobs and housing as well as individual and family factors such as health behaviours, parenting practices and relationships in a family.

Health services in the early years

The historical role of health in young children's services

This section summarises the historical context for the role of health in EYS. Child health services have historically been separate from not only the hospital-dominated NHS and maternity services but also from children's social and educational services. Policy developments in recent years aimed to provide more integration of provision between health and EYS through the development of Sure Start children's centres and more recently with the plans set out in *Supporting Families in the Foundation Years* (DfE/DH, 2011). However, the integration of health and early years services cannot be complete given the important roles taken by hospital and GPs. Originally in the NHS there was a tripartite division between hospital services, primary health care services and those controlled by the Medical Officer of Health (MoH), including provision for young children. Preventive health care for children was outside the NHS, provided by the local authority. The situation was relatively unchanged until the 1997 election, from which time there was a gradual intertwining of health services for young children (and their parents) with other EYS. The then Labour leadership promoted connectedness between departments responsible for health, education, childcare, social services, housing, employment and family support (Anning and Hall, 2008). The Sure Start Local Programmes (SSLPs) initiative aimed to join up the planning and provision of primary and community health care, advice about child health and development, childcare, play, early education and parental support for all families with a child under the age of 4 years, focusing on disadvantaged areas.

By 2002, building on SSLPs, the concept of Sure Start children's centres was developed to bring together health practitioners who focus on maternal and child health (e.g. midwives, health visitors, speech therapists) to work in one location with a range of other services for children such as childcare, early education, play opportunities, child protection and family support (see Chapter 9). They were said to represent a radical shift in the way that services are delivered, offering significant opportunities for improving children's health and ensuring the families are able to access the information, support and services that they need (DCSF, 2007). The National Service Framework for Children, Young People and Maternity Services (DH/DfES, 2004) was another major step in the integration of health with other EYS. It dealt with young people and maternity services together, emphasising preventive services and setting out standards for all organisations providing services to children and their delivery partners, and set a standard for the Child Health Promotion Programme (CHPP; DH, 2008), now the Healthy Child Programme (HCP; DH, 2009a).

Most recently, the role of local authorities has been given more emphasis together with the promotion of a 'diverse sector' with strong roles for private, voluntary, community and social enterprise organisations (DfE/DH, 2011). The overall message of national policy is that central government will set overall policy, the statutory framework and standards but local areas will design services to meet local needs. Systems for joint working between services are promoted as a way to bring together professionals to create partnerships between health, children's centres, childminders, nurseries and schools. To facilitate this in England, Health and Wellbeing Boards together with public health reforms will play an important part in ensuring that the health needs of all young children are met and that integration between health and children's services is maximised. Local councillors will join with clinical commissioning groups, directors of public health, and children's services to assess local needs and develop a shared strategy for commissioning local children's services. The success of integrated working in the future is likely to depend on the effectiveness of information sharing between children's centres and health partners. This will need good agreements to be developed about ways to gain informed consent from families (DfE/DH, 2011). Health and other EY practitioners will need to agree on adequate data security mechanisms so that there can be adequate access to information about children and their families.

Constraints on public spending will continue to have an impact on funding for early years services with an emphasis on investing in services and programmes that are effective in achieving better outcomes and that save money by preventing problems later on, such as reducing youth crime, unemployment and health problems. New funding systems are being introduced to strengthen financial accountability in EYS. Payment by results for children's centres (DfE/DH, 2011) is intended to shift funding to reflect outcomes rather than inputs (see Chapter 9).

Early years health services today

In the past years there has been a significant re-orientation in terms of where health is positioned in relation to pregnant women, infants and young children. There are two programmes: the Healthy Child Programme and the Family Nurse–Partnership programme, that exemplify policy changes promoting the integration of health within early years services

The Healthy Child Programme (HCP)

The HCP is the universal schedule of screening tests, health and development reviews, immunisations and health promotion offered to all parents from pregnancy to 19 years (DH, 2009a). Its purpose is to identify and address health and development problems early, to protect children against serious communicable diseases and guide and support parents to promote their children's health and well-being. In the first five years there are screening tests for a number of diseases and abnormalities. Universal health and development reviews are carried out at key intervals including around 2 weeks after birth, before the first birthday, between 2 and 2½ years (DH, 2009a) and at school entry. The immunisation programme provides protection against serious communicable diseases such as diphtheria, measles, whooping cough, polio, tetanus and meningitis.

The services described in the HCP have been the core of preventive provision for many years. It has a strong evidence base (Hall and Elliman, 2006; DH, 2009a) and adaptations have been made over the years to keep pace with new research. Traditionally this programme been the territory of the NHS in isolation from wider children's services but recent years have seen some major changes, culminating in the updated HCP for pregnancy and the first years of life (DH, 2009a). The value of a more integrated approach between the HCP and EYS can be seen in plans to bring together the EYFS assessment with the HCP review at age 2 (DfE/DH, 2011). It is too early to tell whether this will be possible but for parents it offers an opportunity for one review at a key time in their child's development. The programme is led by health and delivered by health visitors and GPs. Health has the lead responsibility for the HCP for several reasons. First, identification of many of the factors in the assessment requires clinical knowledge and skills. Second, the HCP forms part of the routine care that all families receive during pregnancy and their child's early life from the health visitor which helps to ensure maximum coverage. Finally, being part of the NHS ensures that, through the HCP, children have optimal access to primary care and specialist health services.

Recent years have seen a decline in the number of health visitors which has undermined the coverage and quality of the HCP. This has been recognised by the current government and a programme to increase the number of health visitors by over 4,000 by 2015 is well under way (DH, 2011).

Example: Recent changes to the Healthy Child Programme

- The inclusion of a 'progressive universal' model, i.e. a universal core programme with additional evidence-based preventive services and programmes for children and families socially, emotionally or physically disadvantaged.
- Emphasis on promoting child health in pregnancy.
- Focus on public health priorities such as obesity prevention, breast feeding and accident prevention.
- Recognising the importance of early attachment and positive parenting and relationships within families.
- Giving fathers an equal role in the Healthy Child Programme.
- Delivering the programme through children's centres as well as general medical practices.
- Use of new technologies such as the internet
- Giving the health visitor the lead role with responsibility for the overall delivery of the Healthy Child Programme in terms of quality, coverage and outcomes.

The Family Nurse Partnership programme (FNP)

One of the challenges for preventive services in the first years of life is to find programmes that are known to work for the most disadvantaged children and families. One such is the Family–Nurse Partnership programme (known in the United States as the Nurse–Family Partnership). This intensive preventive home visiting provision for vulnerable first-time young parents is delivered by specially trained nurses from early pregnancy through until the child is 2 years old. FNP was developed in the United States over the past 30 years where three large scale research trials demonstrated significant and consistent short and long term benefits for children and their parents (Olds, 2006). The programme goals are to improve antenatal health, child health and development, and parents' economic self-sufficiency. The benefits are greatest where the mother has low psychological resources and it is these families for whom more intensive interventions are required than the universal HCP. FNP is a manualised and structured programme that works in depth across a range of domains. The nurses, drawn from health visiting, midwifery and other branches of nursing, use high level communication skills, and materials that help the parents to learn. They use a strength-based, future-orientated approach and methods that guide parents to make changes in how they care for themselves and their child. The programme has been tested in England since 2007 (Barnes et al., 2011) and the government wishes to see a doubling in the number of places available for families by 2015 to over 13,000. At the time of writing more than 9,000 families had benefited from the programme in more than half of local authority areas in England with new sites in Scotland and Northern Ireland. FNP has been an important part of the new landscape for children's services, bringing new perspectives and approaches. Its strong commitment to research and building an evidence base means that the future of the programme will always depend on the outcomes of research.

These two programmes are both health-led but delivered in the context of wider early years services where their impact is enhanced by their links to other services provided in Sure Start children's centres and the health work carried out by other early years staff.

Sure Start: working together with health in the early years

The establishment of Sure Start in the late 1990s brought significant changes to early years provision. At the heart of this new service was the integration of health with other services in Sure Start Local Programmes and the evaluation of these early programmes provides some useful learning on how to work together more effectively for children and families (see Chapter 9). The statutory guidance will be less prescriptive, and may change after the 'payment by results' research is completed (DfE/DH, 2011). However integration and collaborative working will still be central, highlighted in the recent report on child protection (Munro, 2011).

Lessons from Sure Start for 'joined-up' working

One of the groundbreaking aspects of the original Sure Start Local Programmes (SSLPs) was that they would typify 'joined-up' services for the early years, bringing together health, childcare and play, early education and parental support. The SSLPs were managed by partnership boards consisting of local stakeholders from the statutory and voluntary agencies and local community members including parents. Health was represented on almost all boards (Tunstill et al., 2002) but was the lead agency in only a small proportion (13%) (Meadows, 2006).

The national evaluation of the early impact on children and parents identified how integrated working between health and other EYS may impact on outcomes. Programmes that were more proficient in the identification of users had greater positive impacts on child development at 36 months old (NESS, 2005). Health-led programmes were better positioned to identify families with young children, because of easy access to birth records (McCallum Layton, 2002; Cordis Bright, 2003). When not the lead agency, information sharing could be a challenge for health services, due to data protection concerns, with health unwilling to take responsibility for sharing information about families with EY outreach staff (Ball et al., 2006).

Barriers to information sharing were also found between health professionals. In some local Sure Start areas community midwives were seen by Sure Start midwives holding pre-birth sessions as gatekeepers, who either referred women too late to take advantage of the additional support or who did not refer them at all to the Sure Start programmes (Pearson and Thurston, 2006). Inclusion of maternity provision with EYS should be strengthened now in children's centres by more recent initiatives such as the HCP and *Preparation for Birth and Beyond*. Information sharing between health and early years services should also be strengthened following the report of a working group to be presented to DfE in the near future (Gross, 2011).

The national evaluation of SSLPs identified ways that the integration of services could be enhanced. These include strong local authority support for shared service delivery; integrated protocols; and multi-disciplinary training and meetings. It further reported that partnerships could be dominated by one member, which could create barriers to an effective partnership (DCSF, 2008). It was necessary to gain high level commitment for each partner organisation for smooth partnership working with all partners setting aside their own interests and concerns about perceived threats to traditional roles and responsibilities. Health agencies and health professionals were sometimes perceived to work within a medical model that was not in accordance with the 'bottom-up' community-led focus core of the original SSLP model of working (Tunstill and Allnock, 2007).

Thus, overall it appears from the initial Sure Start experience that there was a need to develop a good balance of power between health and other agencies, either statutory or from the third sector, in relation to enhancing services in the early years. Attention was also needed to establishing clear understanding about ways to share information so that families could be accessed early and offered appropriate provision. The introduction of Children's Trusts represented one way to smooth this process (O'Brien et al., 2009); co-location of health services within children's centres can also be beneficial not only in enabling more efficient data sharing but also so that different professionals meet regularly and can share some training and other support. The original SSLP model placed a heavy burden on all partnership board members, which was reduced with the local authority led children's centre model.

Supporting the integration of health in early years services

Given the historical context within which early years and health services operate it comes as no surprise that the journey to integrated working is not always smooth. There is much to learn from the early days of Sure Start Local Programmes and many of these early difficulties were addressed as children's centres became established in local communities. Currently, in a period of recession, cuts have been made to those services and integration has to take place in an environment focused on maintaining high quality services which have a positive impact but with reduced resources, which represents a major challenge. The government hopes to establish stronger partnerships between health and EYS, stronger integrated working, with a foundation of effective information sharing in the foundation years (DfE/DH, 2011). The evaluation of Sure Start and experience of delivering the HCP and the FNP suggest that an environment that supports effective integrated working includes the following features:

1 Joint planning, giving partners an equal voice to shape how services are delivered, for whom and by whom with strong local authority support.
2 The development of a common language and agreed framework for services to facilitate commissioning.
3 Providing evidence-based services with systems for ongoing monitoring and evaluation to ensure that they are delivered effectively.
4 Professionals from different disciplines understanding and respecting each other's roles and core purpose.
5 Having the infrastructure in place, such as space for health professionals to work in EY settings with the necessary equipment and privacy, becoming true partners in the EY team.
6 Paying close attention to IT and data management. Health professionals need access to data from GPs and hospitals, with high data security. Rather than simply locating them out of EY into an NHS setting, systems are required to ensure confidential access.
7 Ensuring that multi-agency teams are run in a way that allows all EY staff to have an equal contribution.

All of the points mentioned above need to keep in mind that EYS should focus on the needs of children and families and their hopes and aspirations.

Conclusion

The role of health in EYS will always be a 'work in progress' influenced by wider societal changes and the economic context. Local services and the workforce delivering them will continue to change and finding more cost-effective services will be the key driver over the coming years. At the same time evidence will continue to emerge and new government policies will ensure that the landscape of children's services will continue to develop in the coming years. Nonetheless the recognition that health is everybody's business in the early years and that there is a need for greater service integration will remain driving forces in the future.

In this chapter we have provided the context for health in early years services and shown how health services such as the Healthy Child Programme and the Family Nurse Partnership Programme contribute to the shared goals of all who work with young children and families; to help children to achieve their potential and, for some, to overcome the impact of early disadvantage. The importance of health to the immediate and future outcomes for children is likely to become more significant as we learn more about early childhood development and the influences impacting on a child in pregnancy. This means that the role of health promotion and protection in EYS will become more central both through health services and through the health work of EYS. Moreover, the development of the Early Years Foundation Stage provides an opportunity to link the holistic approach of the HCP to that of EYS.

There is still much to be done to enable parents and children to have access to integrated high quality preventive health services that respond to their individual needs and aspirations. In many parts of the country good progress has been made to make sure that health is a core element in EYS and that EYS are linked to wider health services. Key challenges remain, of which the economic recession is the most significant and it is likely that the reductions in public funding will be the imperative for greater integration and use of programmes such as FNP where there is strong evidence of cost savings. At the same time there is more to be done on working together across both GP services and Sure Start children's centres, developing the lead role of the health visitor for the HCP and the wider health work of EYS and implementing evidence-based preventive services and programmes within children's services. What matters to parents and children will always be access to skilled and knowledgeable practitioners they can trust to act in the interest of the child and with whom they can build a relationship based on respect and partnership.

Key points to remember

- Children's health is the responsibility of all professionals coming into contact with children and families.
- Intervention to enhance child health and diminish inequalities in health outcomes, begins ideally in pregnancy.
- Several recent policies have made integration between health and early years a priority; their successes and challenges provide important learning for the future.
- Much has been learned about how professionals from different disciplines can work together effectively.
- The Healthy Child Programme, while ultimately the responsibility of health professionals, depends on the strong involvement of Early Years Services and parents.

Reflective tasks

- What do you think helps health and early years services to work together and what gets in the way? What could you do to help?
- Thinking about working with a family, when would you make contact with a health professional? Why would you? Whom would you contact? What would you expect from them and delivered how? How would this benefit the child and family?
- Discuss the issues raised by seeking external investment in early years services and 'payments by results' as a means of improving outcomes.

Further reading

Anning, A. and Ball, M. (eds) (2008) *Improving Services for Young Children. From Sure Start to Children's Centres.* London: Sage. Explores the successful and problematic aspects of Sure Start and has practical lessons for practitioners and policymakers.

Belsky, J., Barnes, J. and Melhuish, E. (eds) (2007) *The National Evaluation of Sure Start. Does Area-Based Early Intervention Work?* Bristol: Policy Press. Reviews the history of policies preceding Sure Start and how the programmes were expected to function, how they operated and their impact.

Blair, M., Stewart-Brown, S., Waterston, T. and Crowther, R. (2010) *Child Public Health.* Oxford: Oxford University Press. A comprehensive overview of the public health of children, providing information on how public health actions can make a difference.

Department of Health (DH) (2009) *The Healthy Child Programme. Pregnancy and the First 5 Years of Life.* London: DH. www.gov.uk/government/publications/healthy-child-programme-pregnancy-and-the-first-5-years-of-life. This publication sets out the content of the Healthy Child Programme and how it should be delivered, including joint commissioning and integrated children's services across general medical practice and Sure Start children's centres.

Hall, D. and Elliman, D. (2006) *Health for All Children*, revised 4th edn. Oxford: Oxford University Press. This book pulls together research and provides detailed information on what should be in a preventive child health programme for children.

Useful websites

Child and Maternal Health Observatory: PREview Planning Resources: http://www.chimat.org.uk/preview – planning resources to help commissioners, managers and professionals to target preventive resources, in particular around the Healthy Child Programme.

Center on the Developing Child: http://developingchild.harvard.edu – a range of research evidence on how to enhance child well-being through innovations in policy and practice.

Families in the Foundation Years: www.education.gov.uk/childrenandyoung people/earlylearningandchildcare/early/ – documents on evidence and research, delivery of services and policy.

Preparation for Birth and Beyond: www.gov.uk/government/publications/ preparation-for-birth-and-beyond-a-resource-pack-for-leaders-of-community-groups-and-activities. Gateway ref. 16509 – a resource pack is available which aims to help the NHS, local authorities and the voluntary sector in planning or running groups for expectant and new parents.

To access a variety of additional web resources to accompany this book please visit: **www.sagepub.co.uk/pughduffy**

References

Anning, A. and Hall, D. (2008) 'What was Sure Start and why did it matter?', in A. Anning and M. Ball (eds), *Improving Services for Young Children. From Sure Start to Children's Centres*. London: Sage. pp. 3–15.

Ball, M., Chrysanthou, J., Garbers, C., Goldthorpe, J., Morley A. and Niven, L. (2006) *Outreach and Home Visiting Services in Sure Start Local Programmes*. Sure Start Report 17. London: Department for Education and Skills.

Barker, D. (1998) *Mothers, Babies and Health in Later Life*. Edinburgh: Churchill Livingstone.

Barnes, J., Ball, M., Meadows, P., Howden, B., Jackson, A., Henderson, J. and Niven, L. (2011) *The Family Nurse Partnership Programme in England: Wave 1 implementation in toddlerhood and a comparison between Waves 1 and 2a of implementation in pregnancy and infancy*. London: Department of Health.

Blair, M., Stewart-Brown, S., Waterston, T. and Crowther, R. (2010) *Child Public Health*. Oxford: Oxford University Press.

Bronfenbrenner, U. (1979) *The Ecology of Human Development*. Cambridge, MA: Harvard University Press.

Center on the Developing Child at Harvard University (2007) *A Science-Based Framework for Early Childhood Policy: Using Evidence to Improve Outcomes in Learning, Behavior, and Health for Vulnerable Children*. Cambridge, MA: Center on the Developing Child at Harvard University. http://developingchild. harvard.edu/index.php/resources/reports_and_working_papers/policy_ framework/. (accessed 28 June 2013).

Center on the Developing Child at Harvard University (2010) *The Foundations of Lifelong Health are Built in Early Childhood*. Cambridge, MA: Center on the Developing Child at Harvard University. http://developingchild.harvard.edu/ resources/reports_and_working_papers/foundations-of-lifelong-health/. (accessed 28 June 2013).

Cordis Bright (2003) *Maltby Sure Start Spotlight Project Evaluation: Health Visiting*. Local evaluation report. www.ness.bbk.ac.uk/documents/findings/656. pdf (accessed 12 August 2008).

Cozolino, L. (2006) *The Neuroscience of Human Relationships*. New York: Norton.

Department for Children, Schools and Families (DCSF) (2007) *Sure Start Children's Centres: Phase 3 Planning and Delivery*. London: DCSF. www.education.gov.uk/ publications/standard/Surestart/Page1/DCSF-00665-2007 (accessed 13 April 2013).

Department for Children, Schools and Families (DCSF) (2008) *The Sure Start Journey. A Summary of Evidence*. London: DCSF. www.education.gov.uk/ publications/eOrderingDownload/FINAL%20The%20Sure%20Start%20Journey. pdf (accessed 13 April 2013).

Department for Education and Department of Health (DfE/DH) (2011) *Supporting Families in the Foundation Years*. London: DfE/DH.

Department for Education and Skills (DfES) (2003) *Every Child Matters*. Green Paper. Cm 5860. Norwich: TSO.

Department for Education and Skills (DfES) (2004) *Every Child Matters: Change for Children*. Nottingham: DfES Publications.

Department for Education and Skills (DfES) (2006) *Statutory Guidance on Inter-agency Co-operation to Improve the Wellbeing of Children: Children's Trusts*. London: DfES.

Department of Health and Department for Education and Skills (DH/DfES) (2004) *National Service Framework for Children, Young People and Maternity Services: Core Standard*. London: DH Publications.

Department of Health (DH) (2007) *Review of Health Inequalities Infant Mortality PSA Target*. London: DH.

Department of Health (DH) (2008) *The Child Health Promotion Programme: Pregnancy and the First Years of Life*. London: DH.

Department of Health (DH) (2009a) *The Healthy Child Programme: Pregnancy and the First 5 Years of Life*. London: DH. www.gov.uk/government/

publications/healthy-child-programme-pregnancy-and-the-first-5-years-of-life. (accessed 13 April 2013).

Department of Health (DH) (2009b) *The Healthy Child Programme: from 5 to 19 years old*. London: DH. http://.dera.ioe.ac.uk/11041/1/dh_108866.pdf (accessed 13 April 2013)

Department of Health (DH) (2011) *Health Visitor Implementation Plan 2011 to 2015*. London: DH. www.gov.uk/government/publications/health-visitor-implementation-plan-2011-to-2015. (accessed 28 June 2013).

Department of Health/National Health Service (DH/NHS) (2011, updated 2012) *Preparation for Birth and Beyond: A Resource Pack for Leaders of Community Groups and Activities*. www.gov.uk/government/publications/preparation-for-birth-and-beyond-a-resource-pack-for-leaders-of-community-groups-and-activities. (accessed 28 June 2013).

Glover, V. and O'Connor, T. (2002) 'Effects of antenatal stress and anxiety: Implications for development and psychiatry', *British Journal of Psychiatry*, 180, 389–91.

Graham, H. (2007) *Unequal Lives: Health and Social Inequalities*. Maidenhead: McGraw Hill/Open University Press.

Gross, J. (2011) *Two Years On: Final Report of the Communication Champion for Children*. London: Office of the Communication Champion. www.rcslt.org/speech_and_language_therapy/commissioning/communication_champion_final_report (accessed 8 May 2013).

Hall, D. and Elliman, D. (2006). *Health for All Children*, revised 4th edn. Oxford: Oxford University Press.

HM Government (2006) *Reaching Out: An Action Plan for Social Exclusion*. London: Cabinet Office.

HM Government (2010) *Healthy Lives, Healthy People: Our Strategy for Public Health in England*. CM 7985. London: TSO.

Joseph Rowntree Foundation (2011) *Monitoring Poverty and Social Exclusion*. York: JRF. www.jrf.org.uk/publications/monitoring-poverty-2011. (accessed 28 June 2013).

Kiernan, K. and Mensah, F. (2009) *Maternal Indicators in Pregnancy and Children's Infancy that Signal Future Outcomes for Children's Development, Behaviour and Health: Evidence from the Millennium Cohort Study*. ChiMat (Child and Maternal Health Observatory). www.chimmat.org.uk/resource (accessed April 2013).

Marmot, M. (2010) *Fair Society, Healthy Lives. Strategic Review of Health Inequalities in England Post 2010* (Marmot Review). London: Department of Health.

Meadows, P. (2006) *Cost Effectiveness of Implementing Sure Start Local Programmes: An Interim Report*. Sure Start Report 15. London: Department for Education and Skills.

McCallum, L. (2002) *Survey of Health Visitors. Seacroft Sure Start*. Local evaluation report. www.ness.bbk.ac.uk/documents/findings/118.pdf (accessed 12 August 2008).

Munro, E. (2011) *The Munro Review of Child Protection: Final Report. A Child-Centred System*. Cm 8062. Norwich: TSO.

National Evaluation of Sure Start (NESS) (2005) *Variations in Sure Start Local Programmes' Effectiveness: Early Preliminary Findings*. Sure Start Report 14. London: Department for Education and Skills.

National Scientific Council on the Developing Child (2010) *Early Experiences Can Alter Gene Expression and Affect Long-Term Development: Working Paper No. 10*. www.developingchild.net. (accessed 28 June 2013).

NHS Health Development Agency (2005) *Injuries in Children aged 0–14 years and Inequalities. A Report Prepared for the Health Development Agency*. University of Newcastle: Department of Child Health. www.nice.org.uk/niceMedia/pdf/injuries_in_children_inequalities.pdf. (accessed 28 June 2013).

NHS Information Centre (2012) *Health Survey for England 2010*. www.ic.nhs.uk/statistics-and-data-collections/health-and-lifestyles-related-surveys/health-survey-for-england. (accessed 28 June 2013).

O'Brien, M., Bachmann, M. O., Jones, N. R., Reading, R., Thorburn, J., Husbands, C., Shreeve, A. and Watson, J. (2009) 'Do integrated children's services improve child outcomes?: Evidence from England's Children's Trust Pathfinders', *Children & Society*, 23, 320–35.

Olds, D. (2006) 'The Nurse Family Partnership: an evidence based preventive intervention', *Infant Mental Health Journal*, 27, 2–25.

ONS (1999) *The Mental Health of Children and Adolescents in Great Britain*. London: Office of National Statistics.

ONS (2004) *Report on Mental Health of Children and Adolescents in Great Britain: Summary Report* by Meltzer, H. and Gatward, J. London: Office of National Statistics.

ONS (2010) *Fair Society, Healthier Lives. The Marmot Review*. London: Office of National Statistics. www.ucl.ac.uk/marmotreview (accessed 28 June 2013).

Pearson, C. and Thurston, M. (2006) 'Understanding mothers' engagement with antenatal parent education services: a critical analysis of a local Sure Start service', *Children & Society*, 20, 348–59.

Rutter, M. (2007) *Genes and Behaviour: Nature–Nuture Interplay Explained*. Oxford: Blackwell.

Tierney, C. and Nelson, L. (2009) *Brain Development and the Role of Experience in the Early Years*. Washington, DC: Zero to Three, National Centre for Infants, Toddlers and Families. www.zerotothree.org/reprints. (accessed 28 June 2013).

Tunstill, J. and Allnock, D. (2007) 'Sure Start Local Programmes: an overview of the implementation task', in J. Belsky, J. Barnes and E. Melhuish (eds), *The National Evaluation of Sure Start. Does Area-Based Early Intervention Work?* Bristol: Policy Press. pp. 79–95.

Tunstill, J., Allnock, D., Meadows, P. and McLeod, A. (2002) *Early Experiences of Implementing Sure Start*. Sure Start Report 1. London: Department for Education and Skills.

UNICEF (2008) *The State of the World's Children*. New York: UNICEF.

CHAPTER 11

Diversity, Inclusion and Learning in the Early Years

Iram Siraj-Blatchford

Chapter contents

Introduction

In modern, diverse societies, and a world that increasingly recognises the realities of global interdependence, it is essential that children learn social competence to respect other groups and individuals, regardless of difference. This learning must begin in the earliest years of a child's education. Learning is thus culturally and socially influenced by the context of the child's development. In this chapter I identify groups who are often disadvantaged due to the poor understanding that some early years staff have of them. I argue that there is a need to challenge the hidden assumptions that oppress particular individuals and groups.

Underlying inequality

Research suggests that settings can vary widely in the impact they have on children's outcomes, with some more effective at promoting positive cognitive, social and behavioural outcomes (Sylva et al., 2004). While most early childhood settings appear to be calm and friendly places on the surface, I argue that there may be a great deal of underlying inequality. This may occur through the implementation of differential policies, adult interactions, the use of displays, or through variations (or lack of variation) in the planning, curriculum or programme that the staff offer to individuals or groups.

These are especially important issues to be considered because they concern the early socialisation of *all* children. The notion that the child is an active player in his/her development is now widely accepted and recognised within the domain of early childhood development. However, in the early years children are vulnerable and every adult has the power to affect each child's future actions and behaviour, as well as their intentions, learning outcomes and beliefs.

Children can be disadvantaged on the grounds of diversity in ethnic background, language, gender and socio-economic class in both intentional and unintentional ways. Children with special educational needs are also commonly disadvantaged in early childhood. This is an important area of equity education, but beyond the scope of this chapter (though see Chapter 12).

Although I am concerned with the structural inequalities that create an over-representation of some groups in disadvantaged conditions, I have cautioned elsewhere against the assumption that all members of a structurally oppressed group (for example, all females) are necessarily oppressed by those members of a structurally dominant group (for example, all males). Because of the interplay between social class, gender, ethnicity and disability, our social experience and identities are multifaceted. I therefore argue that children can hold contradictory individual positions with respect to the structural position that their 'group' holds in society. Interactional contexts are also often highly significant.

Multiple identities

Identity formation is a complex process that is never completed. The effects of gender, class and other formative categories overlap, often in very complicated ways, to shape an individual's identity. While I do not attempt to discuss this complexity in detail, it is important for practitioners to be aware of the nature of shifting and changing identities. No group of children or any individual should be treated as having a homogeneous experience with others of their 'type'.

A number of publications related to the development of children's personal, social and emotional education provide very useful strategies for supporting the positive development of children's personal identities (Roberts, 1998), yet few writers relate this work specifically to ethnicity, language, gender or class.

There is now a great deal of research evidence of racial, gender and class inequality at a structural level in education (MacPherson, 1999). Concerning racial identity, culture and 'agency' (the interactions between individuals and groups) there is only an emerging literature, and most of this is about adolescent school children. This is particularly interesting because issues of gender and class identities have received more attention over the years, but again with regard to older children. Recent trends in research on ethnic and racial minority children and families reflect the broader growth in child development to include the influence of neighbourhood (ethnic composition, prevalence of violence, social class) and peer group (sociometric status, racial density, ethnic affiliation) (Quintana et al., 2006).

Working-class and minority ethnic children's poor academic performance has been well documented, and so has girls' performance in particular subjects (Lloyd, 1987). The link between racism, sexism, class prejudice and underachievement has also been thoroughly established (Ladson-Billings and Gillborn, 2004). However, if those who work with young children are able to undermine children's self-esteem (however unintentional this might be) through negative beliefs about children's ability due to their gender, religion, socio-economic status, language or ethnicity, then we have to evaluate these actions very carefully.

A child may be classed, gendered or 'racialised' (language status is also important here) in more than one way. Stuart Hall (1992), for example, discusses not only the discourses of identity between groups but also those of difference *within* ethnic groups. In the very act of identifying ourselves as one thing, we simultaneously distance ourselves from something else. In terms of race and ethnicity, Hall argues that there are often contradictions within these categories as well as between these and other categories such as sexuality, class, dis/ability. The way we perceive identities is very much shaped by how they are produced and taken up through the *practices* of representation (Grossberg, 1994).

Making use of the metaphor of a kaleidoscope in understanding identity based on a range of inequalities, Bailey and Hall (1992) argue that there will be individual differences within any identity-forming category, such as race, language, gender and social class. For instance, in the United Kingdom an

Indian woman who is a first-generation immigrant, and working class, will have a different identity to her daughter who is second-generation British-Indian, and has become a teacher. Their experience will vary because of how others perceive the combination of ethnic background in relation to their gender, socio-economic status, dress, language, even age and so forth. Mother and daughter will certainly not be treated by others in the same way but they might have some shared experiences.

Staff also need to find resources and a shared language with which to work with dual-heritage children and their parents to support a strong identity. But it would be even better if staff worked with all children to make them aware that they all have an ethnic/racial identity and that they all have a linguistic, gendered, cultural and diverse identity. Surely this is the way forward? In being sure of one's own identity as multifaceted, it must be easier for children to accept that others are exactly the same – even when the combinations are different!

Cosmopolitan citizenship

The UK has never been a monocultural society, and calls for the development of any single 'national' identity have therefore always been misplaced. Citizenship, just like identity, must be recognised as a multifaceted phenomenon. Contradictions and controversies are an inevitable consequence of diversity. They are also grist to the mill of progress and creativity. In any event, democracy requires something more than simply an orientation towards common values. From the earliest years we should be preparing children to participate, critically engage and constructively contribute to local, national and global society. An appropriate aim may be to develop the sort of 'cosmopolitan citizenship' that has been identified by Osler and Starkey (2005). In doing so, we should also recognise that:

> Cosmopolitan citizenship does not mean asking individuals to reject their national citizenship or to accord it a lower status. Education for cosmopolitan citizenship is about enabling learners to make connections between their immediate contexts and the national and global contexts. It is not an add-on but rather it encompasses citizenship learning as a whole. It implies a broader understanding of national identity. It also requires recognition that British identity, for example, may be experienced differently by different people. (Osler and Starkey, 2005: 27)

As the Advisory Group on Citizenship (DfEE, 1998: 216) suggested: 'The ethos, organisation, structures and daily practices of schools have a considerable impact on the effectiveness of citizenship education'. A few early childhood settings, particularly those influenced by Dewey (O'Brien, 2002), Freinet (Starkey, 1997) and Niza (Folque and Siraj-Blatchford, 2003), are already providing young children with significant opportunities to learn how to participate. A good deal more could be achieved in this direction.

The landscape of the UK population has changed over the past 20 years, mostly as a result of asylum arrivals in the 1990s and more recently, migration from the new member states of the European Union. While many migrant children have successful school careers in the UK, the evidence prevails of substantial underachievement in some communities. Poverty and low levels of maternal education are two factors that impact on migrant children's achievement as well as factors specific to particular migrant groups, such as interrupted prior education (Gillborn and Mirza, 2000; Tomlinson, 2001).

In the current UK climate, the significance of migrant children in schools is largely an under-researched area (Ackers and Stalford, 2004). A migrant child is anyone under the age of 18 who was born outside the UK and is now residing in the UK (as defined by the UN Convention on the Rights of the Child, 1989). This definition is broad and encompasses a wide range of reasons for migration – including refugees, asylum-seekers, reunified children, EU migrants and economic migrants – and circumstances of migration – whether an unaccompanied minor or migrating family, for example. A child's experience of migration is largely shaped by their experience of the education system, an experience that is palpably different to the experience of non-migrant children (Gillborn, 1995: 2).

Researchers have argued that despite the positive trends in the overall societal acceptance of immigrants, educating children from diverse cultural, linguistic, ethnic and racial or religious backgrounds are perceived as problematic (Adams and Kirova, 2006: 6).

The recent government's New Arrivals Excellence Programme (NAEP) has found, however, that migrant children can be academically beneficial to schools (DfES, 2007).

Vertovec (2006, 2007) proposes that the UK has reached a new stage of diversity where groups are not only distinguished by their country and ethnicity but by a complex 'interplay of variables' including immigration status. He argues that recognition of this 'super-diversity' of identities by UK policymakers can help improve experiences of inclusion and cohesion.

Whilst it is beyond the scope of this chapter to discuss the challenges in depth, it is however a policy challenge in the UK to reframe the way we think about migrant and refugee children, including supporting school life as well as the home environment using the skills of health visitors, outreach workers and volunteers to ensure successful integration into employment, community and society.

The dangers of stereotyping

The sexism, racism and other inequalities in our society explain why at a structural level certain groups of people have less power while others have more. But at the level of interaction and agency we should be critically aware of the danger of stereotyping and should focus on individuals. This is not to suggest that we should ignore structure, far from it, we need to engage in developing the awareness of children and staff through policies and practices, which explain and counter group inequalities.. What I am suggesting is that educators need to work from a number of standpoints to empower fully the children in their care. Children need to be educated to deal confidently and fairly with each other and with others in an unjust society; in this way our values will be reflected in our children (Siraj-Blatchford and Clarke, 2000).

The experiences and values of children can come from parents' views, media images and the child's own perceptions of the way people in their own image are seen and treated. Research (Bates and Pettit, 2007) shows the need for positive interaction between a child and caregiver is particularly crucial for children from disadvantaged backgrounds in the child's socialisation. In the absence of strong and positive role models children may be left with a negative or a positive perception of people like themselves. This bias can start from birth. In the Effective Provision for Pre-School Education (EPPE) project, the largest project on early years education in the UK, we have found some marked differences in equity issues. For instance, we know that most providers create a poor environment for children in terms of diversity (Sylva et al., 1999) with the exception of combined centres and some nursery schools (see also Chapter 4 and Siraj-Blatchford et al., 2003). The EPPE study also found that the provisions for diversity were associated with as many as five of the nine attainment outcomes measured. This was higher than for any of the other Early Childhood Environmental Rating Scale subscales that were applied to evaluate the quality of the learning environment that was offered. EPPE showed that minority ethnic workers were better represented in social services-type daycare and combined centres, and very few were employed in other sectors (Taggart et al., 2000). Managers and staff in settings need to be challenged by such data and think about how this has come about and, indeed, how it might be changed.

Many parents and staff conclude from children's behaviour that they are naturally different, without considering their own contribution to the children's socialisation, or considering the impact of role-modelling. Difference, apart from physiology, is therefore a matter of social learning. This has implications for practice and the kinds of activities that we should make sure all children have access to, regardless of their gendered or other previous experiences.

Diversity and achievement

Cultural identity should be seen as a significant area of concern for curriculum development and values education. All children and adults identify with classed, gendered and racialised groups (as well as other groups) but what is especially significant is that some cultural identities are seen as less 'academic' than others (often by the staff and children). We know that children can hold views about their 'masterful' or 'helpless' attributes as learners (Dweck and Leggett, 1988). Dweck and Leggett (1988) therefore emphasise the importance of developing 'mastery' learning dispositions in children. There is evidence that children who experience education through taking some responsibility for their actions and learning become more effective learners. They are learning not only the content of the curriculum, but also the processes by which learning takes place (Siraj-Blatchford and Clarke, 2000). Roberts (1998) argues that the important area of personal and social education should be treated as a curriculum area worthy of separate activities, planning and assessment.

The 'helpless' views adopted by some children can be related to particular areas of learning and can lead to underachievement in a particular area of the curriculum. Children construct their identities in association with their perceived cultural heritage. Recent research shows us that the use of ethnic minority status as a proxy for culture should only be a preliminary step in evaluating an individual's cultural framework (Hill et al., 2005). Researchers have been attempting to disentangle the various components associated with ethnic and racial minority children (e.g. race, culture, social class etc.) as well as the interactions of multiple sociocultural features (Quintana et al., 2006).

Recently we have heard a good deal in educational debates about (working-class) boys' underachievement. The results from the school league tables suggest that some boys do underachieve in terms of basic literacy, but it is important to note that this is only certain groups of boys and not all boys. In the UK working-class white boys and African-Caribbean boys are particularly vulnerable (Siraj-Blatchford, 1998). Similarly, children from some minority ethnic groups perform poorly in significant areas of the curriculum while other minority ethnic groups achieve particularly highly (Gillborn and Gipps, 1997).

It is apparent that certain confounding identities, for instance, white/working class/male, can lead to lower outcomes (in the UK and some other societies) because of expectations held by the children and adults. In asserting their masculinity, white working-class boys might choose gross-motor construction activities over reading or pre-reading activities. Similarly, some girls may identify more strongly with home-corner play and favour nurturing activities over construction choices.

Class, gender and ethnicity are all complicit here and the permutations are not simple but they do exist and do lead to underachievement. The answer is to avoid stereotyping children's identities but also requires educators to take an active role in planning for, supporting and developing individual children's identities as masterful learners of a broad and balanced curriculum (Siraj-Blatchford, 1998).

Diversity and learning

Children need to be in a state of emotional well-being, secure and to have a positive self-identity and self-esteem. The curriculum must be experiential, social/interactional and instructive and children need to be cognitively engaged (Siraj-Blatchford and Clarke, 2000). There is considerable interaction between emotion and cognition in seeking to understand children's social behaviour (Lemerise and Arsenio, 2000).

It is widely recognised that an integrated, holistic and developmental approach is needed to learning, teaching and care with children from birth to 7. They learn not only from what we intend to teach but from all their experiences. For example, if girls and boys, or children from traveller families, are treated differently or in a particular manner from other people, then children will learn about the difference as part of their world-view. To deny this effect is to deny that children are influenced by their socialisation. The need for emotional, social, physical, moral, aesthetic and mental well-being all go hand in hand. This is also true of our youngest children, hence the references to equal opportunities in the Early Years Foundation Stage (EYFS) (DfE, 2012) where the revised framework of the EYFS emphasises the overall holistic development of the child. This includes stronger emphasis on communication, language, physical and personal, social and emotional development, and stronger partnerships between parents and professionals. It also separates out language and literacy and hence promotes greater emphasis on language development especially for children under 3.

The early years curriculum should therefore incorporate work on children's awareness of similarities and differences, and help them to see this as 'normal'. Some children can be limited in their development by their view that there are people around them who do not value them because of who they are. This would suggest that early years staff need to offer *all* children guidance and support in developing positive attitudes towards all people. A focus on similarities is as important as dealing with human differences. The early years are an appropriate time to develop this work with young children.

Students, teachers, childminders and playgroup workers have often asked how they can deal with class, gender and ethnic prejudice. It would be a great mistake to assume that this is only a 'problem' in largely multi-ethnic settings. Strategies that allow children to discuss, understand and deal with oppressive behaviour aimed at particular groups, such as minority ethnic children, girls, the disabled and younger children, are essential in all settings. I suggest that educators should always make opportunities for stressing similarities as well as differences.

Promoting positive self-esteem

Findings from EPPE and related Researching Effective Pedagogy in the Early Years (REPEY) (Siraj-Blatchford et al., 2002) emphasise the importance of adult–child relationships as an indicator of quality within the most effective settings. The NICHD study also states the importance for positive caregiving of staff who were 'more educated' and held more child-centred beliefs about child-rearing (NICHD, 2000). Thus, staff need to help children learn to guide their own behaviour in a way that shows respect and caring for themselves, other children and adults, and their immediate and the outside environment. Values education goes hand in hand with good behaviour management practices. The way that adults and children relate to each other in any setting is an indication of the ethos of that setting. To create a positive ethos for equity practices, staff in every setting will need to explore what the ethos in their setting feels like to the users, for example, parents, children and staff. Staff need to explore what behaviours, procedures and structures create the ethos, which aspects of the existing provision are positive and which are negative, and who is responsible for change.

Children need help from the adults around them in learning how to care for each other and to share things. Young children's capacity to reflect and see things from another person's point of view is not fully developed. Most small children find it difficult to see another person's view as equally important. Children need a lot of adult guidance to appreciate the views and feelings of others. This can be learnt from a very early age. In her research on the relationship between mothers and their babies, and relationships between very young siblings, Dunn (1987: 38) suggests that mothers who talk to their children about 'feeling states' have children who themselves 'become particularly articulate about and interested in feeling states'. Laible and Thompson (2007) in their work on early socialisation, offer further support for the evidence of warm and mutually responsive relationships to enhance a child's conscience development. Furthermore, they discuss the power of content and structure for young children '*who are seeking predictability and control to everyday experience*' (p. 194). Consideration for others has to be learnt.

Of course educators cannot expect children to behave in this way if they do not practise the same behaviour themselves. If children see us showing kindness, patience, love, empathy, respect and care for others, they are more likely to want to emulate such behaviour. For many educators the experience of working actively with children in this way may be underdeveloped, especially when it comes to dealing with incidents of sexism or racism. Each setting, as part of their equality policy, will need to discuss the issue of harassment and devise procedures for dealing with it.

Example: Dealing with discrimination

Short-term action

- If you hear sexist, racist or other remarks against another person because of ethnicity, class or disability you should not ignore it or you will be condoning the behaviour and therefore complying with the remarks.
- As a 'significant' other in the child's life, she/he is likely to learn from your value position. Explain clearly why the remarks made were wrong and hurtful or offensive, and ask the abused child how she/he felt so that both children can begin to think actively about the incident.
- Do not attack the child who has made the offending remarks in a personal manner or imply that the child as a person is wrong, only that what was said is wrong.
- Explain in appropriate terms to the abuser why the comment was wrong, and give both children the correct information.
- Support and physically comfort the abused child, making sure that she knows that you support her identity and that of her group and spend some time working with her on the activity she is engaged with.
- At some point during the same day, work with the child who made the offending remarks to ensure that she knows that you continue to value her as a person.

Long-term action

- Target the parents of children who make offensive discriminatory comments, to ensure that they understand your policy for equality and that you will not accept abuse against any child. Point out how this damages their child.
- Develop topics and read stories which raise issues of similarities and differences in language, gender and ethnicity, and encourage the children to talk about their understandings and feelings.
- Create the kind of ethos that promotes and values diverse images and contributions to society.
- Involve parents and children (depending on the age of the children) in decision-making processes, particularly during the development of a policy on equality.
- Talk through your equality policy with all parents as and when children enter the setting, along with the other information parents need.
- Develop appropriate teaching and learning strategies for children who are acquiring English so that they do not get bored, frustrated and driven to poor behaviour patterns.

(adapted from Siraj-Blatchford, 1994)

Social competence

The significance of emotional warmth and affection in the development of young children is a recurring theme (Roberts, 2002). Developing the social skills that assist children to get along with their peers and adults will have a significant impact on their lives. Social skills are used to enter and maintain interactions, to engage others in conversation, to maintain friendships and to cope with conflict. Non-verbal skills involve smiling, nodding, eye contact and the development of listening skills. All of these non-verbal strategies form foundations for language interactions.

All babies and toddlers in childcare and nursery settings need opportunities for warm interactions with adults. Young children need consistency, familiarity and the presence of caring adults, and those children who come from language backgrounds other than English need support on a consistent basis from staff who speak their first or home languages. The children need to receive messages that say they are important to their caregivers. They need to develop a feeling of trust in their new environment. Staff need to respect all the children in their care. This means taking particular care to understand and acknowledge the different cultural and socio-economic backgrounds of the children and to make special efforts to work with families to assist the children to settle into a new environment (Siraj-Blatchford and Clarke, 2000).

Boys and girls can have different language experiences within the same household. Dunn (1987) studied the relationship between mothers' conversation styles with their children aged 18–24 months. She states:

> The analysis also showed marked and consistent differences in the frequency of such conversations in families with girls and with boys. Mothers talked more to 18-month-old daughters about feeling states than they did to their 18-month-old sons. By 24 months the daughters themselves talked more about feeling states than did the sons. (Dunn, 1987: 37)

In multicultural or diverse societies there is a great variety of family values and traditions and it is important that children are brought up to balance the tensions and handle the adjustments of being reared in one way and being educated in another. Children need to become socialised into the new practices and society. Early childhood staff need to be patient, caring, tolerant, flexible and need to be able to communicate effectively with parents and other staff about their work.

The EYFS provides children with a range of first-hand experiences that promote equality, interactive learning, foster children's self-esteem and support individual children in their construction of knowledge. They also recognise the key role of play in young children's development and learning. Central to this is the role of the early childhood staff in establishing the learning environment, structuring interactions and supporting learners in their development.

Young, developing children do not compartmentalise their learning, so an integrated environment suitable for the development of cognitive, social, emotional, aesthetic, linguistic/communicative and physical dimensions needs to be created. Therefore, the approaches highlighted in this chapter must go across the whole of the curriculum.

All children have the right to an early childhood curriculum that supports and affirms their gender, cultural and linguistic identities and backgrounds. From an early age, young children are beginning to construct their identity and self-concept and this early development is influenced by the way that others view them and respond to them and their family. Within today's society, the prejudice and racist attitudes displayed towards children and families can influence their attitudes towards themselves and others (MacPherson, 1999). Early childhood educators need to examine their own values, attitudes and prejudices, and learn to deal with them in positive ways.

A culturally responsive curriculum and staff who understand and respect the cultural and linguistic backgrounds of the children in their care can make a difference. Children can grow up with the ability to retain their home language and culture, and to have pride in their gender and class identity as well as adapting to the new cultures and languages of any early childhood setting they enter.

Curriculum for children in the early years should:

- foster children's self-esteem
- acknowledge the cultural and linguistic backgrounds of all children
- actively maintain and develop the children's first or home languages
- promote the learning of English as an Additional Language
- value bilingualism as an asset
- value what boys and girls can do equally
- support families in their efforts to maintain their languages and culture
- foster an awareness of diversity in class, gender, ability and culture
- promote respect for similarity and difference
- challenge bias and prejudice
- promote a sense of fairness and justice
- promote principles of inclusion and equity
- support the participation of the parents in the children's learning.
(Siraj-Blatchford and Clarke, 2000)

All those working with young children can discuss with parents and community members issues which concern both parents and staff. The following list covers some of the aspects of family and community life which should be explored and so enhance understanding:

- family history
- religious beliefs and practices (including important cultural events)
- children's everyday life at home
- language practices
- parents' theories about learning
- parents' views on schooling and early education
- community events and contacts.

Involving parents

Reference has already been made to the data that were collected in the EPPE project (Siraj-Blatchford, 2004) on early years provisions for 'diversity'. The EPPE project also looked particularly closely at the quality of the early home learning environment (HLE) (Melhuish et al., 2001) provided by parents. Although the parents' socio-economic status and levels of education were found to be related to child outcomes, the quality of the home learning environment was found to be even more important. At the age of 3 years and onwards a strong association was found between poor cognitive attainment and less stimulating HLEs. By comparison there was only a moderate, positive association between the HLE and parents' social class and qualifications. For example, the children of parents who reported that they regularly taught/played with the alphabet had pre-reading scores 4.5 points higher than children whose parents did not teach/play with the alphabet. This could be compared to the impact of social class, where the difference between lowest class (IV and V) and highest (I) was only 2.4 points. In other words, EPPE found that it is what parents did that is more important than who they were (Melhuish et al., 2001). Thus parental involvement can be particularly significant in breaking the cycle of disadvantage and children's underachievement (Feinstein, 2003, 2004).

However, as Melhuish et al. (2008) note, responsibility should not be placed solely on parents. The provision of good quality pre-school education from 3 years is likely to produce further benefits when the pre-school centre works closely with parents (Siraj-Blatchford et al., 2003).

Research on pre-school education in five countries evaluated by Sylva and Siraj-Blatchford (1995) also considered the links between home and school. The authors report the importance of involving parents and the local community in the construction and implementation of the curriculum. When they begin school or early childhood education, children and their parents 'bring to the school a wealth of cultural, linguistic and economic experience which the school can call upon' (1995: 37).

> It therefore becomes the responsibility of the teacher to localise the curriculum and to enlist the support of the local community and families in framing school policy and practice and making the school and educational materials familiar and relevant to the children's experience. (p. 37)

Parents need to be given information about the curriculum and learning outcomes and about the achievement of their children. They may also require support in improving their home learning environment. Early years practitioners will need to establish a dialogue with parents that is meaningful to them. Observations of children can be exchanged between staff and parents. To achieve values of true inclusiveness, everyone has to be part of the process of education and care.

There is more on partnership with parents in Chapter 13.

Key points to remember

- Early years practitioners need to actively challenge the hidden assumptions that oppress particular individuals and groups.
- While most early childhood settings appear to be calm and friendly places on the surface there may be a great deal of underlying inequality, and children disadvantaged in both intentional and unintentional ways.
- It is important for practitioners to be aware of the nature of shifting and changing identities. The UK has never been a monocultural society, and calls for the development of any single 'national' identity have therefore always been misplaced.
- Cultural identity should be seen as a significant area of concern for curriculum development and values education. The EPPE study found that the provisions for diversity were associated with as many as five of the nine attainment outcomes measured.
- Each setting needs to discuss the issue of harassment and devise procedures for dealing with it as part of their equity policy.
- All children have the right to an early childhood curriculum that supports and affirms their gender, cultural and linguistic identities and backgrounds.

 Points for discussion

- When was the last time an audit of equity issues (SEN, gender and racial equality and so on) was conducted in your setting and what were the outcomes?
- How can the English *Early Years Foundation Stage* (DfE, 2012) and the Welsh *Foundation Phase* (DCELLS, 2006) be truly inclusive to all children – and their parents?
- How are parents involved in informing your inclusive practice and how do they remain partners in its implementation?

Further reading

Siraj-Blatchford, I. (2004) 'Educational disadvantage in the early years: how do we overcome it? Some lessons from research', *European Early Childhood Education Research Journal*, 12 (2), 5–20.

Siraj-Blatchford, I. and Clarke, P. (2000) *Supporting Identity, Diversity and Language in the Early Years*. Buckingham: Open University Press.

To access a variety of additional web resources to accompany this book please visit: **www.sagepub.co.uk/pughduffy**

References

Ackers, H. L. and Stalford, H. (2004) *A Community for Children?* Aldershot: Ashgate.

Adams, L. D. and Kirova, A. (2006) *Global Migration and Education: Schools, Children and Families.* Brunswick, NJ and London: Lawrence Erlbaum Associates.

Bailey, D. and Hall, S. (eds) (1992) *Critical Decade: Black British Photography in the 80s. Ten.8,* 2(3).

Bates, J. E. and Pettit, G. S. (2007) 'Temperament, parenting and socialization', in J. E. Grusec and P. D. Hastings (eds), *Handbook of Socialization Theory and Research.* New York/ London: The Guilford Press. pp.152–77.

Department for Children, Education and Life Long Learning (DCELLS) (2006) *The Foundation Phase in Wales 3–7.* Cardiff: National Assembly for Wales.

Department for Children, Schools and Families (DCSF) (2008) *Statutory Framework for the Early Years Foundation Stage.* Nottingham: DCSF Publications.

Department for Education (DfE) (2012) *Statutory Framework for the Early Years Foundation Stage 2012: Setting the Standards for Learning, Development and Care for Children from Birth to Five.* Runcorn: DfE Publications.

Department for Education and Employment (DfEE) (1998) *Education for Citizenship and the Teaching of Democracy in Schools* (The Crick Report). London: QCA.

Department for Education and Skills (DfES) (2007) *New Arrivals Excellence Programme.* London: DfES.

Dunn, J. (1987) 'Understanding feelings: the early stages', in J. Bruner and H. Haste (eds), *Making Sense: The Child's Construction of the World.* London: Routledge. pp. 26–40.

Dweck, C. S. and Leggett, E. (1988) 'A social-cognitive approach to motivation and personality', *Psychological Review,* 95 (2), 256–73.

Feinstein, L. (2003) 'Inequality in the early cognitive development of British children in the 1970 cohort', *Economica,* 70, 73–97.

Feinstein, L. (2004) 'Mobility in pupils' cognitive attainment during school life', *Oxford Review of Economic Policy,* 20 (2), 213–29.

Folque, M. and Siraj-Blatchford, I. (2003) *Children and Pedagogues Learning Together in the Early Years: The Collaborative Process of the Portuguese MEM Pedagogy.* European Early Childhood Educational Research Association Conference, 3–6 September, University of Strathclyde.

Gillborn, D. (1995) *Racism and Antiracism in Real School: Theory, Policy and Practice.* Buckingham: Open University Press.

Gillborn, D. and Gipps, C. (1997) *Recent Research on the Achievements of Minority Ethnic Pupils.* London: HMSO.

Gillborn, D. and Mirza, H. (2000) *Educational Inequality: Mapping Race, Class and Gender.* HMI 232. London: Ofsted.

Grossberg, L. (1994) 'Introduction: Bringing it all back home – pedagogy and cultural studies', in H. A. Giroux and P. McLaren (eds), *Between Borders:*

Pedagogy and the Politics of Cultural Studies. London: Routledge. pp. 1–28.

Hall, S. (1992) 'Race, culture and communications: Looking backward and forward in cultural studies', *Rethinking Marxism*, 5, 10–18.

Hill, N. E., McBride Murry, V. and Anderson, V. D. (2005) 'Sociocultural contexts of African American families', in V. C. McLoyd, N. E. Hill and K. A. Dodge (eds), *African American Family Life: Ecological and Cultural Diversity.* New York: Guildford. pp. 21–44.

Ladson-Billings, G. and Gillborn, D. (2004) *The Routledge Falmer Reader in Multicultural Education.* London: RoutledgeFalmer.

Laible, D. J. and Thompson, R. A. (2007) 'Early socialisation: a relationship perspective', in J. E. Grusecm and P. D. Hastings (eds), *Handbook of Socialisation Theory and Research.* New York/London: The Guildford Press. pp. 181–207.

Lemerise, E. A. and Arsenio, W. F. (2000) 'An integrated model of emotion processes and cognition in social information processing', *Child Development*, 71 (1), 107.

Lloyd, B. (1987) 'Social representations of gender', in J. Bruner and H. Haste (eds), *Making Sense: The Child's Construction of the World*, London: Routledge. pp. 147–62.

MacPherson, W. (1999) *Report of the Stephen Lawrence Enquiry.* London: HMSO.

Melhuish, E., Sylva, K., Sammons, P., Siraj-Blatchford, I. and Taggart, B. (2001) *The Effective Provision of Pre-School Education (EPPE) Project: Technical Paper 7 – Social/Behavioural and Cognitive Development at 3–4 Years in Relation to Family Background.* London: Department for Education and Employment/ Institute of Education, University of London.

Melhuish, E., Sylva, K., Siraj-Blatchford, I., Taggart, B. and Phan, M. (2008) 'Effects of the Home Learning Environment and preschool center experience upon literacy and numeracy development in early primary school', *Journal of Social Issues*, 64, 95–114.

NICHD Early Childcare Research Network (2000) 'Characteristics and quality of child care for toddlers and preschoolers' *Applied Developmental Science 4.* https://secc. rti.org/abtarcts.cfm?abstracts=17 (accessed 22 May 2009).

O'Brien, L. (2002) 'A response to "Dewey and Vygotsky: Society, Experience, and Inquiry in Educational Practice"', *Educational Researcher*, June/July, 31 (5), 21–3.

Osler, A. and Starkey, H. (2005) *Learning for Cosmopolitan Citizenship Ad-Lib.* University of Cambridge Institute of Continuing Education, Issue 28. www. Cont-Ed.Cam.Ac.Uk/BOCE/Adlib28/Article1.html.

Quintana, S. M, Aboud, F. E., Chao, R. K., Contreras-Grau, J., Cross, W.E., Hudley, C., Hughes, D., Liben, L. S., Nelson-Le Gall, S. and Vietze, D. L. (2006) 'Race, ethnicity, and culture in child development: contemporary research and future directions', *Child Development*, 77 (5), 1129–41.

Roberts, R. (1998) 'Thinking about me and them: personal and social development', in I. Siraj-Blatchford (ed.), *A Curriculum Development Handbook for Early Childhood Educators.* Stoke-on-Trent: Trentham. pp. 155–74.

Roberts, R. (2002) *Self-Esteem and Early Learning*, 2nd edn. London: Paul Chapman.

Siraj-Blatchford, I. (1994) *The Early Years: Laying the Foundations for Racial Equality*. Stoke-on-Trent: Trentham.

Siraj-Blatchford, I. (ed.) (1998) *A Curriculum Development Handbook for Early Childhood Educators*. Stoke-on-Trent: Trentham.

Siraj-Blatchford, I. (2004) 'Educational disadvantage in the early years: how do we overcome it? Some lessons from research', *European Early Childhood Education Research Journal*, 12 (2), 5–20.

Siraj-Blatchford, I. and Clarke, P. (2000) *Supporting Identity, Diversity and Language in the Early Years*. Buckingham: Open University Press.

Siraj-Blatchford, I., Sylva, K., Muttock, S., Gilden, R. and Bell, D. (2002) *Researching Effective Pedagogy in the Early Years*. London: Department for Education and Skills, Research Report 356.

Siraj-Blatchford, I., Sylva, K., Taggart, T., Sammons, P., Melhuish, E. and Elliot, E. (2003) *Case Studies of Practice Across the Foundation Stage, Technical Paper 10*. London: Department for Education and Employment/Institute of Education, University of London.

Starkey, H. (1997) 'Freinet and citizenship education, pleasure of learning et Travail Coopératif: Les méthodes éducatives et la philosophie pratique de Célestin Freinet', *Séminaire International à l'alliance Française de Londres*, June.

Sylva, K. and Siraj-Blatchford, I. (1995) *The Early Learning Experiences of Children 0–6: Strengthening Primary Education through Bridging the Gap between Home and School*. Paris: UNESCO.

Sylva, K., Siraj-Blatchford, I., Melhuish, E., Sammons. P. and Taggart, B. (1999) *Effective Provision for Pre-School Education Project, Technical Paper 6*. London: Department for Education and Employment/Institute of Education, University of London.

Sylva, K., Melhuish, E.C., Sammons, P., Siraj-Blatchford, I. And Taggart, B. (2004) *The Effective Provision of Pre-School Education (EPPE) Project: Final Report*. London: DfES/Institute of Education, University of London.

Taggart, B., Sylva. K., Siraj-Blatchford, I., Melhuish, E. and Sammons, P. (2000) *Characteristics of the Centres in the EPPE Sample: Interviews. Technical Paper 5*. London: Department for Education and Employment/Institute of Education, University of London.

Tomlinson, C. A. (2001) *How to Differentiate Instruction in Mixed-Ability Classrooms*, 2nd edn. Alexandria, VA: ASCD.

Vertovec, S. (2006) 'The emergence of super-diversity in Britain', COMPAS Working Paper No.25, University of Oxford.

Vertovec, S. (2007) 'New complexities of cohesion in Britain: super-diversity, transnationalism and civil-integration'. A Thinkpiece for the Commission on Integration and Cohesion, Department for Communities and Local Government.

CHAPTER 12

Inclusion and Entitlement in the Early Years for Disabled Young Children and Young Children with Special Educational Needs

Philippa Stobbs, Elizabeth Andrews and Julie Revels

Chapter contents

- Disabled children and children with special educational needs – who are we talking about?
- Early identification and action
- Access and entitlement
- Sharing information and decision-making with families
- Professional skills, support for settings and workforce development

Considering disabled children and children with special educational needs (SEN) in a separate chapter runs many of the risks associated with current policymaking and professional practice: it feeds the perception that these children are separate or different from their peers and that they therefore require different treatment. Such a mindset works against the best interests of many children, particularly when factors influencing learning and development are relatively mild. There is a time and a place for focusing sharply on the nature of additional or specialist support required by an individual child, but a general presumption of difference erodes understanding that the Early Years Foundation Stage (EYFS) and universal services provide the bedrock on which any additional support should be built and can, in consequence, undermine the confidence of practitioners in their ability to support the learning and development of disabled children and children with SEN. An assumption of difference also subtly and dangerously lowers expectation of what a child may be able to achieve and distracts early years practitioners from the task of supporting the learning and development of all the children in their care.

Yet two very different sets of legislation require early years practitioners to do things differently: children with SEN are defined, in the 1996 Education Act, by the requirement to do things that are *additional to or different from* what is generally available; and the Equality Act requires settings and practitioners to make *reasonable adjustments* for disabled children, in effect: to do things differently to prevent disabled children being at a disadvantage.

In this chapter we first describe the population of children involved and then consider the *same yet different* tension in the context of changing national policy in relation to the following themes:

- early identification and action
- access and entitlement
- sharing information and decision-making with families
- professional skills, support for settings and workforce development.

Disabled children – who are we talking about?

The definition of disability is set out in the Equality Act 2010: a disabled person is someone who has

> *a physical or mental impairment which has a substantial and long-term adverse effect on his or her ability to carry out normal day-to-day activities.*

This definition is wide and it includes many more young children than those with a known sensory or physical impairment or learning difficulty. It includes children with conditions that may not be apparent at birth, such as autism and speech, language and communication impairments and children with a range of medical conditions such as diabetes, epilepsy and more severe forms of common conditions such as asthma and eczema. Some progressive conditions, such as cancer and HIV/AIDS, are also included even if they do not yet have an effect on the child's ability to carry out normal day-to-day activities.

For young children, normal day-to-day-activities are playing, communicating, interacting, running around. If an impairment has *more than a minor or trivial* effect on such activities for *a year or more*, a child is likely to be covered by the disability discrimination duties in the Equality Act.

Some of the duties in the Equality Act only apply to disability. Of these, practitioners are most likely to be familiar with the *reasonable adjustments* duty. This requires early years settings to adopt an anticipatory approach, foreseeing potential barriers and taking pre-emptive action to prevent a disabled child being at a disadvantage compared with their peers.

There is no compulsory collection of disability data and estimates of the number of disabled children vary with the methodology and the definitions used. Research undertaken by Thomas Coram Research Unit (Mooney et al., 2006), was designed to estimate the number and the characteristics of disabled children using local services. It highlighted a dearth of data, both locally and nationally, and pointed to the limitations this placed on effective planning. The government draws on the Family Resources Survey, which indicates about 700,000 disabled children in England and 800,000 in the United Kingdom, though this is recognised as being an underestimate of those who are covered by the Equality Act definition (Hansard, 2012).

Children with special educational needs – who are we talking about?

The definition of special educational needs is set out in the Education Act 1996. Children are defined as having SEN if they have a learning difficulty; and they have a learning difficulty if they have *a significantly greater difficulty in learning than other children of the same age* and they require *special educational provision*. Special educational provision is defined as provision that is *additional to, or otherwise different from, provision that is normally available* to children of that age.

The definition is relative, in two key ways: children's needs are defined in relation to other children and in relation to the provision available locally. One consequence of this relative definition is that the number of children identified as having SEN is highly variable across different settings, schools and local authorities.

About 20% of children of school age are identified as having SEN, 2.8% with a statement and 17.0% without (DfE, 2012a). Data by age group[1] show that the percentage of children identified as having SEN is significantly smaller for younger children: under the age of 3, 3.5% of the age group is identified as having SEN, including just 225 children with a statement. By the age of 6, the percentages rise significantly to over 20% of children, 1.9% with a statement and 18.7% without. This period from birth to 5 is a time of significant development for children and a period in which many factors affecting learning and development begin to show. It is a key period for identifying and addressing SEN.

The Early Years Census and the School Census provide data on 3- and 4-year-old children taking up free early education places, but not about children identified with SEN within this group. There is, however, information on children taking up some of their entitlement in a special school: about 4,000 children, or 0.3% of all children who take up the free offer.

The Department for Education's annual analysis of SEN data shows a year-on-year increase in both the number and percentage of children identified as having SEN. Between 2008 and 2012 this rose from 11.3 to 13.1% (DfE, 2012b). The same analysis provides data on attainment in the Early Years Foundation Stage Profile (EYFSP). Within an overall increase in children with SEN, this shows that between 2007 and 2011, children with identified speech, language and communication needs (SLCN) increased by about 4% to about half of children with SEN[2] and to about 2.5% of all children in the same age cohort.

Overlapping populations

Though there are two different definitions, in the Equality Act 2010 and the Education Act 1996, there is significant overlap between disabled children and children identified as having SEN. The definition of SEN includes disabled children who require special educational provision, that is: something *additional or different* to be provided for them. Research at Bath and Bristol Universities estimates that about three-quarters of disabled children are also covered by the definition of SEN (Porter et al., 2008). This leaves a quarter of disabled children who may not be identified as having SEN. Children who have a range of health conditions, for example epilepsy or diabetes, are likely to be covered by the definition of disability but often do not have SEN.

There are also significant overlaps with other vulnerable groups: the data show that more disabled children grow up in poverty. A report for the Disability Rights Commission identified a two-way relationship between disability and poverty in childhood, with more poor children likely to become disabled and more disabled children likely to live in poverty (IPPR, 2007).

The terms *disabled* and *SEN* are often linked, through usage, to particular service areas, with *disabled* being used more in relation to social care and *SEN* in relation to education. This can distract from the fact that disabled children go to school and the day-to-day activities of children with SEN at home promote development and well-being. Additional, personalised support is needed in educational settings, at home and in the local community to achieve a holistic approach that enables families with disabled children and children with SEN to live as other families do – in effect, to *live ordinary lives* (HM Treasury and DfES, 2007).

Early identification and action

Early years practitioners are key to identifying needs early and taking appropriate action. The revised EYFS (DfE, 2012c) emphasises the responsibility of practitioners for considering the individual needs, interests and stage of development of each child in their care. It highlights practitioners' responsibility for considering, with the child's parents or carers, any concerns about the child's development and learning, whether the child may have an SEN or a disability and, if so, practitioners' responsibility for arranging appropriate support from services and agencies beyond the setting.

For all children, but particularly for children with emerging needs, the EYFS progress check at two provides a well-timed opportunity to share views between practitioners, parents and carers and any professionals involved with the child. The check is intended to link with the health visitor check, but the proposals for an integrated education and health review from 2015 should provide a more comprehensive basis for sharing information and agreeing actions.

Early identification and action are based firmly in the mainstream processes of early years settings, and are rooted in confident knowledge of child development. The Nutbrown Review of early education and childcare qualifications (Nutbrown, 2012) identifies an understanding of typical patterns of development as being crucial to noticing signs of slower or different development and to whether any such differences may indicate SEN or disability.

The same knowledge and expertise also informs understanding of the next steps in a child's learning and development and how to support progress. The more detailed an assessment of development becomes, the more important it is to broker a two-way exchange of information with the family and home so that a rich, shared picture can develop of how a child is doing at home and in the setting, how they are changing and what might happen next. This two-way communication and sharing of information is critical to the early stages of joint planning and agreement of next steps. The Early Support Developmental Journal can help with this.

Effective early identification depends on the professional skills of practitioners. A number of reports have indicated how, where practitioners lack the skills or the confidence to respond appropriately, needs may be identified without action being taken (DCSF, 2009a; Ofsted, 2010; DfE, 2011a). A disastrous cocktail of slow progress, lowered expectations and parental loss of confidence can follow. This can limit children's achievements and later difficulties can become overlaid on earlier ones.

The point of early identification is to take purposeful action, to remove barriers and to make different or additional provision to meet a child's needs. Such action must follow hard on the heels of the identification of need.

All early years settings in receipt of government grant are required to *have regard to* the SEN Code of Practice (DfES, 2001). The Code sets out a graduated response to children's SEN – *Early Years Action* – where settings take purposeful action to provide additional support for individual children. Where children do not make adequate progress, settings are advised to seek advice from relevant specialist services outside the setting at *Early Years Action Plus*. When more significant additional support is required, the local authority can be asked to carry out a statutory assessment. This may lead to a statement being issued. Local authorities are required to identify, assess and, where necessary, make provision for a child, through a statement of a child's SEN.

The graduated approach is designed to address an underlying continuum of need ranging from children with milder needs that are more likely to emerge or become apparent around the time of going into group provision at the age of 3 or 4; to the much smaller number of children with more complex needs and who may be identified at or shortly after birth. A graduated approach implies a gradual intensification of focus and action: more detailed assessment of a child's learning and development; a more detailed planning process to design objectives or next steps; consideration of a range of options for supporting the child's learning and development; and more detailed monitoring of progress towards objectives or next steps. Crucial to the success of this approach are:

- a closer working partnership with parents than might be required for other children;
- increased engagement with specialist services in the local area so that working practices in the setting can be adjusted and, where necessary, more expert support accessed.

The graduated approach should not be taken to mean delay in seeking a specialist opinion if a child is not developing as expected or is not responding to purposeful action taken by the setting. Equally, for some young children, specialist support may be in place before they arrive in a setting, for example, where a specialist teacher for visual impairment has been involved from an early age.

The graduated approach within early years settings should be led and coordinated by the setting's SEN Coordinator (SENCO). The Code specifies that setting SENCOs are responsible for ensuring close working with parents and with any professionals involved with the child; advising and supporting colleagues; ensuring that Individual Education Plans are in place; and ensuring that relevant information is brought together, reviewed and updated (DfES, 2001). However, while SENCOs lead the work, it remains the responsibility of all staff working in early years settings to identify and meet the SEN of young children (DCSF, 2009b).

In March 2011, the government published proposals for the reform of the SEN system (DfE, 2011a). Statutory assessment and statements would be replaced by a single assessment process and an Education, Health and Care

Plan (EHCP) available from birth to the age of 25. It is intended that an EHCP would focus more on outcomes and less on SEN processes. There are accompanying proposals for the closer integration of education, health and care systems that support disabled children and children with SEN. Measures to implement the SEN reforms were included in the Children and Families Bill which was introduced in to Parliament in February 2013 (HC Bill, 2012–2013).

The measures themselves would not make a significant difference for early years settings: the definition, whilst amended to take account of young people over the age of 16, would retain its relative nature; a statutory process would cut in at a similar point. The more significant change for settings would be a new SEN Code of Practice which would change the advice about the graduated approach, removing Early Years Action and Early Years Action Plus and replacing them with a single stage.

In summary, it is important that:

- early identification is followed by early action;
- children are not labelled in a way that encourages low expectations;
- we do not label children in a way that leads to their being seen as essentially different from their peers;
- an understanding of the learning and development of all children informs decisions about when to identify and how to respond to young children identified with SEN;
- an integrated approach to the identification of children's needs is developed, first with parents and carers and supported where necessary by expertise from beyond the setting; and
- this process is supported by current and new structures for checking children's development and their early progress.

Access and entitlement

High quality childcare and early years settings have a positive impact on children's learning and development as well as providing contact with other young children, facilitating transition into school and increasing opportunities for mothers and fathers to work. Government has recognised the importance of children with SEN and disabilities enjoying the same access to such opportunities as others (DCSF, 2009c).

Any evidence that access to childcare and education for disabled young children and young children with SEN is limited is therefore disturbing. In 2004, the National Audit Office (NAO) found that many providers of high quality childcare and early education did not offer services for disabled children and children with SEN. Childminders were least able to offer services: 19% offered services for children with SEN; only 10% offered services for disabled children. Amongst the providers who did offer provision, the majority offered only one place for a disabled child. The barriers that were most frequently cited by providers were lack of suitable provision, lack of trained staff, and the need for funding to pay for extra staff (NAO, 2004).

The evaluation of the Disabled Children's Access to Childcare (DCATCH) programme (DfE, 2011b) shows that the cost and availability of appropriate childcare provision continue to limit access for families of disabled children. Parents talked openly to the evaluators about their need for childcare in order to work and their child's need for social activities, inclusion and the opportunity to interact and develop friendships. The very children who might benefit most from provision are amongst those least likely to be able to access it and the limitations on access relate back directly to the nature of the child's disability or SEN.

A careful reading of the evaluation of the *Early Education Pilot for Two Year Old Children* provides further insights. Although specifically targeted, along with other groups, disabled children and children with SEN were significantly more likely than their peers to drop out of the pilot early, 17% of children compared with 9% of children with no SEN or disability (Smith et al., 2009). Qualitative findings from the evaluation showed that parents of disabled children and children with SEN had more mixed views about the provision than parents overall. Where the provision met their child's needs, the benefits were felt more strongly; where it did not, parents were more dissatisfied. There was also evidence that those parents who were not satisfied were more likely to change settings when their child reached the age of 3, and a significant number of these parents were parents of children with SEN who then sought a special school place for their child as they became eligible for the universal 3- and 4-year-old offer – an outcome that doesn't reflect well on the quality of inclusive provision.

Only rarely are barriers to inclusion physical, though the design of the physical environment can be an important enabler of access and full participation. Attitudinal factors are also important, including resistance to inclusive practice in some settings and lack of confidence amongst parents that settings can meet their child's needs and keep them safe.

Between 2005 and 2007 the Council for Disabled Children worked with local authorities, services, children's centres and families to identify the barriers faced by families and to explore the creative solutions that had been put in place (Stobbs, 2008). Some barriers were simple, practical and relatively easy to deal with; others were more complicated and their resolution required sensitive planning and partnership working:

> Tinsley Children's Centre in Sheffield includes a number of disabled children with a range of impairments and medical conditions. The Centre uses a discussion of risk assessments around children's medical conditions to both engage and re-assure parents about the ability of the Centre to provide for their child. One parent, who was originally very reluctant to leave her child and thought she would have to give up work, is now leaving her child at the Centre.

Early Days Children's Centre in Sheffield has a welcoming room for childminders. This is well-used, but childminders also integrate into the drop-in and other facilities at the Centre. It is through this route that a number of parents of disabled children have seen their child engaging in activities at the Centre and have become comfortable with their child progressing to provision at the Centre.

(Stobbs, 2008)

The successful inclusion of children with more complex needs depends on close working with a range of different agencies beyond the setting: health, social care and education teams with particular and, sometimes, impairment-specific expertise. Early Support, an approach that supports integrated working in partnership with families, has an important role to play in promoting access and inclusion in these circumstances.

Recent initiatives have been focused more on disadvantaged groups of young children and the question arises as to whether including disabled children and children with SEN in the target group for the new free 2-year-old offer, without looking at the specific aspects of quality that need to be in place in order to include them, is acceptable as an overall strategy.

In 2010 a number of funding streams, including early years funding for sustainability, access and workforce development, were brought together into the Early Intervention Grant. Within the same financial year £311 million was taken out of the new aggregated grant, with further percentage cuts in subsequent years. Reductions in the Early Intervention Grant and the fact that it is not ring-fenced have a direct impact on the capacity of local authorities to sustain the range and level of support to settings, they risk further compromising access for young children who are dependent on reasonable adjustments or additional or different provision in order to be able to benefit from the opportunities available to other young children.

Sharing information and decision-making with families

The importance of working with families is a consistent thread running through current policy statements. The EYFS embeds an expectation of partnership with families. This mirrors a strong, overarching recognition of the importance of families, coming from both the Department of Health and the Department for Education (DfE/DH, 2011). Current proposals for reform of the SEN framework also focus on improving relationships between parents and the services they use.

Early years settings are required to identify a *key person* for each child in their care. Providers must inform parents and/or carers of the name of the key person and explain their role, when a child starts attending their setting. The role of the key person is to:

- ensure that children's learning and care is tailored to meet their individual needs;
- build a relationship with parents;
- engage and support them in guiding their child's development at home. (DfE, 2012c)

The more significant or complex a child's SEN or disability, the more important it becomes to build on this foundation and do more. More interaction and exchange of information with families is required, and it becomes important to develop joint planning and decision-making with mothers and fathers sitting alongside practitioners. In some cases, key working is also required to help families navigate the system. It may be helpful to think of this *sliding scale* of partnership with families as a necessary, complementary aspect of the graduated response to children's learning.

The need for effective partnership working with families is most obvious when known, significant and possibly multiple factors affect a child's development and well-being. It is recognised (DfE/DH, 2011) that in these circumstances:

- more people are likely to be involved with a family to provide therapy, treatment and support for learning;
- more coordination including key working may be required; and
- better communication is needed to avoid duplication or confusion.

Government identifies Early Support as an approach with an established track record that is known to work (DfE, 2012d). Early Support provides information; supports parents and carers in making informed choices; and brokers joint decision-making between families and settings, using a single plan. At an operational level, it promotes the use of regular, family-centred or *team around the child* meetings to share information and agree next steps, supported by key working. It also provides an Early Years Developmental Journal, a shared record that makes it easier for families and practitioners to talk about what they know about what a child can do, using the framework of *Development Matters* (Early Education, 2012).

Many children with identified SEN do not need such a structured, integrated approach. However, a complete picture of any child's development depends on the full participation of parents and all the practitioners and professionals who have been involved (NCB/DfE, 2012). Whenever there is concern about a child's development, normal expectations of contact, communication and joint working with families should be revisited. These interactions reflect the same underlying processes for all children but may need to be more frequent, more detailed and more collaborative in nature in order to provide a sound basis for shared planning and decision-making.

There is an overlap between the early identification of special educational needs and *risk* factors associated with social deprivation, particularly in relation to high incidence factors such as language and communication needs. However, it is not yet clear whether a strong enough focus is being maintained on the distinctive nature of working with families when children are disabled or have SEN.

In summary, increased engagement between settings and families is required when children have SEN. Some of the characteristics of effective partnership working in this context are:

- more frequent contact and discussion;
- continuity in the personnel building a relationship with families;
- mutual respect;
- regular information exchange that operates as a two-way street and values what families have to say about their child;
- discussion and agreement of shared priorities and goals; and
- joint planning with families.

Professional skills, support for settings and workforce development

The attributes, training and commitment of the workforce are the most frequently cited factors influencing the quality of early years provision and workforce development is particularly important in making high quality provision for young children with SEN and disabilities. Through the last decade, government guidance assumed SENCOs working in early years settings would be supported by an Area SENCO and SENCO network. Sure Start guidance published in 2002 set out the anticipated role of Area SENCOs as being: to enable early years practitioners to develop inclusive practices and to remove any barriers to learning (DfES/DWP, 2002).

In 2004, *Removing Barriers to Achievement* (DfES, 2004) identified a gap in workforce development and concerns about the availability of specialist advice and support. Since then, the need for a strategic approach to developing expertise has been recognised and some positive action has been taken to invest in workforce development. Ambitious targets for the provision of one Area SENCO to every 20 settings were established and there was a focus on building improved capacity and professional skills across the early years.

In 2006, funding was made available, through the Transformation Fund, to improve the qualifications and training of the early years workforce. In 2007, this was replaced by the Graduate Leader Fund, designed to increase the number of graduates leading the workforce. Professional development for SENCOs was one of the priorities identified by local authorities. This led to the establishment of Early Years Lead Practitioners for SEND, who share good practice within and beyond their setting.

Through the DCATCH programme and roll-out, training and development was highlighted as part of the solution to improving quality and removing barriers for young disabled children (DCSF, 2009d). More recently, some of the key concerns raised by the Nutbrown Review relate to whether qualifications equip those who hold them to work with children with SEN and disabilities, whether they have a sharp enough focus on inclusion, and whether they equip those qualifying to work with parents as well as children (DfE, 2012d). The final report places a strong emphasis on the importance of workforce development in SEN and disability.

The professional skills and knowledge required to make high quality, inclusive early years provision must be a priority for all practitioners, whether in initial training or as part of continuing professional development. In addition to targeted professional development, a wide range of resources is available to support early years practitioners in developing inclusive practice. Some of these are listed at the end of the chapter.

The quality of leadership is considered key: under Ofsted's revised framework, inspectors are required to evaluate and report on the effectiveness of leadership and management in implementing the requirements of the EYFS. Leaders are expected to support practitioners through professional supervision and to offer a targeted programme of professional development. The approach needs to start with a regularly updated audit of the knowledge, skills and experience of all practitioners. During regular supervision meetings with leaders, each practitioner's development needs would be discussed and opportunities to meet these needs identified. At the level of the setting there should be opportunities for all practitioners to:

- gain skills in identifying additional need early and taking action;
- become confident in applying whole setting strategies that support inclusive practice, such as Makaton signing, visual timetables; and
- develop skills in making adjustments to policies and practices in the setting.

Beyond the level of the individual setting, where there is a need to call upon external advice for guidance and support, the role of the Area SENCO remains key. However, there is evidence that local support, training and advisory services are being eroded. In this context, the omission of any reference to the role of the Area SENCO in the revised EYFS (DfE, 2012c) seems significant. As centrally funded support services have shrunk, practitioners have been encouraged to set up local networks to support each other.

Current approaches to professional development and enhanced practice in the early years include the establishment of Early Years Teaching Centres (EYTCs). Centres work together to raise standards and improve children's outcomes across foundation years settings within each centre's area of reach. Between 2011 and 2013, Pen Green Research Centre were setting up a national network of EYTCs. The Department for Education and the Department of Health committed to sharing the evaluative research from this work in order to plan next steps (DfE/DH, 2011). While the main focus of EYTCs is on disadvantage rather than on SEN and disability, the proportion of children in EYTCs with SEN is higher than in other settings.

There is also a need for specific support, advice and professional development for setting SENCOs. Such opportunities rely on external expertise; they are predicated on the SENCO's own commitment to professional development; they draw on nationally available training and resources from disability-specific organisations. Specific, in-depth training should include:

- promoting and supporting inclusion, especially social inclusion;
- adapting pedagogical approaches to improve the development and learning of young children;
- working with parents in the context of diagnosis, this could be based on the Early Support approach and use the materials;
- multi-agency and integrated working including knowledge of where to get specialist support.

Over and above the expertise developed by SENCOs, there is a need for specialist support and training such as that required for children with hearing and visual impairments, for children with health needs, and for children identified as having complex learning difficulties and disabilities (Specialist Schools and Academies Trust, 2011).

Much specialist support and training relies on expertise that is not available in individual settings. As many local authorities face difficult decisions about budget priorities, there is increasing evidence of the demise of teams that have evolved since the introduction of Area SENCOs. This is leaving settings and SENCOs with little or no access to support and training beyond their walls and puts at risk their ability to provide an effective service for disabled children, children with SEN and their families. This is a growing concern. At the same time local authorities are planning more places for 2-year-olds and some of those children will have identified SEN, delayed development, or may be disabled. Having the training and support in place to meet the needs of this group of young children is vital to their being able to benefit from the provision.

In summary, a model of support and training that contributes to high quality inclusive provision in the early years needs to be offered at a variety of levels. This should include:

- setting-based support, advice and development: based on careful planning to ensure that all practitioners have the relevant skills;
- locality or area based support, advice and development: based on sharing good practice across settings to improve outcomes; such support needs to have a clear SEN and disability focus;
- specific, in-depth support, advice and development for setting SENCOs, drawing on local and national expertise; and
- specialist support and training required to enable settings to include young children with specific low incidence needs.

This approach holds the potential to increase the capacity of practitioners to work effectively with a wide range of children with diverse needs, and with their families. As with other aspects of SEN and disability in the early years, what we do for this group of children needs to be based firmly in the very best of what we do for all children. However, we need to go further: where mainstream policies and practices do not fully accommodate the children who are the focus of this chapter, we need to make adjustments to what we do and do things that are additional to or different from what we do for all children.

Key points to remember

- Children with special educational needs are everyone's business.
- Practitioners must consider the individual needs, interests and stage of development of each child, and use this information to plan enjoyable and challenging experiences. When a child is identified as having SEN, the job remains the same: to provide an enabling environment for a unique child, but practical help and training may be needed to extend your practice.
- You are likely to meet a few children with known special educational needs, but many more whose need for additional support will become more obvious during the time they are with you.
- Assessment and identification of a special educational need is a starting point. The action taken in response to identification is likely to be more important for a child and their family.
- Early identification of a SEN requires you to be confident in your understanding of typical patterns of child development. It depends on you being able to recognise when a child's learning or behaviour falls outside the expected range for their age.
- Talk with parents and carers. They have useful information to share about their child and are critical partners in the processes of assessing need, discussing options and taking action.
- A proactive, 'can do' attitude may be required to find and access advice, support and training about working with children with special educational needs in your local area.

 Points for discussion

- What does the two year progress check add to the early identification of children with special educational needs?
- Where can early years settings look for support in developing their practice with children with special educational needs and disabilities?

> - What might Education, Health and Care Plans look like for young children and how will additional support be agreed for children who do not meet the thresholds for such plans?

Reflective tasks

- What is involved in working well with parents and carers of disabled children and children with SEN? Is this the same as working with the parents and carers of other 'vulnerable' families?
- What do you think a good pathway looks like for a child who has SEN identified during the foundation years? Is it available in your setting?

Notes

1. This dataset relates to children in state-funded schools only.
2. The nature of children's special educational needs is recorded only at Early Years Action Plus, or School Action Pus, and for children with a statement.

Further reading

Department for Education (DfE) (2012) *2013 Early Years Foundation Stage Handbook*. Standards & Testing Agency. www.education.gov.uk/schools/teachingandlearning/assessment/eyfs/a00217599/eyfs-handbook.

Department for Education and Skills (DfES) (2001) *SEN Code of Practice*. London: DfES. www.education.gov.uk/publications/standard/publicationDetail/ Page1/DfES%200581%202001.

Council for Disabled Children (forthcoming) *Early Years, Disability Discrimination and the Equality Act 2010: What Providers Need To Know*.

Useful websites

www.ncb.org.uk/earlysupport – Early Support information and resources, including the Developmental Journal

www.thecommunicationtrust.org.uk/early-years.aspx – Communication Trust information and resources

http://webarchive.nationalarchives.gov.uk/20110202093118/http://nationalstrategies.standards.dcsf.gov.uk/search/inclusion/results/nav%3A46335facets%3A24717 – Inclusion Development Programme materials http://www.council for disabled children.org.uk/resources/cdcs-resources – Council for Disabled Children resources

To access a variety of additional web resources to accompany this book please visit: **www.sagepub.co.uk/pughduffy**

References

Department for Children, Schools and Families (DCSF) (2009a) *Lamb Inquiry: Special Educational Needs and Parental Confidence.* Nottingham: DCSF Publications.

Department for Children, Schools and Families (DCSF) (2009b) *Inclusion Development Programme – Supporting Children on the Autism Spectrum: Guidance for Practitioners in the Early Years Foundation Stage.* https://www.gov.uk/government/uploads/system/uploads/attachment_data/file/190536/00040-2009BKT-EN.pdf. (accessed July 2013)

Department for Children, Schools and Families (DCSF) (2009c) *Next Steps for Early Learning and Childcare: Building on the 10 Year Strategy.* http://webarchive.nationalarchives.gov.uk/20130401151715/https://www.education.gov.uk/publications/eOrderingDownload/00173-2009DOM-EN.pdf. (accessed July 2013)

Department for Children, Schools and Families (DCSF) (2009d) *Disabled Children's Access to Childcare (DCATCH) Pilot Activity: Information for Local Authorities.* http://webarchive.nationalarchives.gov.uk/20130401151715/https://www.education.gov.uk/publications/eOrderingDownload/DCATCH-Report.pdf. (accessed July 2013)

Department for Education (DfE) (2011a) *Support and Aspiration: A New Approach to Special Educational Needs and Disability.* http://webarchive.nationalarchives.gov.uk/20130401151715/https://www.education.gov.uk/publications/eOrderingDownload/Green-Paper-SEN.pdf (accessed July 2013)

Department for Education (2011b) *Disabled Children's Access to Childcare (DCATCH): A Qualitative Evaluation.* https://www.gov.uk/government/uploads/system/uploads/attachment_data/file/182117/DFE-RR146.pdf. (accessed July 2013)

Department for Education (DfE) (2012a) Statistical First Release: Special Educational Needs in England, January 2012. http://www.education.gov.uk/rsgateway/DB/SFR/s001075/sfr14-2012.pdf. (accessed July 2013)

Department for Education (DfE) (2012b) *Children with Special Educational Needs 2012: An Analysis.* http://www.education.gov.uk/rsgateway/DB/STR/d001092/index.shtml. (accessed July 2013)

Department for Education (DfE) (2012c) *Statutory Framework for the Early Years Foundation Stage 2012: Setting the Standards for Learning, Development and Care for Children from Birth to Five.* Runcorn: DfE.

Department for Education (DfE) (2012d) *Support and Aspiration: A New Approach to Special Educational Needs and Disability: Progress and Next Steps.* https://www.gov.uk/government/uploads/system/uploads/attachment_data/file/180836/DFE-00046-2012.pdf (accessed July 2013)

Department for Education and Department of Health (DfE/DH) (2011) *Supporting Families in the Foundation Years.* London: DfE/DH.

Department for Education and Skills (DfES) (2001) *SEN Code of Practice.* London: DfES. www.education.gov.uk/publications/standard/publicationDetail/ Page1/DfES%200581%202001.

Department for Education and Skills (DfES) (2004) *Removing Barriers to Achievement: The Government's Strategy for SEN.* http://webarchive.nationalarchives.gov.uk/20130401151715/https://www.education.gov.uk/publications/eOrderingDownload/DfES%200117%20200MIG1994.pdf. (accessed July 2013)

Department for Education and Skills and Department for Work and Pensions (DfES/DWP) (2002) *Area Special Educational Needs Coordinators (SENCOs): Supporting Early Identification and Intervention for Children with Special Educational Needs: Guidance for Local Education Authorities and Early Years Development and Childcare Partnerships.* Nottingham: Department for Education and Skills and Department for Work and Pensions.

Early Education (2012) *Development Matters in the Early Years Foundation Stage.* London: British Association for Early Childhood Education. www.early-education.org.uk/sites/default/files/Development%20Matters%20FINAL%20PRINT%20AMENDED.pdf. (accessed July 2013)

Hansard (2012) House of Commons Written Answers for 28 June 2012. Column 358W. www.publications.parliament.uk/pa/cm201213/cmhansrd/cm120628/text/120628w0002.htm#120628101000054. (accessed July 2013)

HC Bill (2012–2013) *Children and Families Bill* [5]

HM Treasury and Department for Education and Skills (HT/DfES) (2007) *Aiming High for Disabled Children: Better Support for Families.* http://webarchive.nationalarchives.gov.uk/20130401151715/https://www.education.gov.uk/publications/eOrderingDownload/PU213.pdf (accessed July 2013).

IPPR (2007) *DISABILITY 2020: Opportunities for the full and equal citizenship of disabled people in Britain in 2020.* A report by IPPR Trading Ltd for the Disability Rights Commission. http://www.ippr.org/images/media/files/publication/2011/05/Disability_2020_full_1568.pdf (accessed July 2013).

Mooney, A., Owen, C. and Statham, J. (2006) *Disabled Children: Numbers, Characteristics and Local Service Provision.* Department for Children, Schools and Families, Research Report DCSF–RR042. http://webarchive.nationalarchives.gov.uk/20130401151715/https://www.education.gov.uk/publications/eOrderingDownload/DCSF-RR042.pdf. (accessed July 2013)

National Audit Office (NAO) (2004) *Early Years: Progress in Developing High Quality Childcare and Early Education Accessible to All.* London: TSO.

National Children's Bureau and Department for Education (NCB/DfE) (2012) *A Know How Guide: The EYFS Progress Check at Age Two.* London: NCB/DfE. www.education.gov.uk/publications/eOrderingDownload/EYFS%20-%20know%20how%20materials.pdf. (accessed July 2013)

Nutbrown, C. (2012) *Foundations for Quality. The Independent Review of Early Education and Childcare Qualifications: Final Report* (Nutbrown Review). London: Department for Education.

Office for Standards in Education (Ofsted) (2010) *The Special Educational Needs and Disability Review: A Statement Is Not Enough.* http://www.ofsted.gov.uk/resources/special-educational-needs-and-disability-review.

Porter, J., Daniels, H., Georgeson, J., Hacker, J., Gallop, V., Feiler, A., Tarleton, B. and Watson, D. (2008) *Disability Data Collection for Children's Services Research Report.* Department for Children, Schools and Families, Research Report DCSF – RR062. https://www.gov.uk/government/uploads/system/uploads/attachment_data/file/189688/DCSF-RR062-report.pdf.pdf (accessed July 2013).

Smith, R., Purdon, S., Schneider, V., La Valle, I., Wollny, I., Owen, R., Bryson, C., Mathers, S., Sylva, K. and Lloyd, E. (2009) *Early Education Pilot for Two Year Old Children.* Department for Children, Schools and Families, Evaluation Research Report – DCSF-RR134. https://www.gov.uk/government/uploads/system/uploads/attachment_data/file/189524/DCSF-RR134.pdf.pdf. (accessed July 2013).

Specialist Schools and Academies Trust (2011) *The Complex Learning Difficulties and Disabilities Research Project: Developing Pathways to Personalised Learning: Final Report.* http://complexld.ssatrust.org.uk/uploads/CLDD_project_report_final.pdf. (accessed July 2013)

Stobbs, P (2008) *Extending Inclusion: Access for Disabled Children and Young People to Extended Schools and Children's Centres: A Development Manual.* The Council for Disabled Children. Nottingham: DCSF Publications. www.councilfordisabledchildren.org.uk/media/56642/extending_inclusion.pdf. (accessed July 2013)

CHAPTER 13

Working with Parents in the Early Years

Mary Crowley and Helen Wheeler

Chapter contents

- A brief history of the development of services for parents and current policy
- The importance of what parents do at home to support children's early learning and development
- The benefits of building relationships with parents, fathers as well as mothers
- The range of help for parents around the parent–child relationship and how to access this
- Recruiting parents and involving them in the work of the early years setting and in governance

Developing awareness of the importance of working with parents

In recent years there has been a growing awareness of the importance of supporting parents in the vital but sometimes challenging task of bringing up their children. At the same time, research has shown not only how important parents' interactions with their children are to children's development and emotional health, but also how the involvement of parents in their children's early learning can have a powerful impact on their progress.

Policymakers were surprisingly slow to recognise the impact of parents on outcomes for children and the importance of offering parenting support and advice in their parenting role. In the 1970s, Sir Keith Joseph, then Secretary of State for Social Services, in a widely cited speech, referred to the 'cycle of deprivation' and the need to break the intergenerational cycle of poor parenting which contributes to mental health problems, crime, domestic violence and educational underachievement (see Rutter and Madge, 1976). He commissioned a review into how to raise standards of parenting (Pugh, 1980) which led to a number of further studies and initiatives intended to raise the importance of parenting and the need to support parents and prospective parents at every stage of the life cycle (see Pugh and De'Ath, 1984). Further studies (Pugh and De'Ath, 1989) described a range of possible levels of involvement and partnership between parents and early years settings and a final study in 1994 provided an updated national picture of education and support for parents and stressed the importance of providing services 'to help parents and prospective parents to understand their own social, emotional, psychological and physical needs and those of their children and to enhance the relationship between them' (Pugh et al., 1994).

Service development

As the pressure to provide better support for parents grew, a new forum – The Parenting Education and Support Forum[1] – was set up by the National Children's Bureau in 1995 to bring together those who were working across the country to provide education and support for parents. The Forum worked with partners from a range of national and local organisations to urge government to put in place universal parenting services. Whereas up to this point bringing up children had been seen as a largely private matter and the state only took an interest and intervened when something went wrong, the government finally saw that it had a role to play in supporting parents and parenting. The publication by the Home Office (at that time responsible for family policy) of the policy document *Supporting Families* (Home Office, 1998), the establishment of the Parenting Education and Support Forum and the setting up of the National Family and Parenting Institute in 1999 were indicative of a growing awareness of the impact of parenting on outcomes for children. A focus on the importance of parents was central to the Labour government's Every Child Matters agenda, and in 2002 the government's spending review allocated a £25 million Parenting Fund to be spent on parenting support across the country.

The policy on parenting was summarised in *Every Parent Matters*: 'Parents and carers are a crucial influence on what their children experience and achieve' (DfES, 2007a: 2). Provision of services for parents was a central feature of Sure Start children's centres which were initially conceived as universal hubs offering access to a range of help for all parents in their local areas (for further discussion of children's centres see Chapter 9).

The Coalition government that took office in 2010 was also convinced of the importance of parenting to improving outcomes for children. The policy document *Supporting Families in the Foundation Years* (DfE/DH, 2011) responded positively to recommendations for improved support for parenting. Ministers expressed a commitment to promoting a greater awareness of the importance of high quality parenting skills and building strong families in the foundation years. Launching the document, the government said that it

> wants to make asking for parenting support the norm rather than the exception … Early parenting experiences are especially critical in the development of the child's emotional regulatory system and a large proportion of adult mental health problems are thought to have their origin in early childhood. A poor parental relationship can be a significant barrier to good parenting. More parents split up in the first years after the birth of a child than at any other time. When the father is involved in the care of a child early on couples are almost a third less likely to split up. (DfE Press Release, 2011)

There was also an acknowledgement that 'mothers and fathers are their children's first and most important educators'.

A range of new interventions

The focus on support for parents has not been limited to the Department for Education. In October 2011, the Department of Health launched *Preparation for Birth and Beyond*, a resource pack for leaders of community groups in order to help the NHS, local authorities and the voluntary sector in planning or running groups for expectant and new parents (DH, 2011). The pack is a practical tool that aims to improve outcomes for babies and parents through a refreshed approach to antenatal education that covers the physiological aspects of pregnancy and birth, but also addresses the emotional transition to parenthood in greater depth and recognises the need to include fathers and other partners in groups and activities.

Three areas are testing the efficacy of offering parents vouchers to enable them to access free parenting support. These are distributed through high street outlets including Boots the Chemists and health centres or online from CANparent. They enable parents to access up to 10 two-hour sessions of free parenting services. Parents can use the vouchers to buy lessons from local parenting service providers, online or a blend of the two. This high street access is in line with the stated intention to remove the stigma and enable parenting support to be accessed by all parents instead of so-called 'responsible' parents. Early results show a higher take-up by mothers who constitute 94% of attendees (DFE, 2013). It will be difficult to assess the effectiveness of these interventions since they will not be comparing like with like, however, they may go some way to removing any perceived stigma from accessing parenting support.

These non-targeted initiatives contrast with programmes focusing specifically on families seen to be at risk, which include some of the more intensive interventions. Professor Judy Hutching led a randomised control trial of the Incredible Years model of parenting intervention in 11 areas across north and mid-Wales with parents of identified high-risk children; the results demonstrated significant improvements in child behaviour from blind observation and parent report (Hutchings and Bywater, 2010). In the Family Nurse Partnership model (discussed in detail in Chapter 10) a specially trained nurse or midwife works with young parents for two years to help them develop a strong relationship with their child and good parenting skills. Information about a range of other evidence-based programmes can be found in the *Commissioning Toolkit* of the National Academy for Parenting Research, which currently includes over 150 programmes, more than 100 of which have been evaluated by the NAPR (http://www.education.gov.uk/commissioning-toolkit).

The Department of Communities and Local Government has now also become involved, setting up the Troubled Families Unit in 2011 with the specific objective of turning around the lives of 120,000 'troubled families' by 2014. The families' problems may of course be limited to crime, prison, physical and mental illness, debt, disability or poor housing, but there is a perception that poor parenting is often a strong contributory factor. It is to be hoped that offering an appropriate parenting intervention will help, though the problems that these families are grappling with will need a sustained multi-pronged response delivered by well-trained practitioners with local knowledge.

Why the emphasis on supporting parents with parenting? The evidence from research

Our raised awareness of the importance of parents is directly attributable to research findings which spell out their impact on outcomes for children. The Canadian National Longitudinal Study of Children and Youth (Sheridan, 1994–5) found that it was the style of parenting rather than family income which had the greatest impact on children's behaviour and success in school. If they were negatively parented, there was twice the chance of delayed development of motor and social skills and an even greater delay in acquiring vocabulary.

Nearer home, Charles Desforges carried out a review of research findings for DfES (Desforges and Abouchaar, 2003: 4) and concluded that:

Parental involvement in the form of 'at-home good parenting' has a significant positive effect on children's achievement and adjustment even after all other factors shaping attainment have been taken out of the equation. In the primary age range the impact caused by different levels of parental involvement is much bigger than differences associated with variations in the quality of schools. The scale of the impact is evident across all social classes and all ethnic groups.

Working with parents as partners to support children's early learning and development

What parents do at home with their babies and young children has the greatest impact on social, emotional and cognitive outcomes. The Effective Provision of Pre-School Education (EPPE) study (Sylva et al., 2004) concluded 'what parents do is more important than who parents are'. Social class, income, living conditions and parents' own education levels are clearly directly related to child development outcomes. However, the quality of the early home learning environment (from birth) can act as a significant modifying factor. Parents (all mothers, fathers and carers) who engage in activities that encourage thinking and 'stretch a child's mind' as part of everyday life at home can enhance their child's progress significantly. The play activities seen to have the most impact are reading and sharing books, going on visits, playing with print (letters and numbers), singing songs and rhymes, drawing, mark making and playing with friends. Children with strong early home learning environments are ahead in both social and cognitive development at the age of 3, and this advantage continues as children progress through school to the age of 7. The quality of the early home learning environment continues to be a predictor of higher attainment at the age of 11 (Sammons et al., 2007) and retains a strong association with differences in achievement at the age of 14 (Sylva et al., 2012).

The evidence of the power that parents have on their children's learning and development has been increasingly reflected in early education policy. Working with parents to support learning has been a long-established principle in the best early education and care settings, and was a central commitment of the Early Years Foundation Stage (DfES, 2007b), which stated that parents are a child's 'first and most enduring educators'. The Tickell Review of the EYFS (2011) recommended a much greater emphasis on the role of parents as partners in learning and more consistency, with all schools and settings learning from the most effective practice.

The revised EYFS (DfE, 2012) confirms partnership with parents as a firm, legal requirement. It requires settings to assign a key person to each child who must seek to engage with and support parents in guiding their child's learning and development at home. This requires the establishment of a warm, respectful relationship with the child and their family, and an ongoing two-way exchange of information with parents on their individual child's progress. This shared observational assessment process should inform both planning in the setting and support enhanced learning opportunities at home.

Supporting a strong early home learning environment

Research consistently shows that settings and schools that develop effective partnership with parents achieve the best cognitive and social outcomes for children. They do this by establishing respectful relationships, encouraging parents, and building confidence in what they already do at home to help their children learn. They extend parents' knowledge and skills and share education theory and practice.

The most effective schools and settings:

- have designated staff with responsibility for parent partnership
- know their community well
- work hard at building trusting relationships
- break down barriers to involvement and reach out to families
- loan equipment to support learning at home
- share education knowledge and theory
- listen to what parents say about their own child's development
- share observations and information with parents regularly
- encourage parents to be active partners in decision-making about their child

Siraj-Blatchford et al, (2003), Desforges and Abouchaar (2003), Sylva et al. (2004), Siraj-Blatchford and Manni (2007)
(adapted from Wheeler and Connor, 2009)

Getting to know each other – forming relationships

Parents welcome confident, well-informed practitioners with relevant valuable expertise. They are intrigued and fascinated to know more about the ways practitioners provide learning opportunities and the particular way their own child responds. However, they also want to be listened to and have their views and knowledge taken seriously. Parents enjoy sharing information and observations about their child, and helping to make decisions about their child's learning (Moran et al., 2004; Quinton, 2004; Tunstill et al., 2005).

Practitioners bring a broader view of the different developmental stages young children go through, what is 'expected' and, perhaps, what really is concerning, and parents are grateful to learn from this. They hear details of a child's life in the setting, and the sometimes familiar and sometimes entirely new facets of a child's personality that reveal themselves. They also have deep knowledge about their own child which needs to be valued and included in planning for the child's future learning and development.

All parents need to feel included in this two-way process and confident that their contribution is welcome. This involves practitioners getting to know families and showing an interest (without being unnecessarily intrusive) in a child's home circumstances and life history to date, in their interests and achievements, hopes and fears, likes and dislikes.

Establishing trusting relationships can be challenging as both parents and practitioners may have anxieties. Practitioners may perhaps see themselves as the experts on children's learning and find it difficult to value the parents' views. They may lack confidence in their work with parents, especially with parents who are very different from them. Likewise, many parents lack confidence in talking to practitioners, they may have had negative experiences of education or simply not share an understanding about how children learn in early education settings – for instance, through play or the outside environment.

Developing relationships and promoting regular dialogue requires concerted time and effort. The 'settling-in' process and creating time to talk are crucial.

Example: Settling in and time to talk

At **Thomas Coram Children's Centre** the family are offered visits to the centre, home visits by the key person, and then a 'settling in' period for their child. Part of this process is a detailed parent meeting during which parents are asked to talk about their child in a semi-structured interview. This covers all areas of the child's development, and provides the foundation for planning for the individual child. Parents and children start to make a relationship with their key person – if they feel that they like and trust them (which often comes from feeling that the key person has a genuine and open interest in the child), this is a sound basis for good communication in the future. Sessions are organised to ensure the key person is regularly free at entry and exit times to welcome families and exchange information. As well as this daily informal contact, there are regular times for parent and key person to meet and review the progress of each child. As part of this review, joint decisions are taken on the next priorities and support for learning at home and at nursery. The key person in each base room also holds regular meetings with parents to discuss what is going on in the room and possible new developments.

At the **Pen Green Centre** for Under Fives there are staggered start times. Families are able to arrive at the centre at any time between 8.15 and 9.45am. This means there is a steadier flow of families into the nursery with more time to converse, exchange information and share learning observations with individual parents.

(PEAL[2] practice examples: Settling In and Time to Talk. www.peal.org.uk)

Sharing regular observations – and supporting learning at home

Parents and practitioners who focus together on a child's learning and talk regularly are able to share insights, understand the child more fully, and plan future learning experiences together based on a child's individual needs and interests. This can be achieved in a variety of ways. Many settings realise the value of an easily accessible portfolio, record of development or learning journal. These display books or files include drawings, paintings, early writing, photographs, and written narratives of children's play and talk. Parents and children enjoy looking through them. They can be taken home to share with the family, and parents are encouraged to contribute their own observations. Children are involved in helping to decide what should be recorded. In this way, a child's step-by-step progress is made very clear and can be recalled and celebrated by child, parent and practitioner alike.

Example: Stop, look and listen

Stop, Look and Listen is an approach used in **Camden** settings that encourages practitioners and parents to take time out to observe children as they play, and listen to what they say on a regular basis. The observations – called Learning Stories – are then shared and plans made together to encourage children's future learning. Parents describe the benefits of this process:

'It has made me realise how wise she is.'
'I talk more about what she is interested in now.'
'I'm more aware of what she's doing and saying. Sometimes I'm busy and I answer her without really listening to what she was saying. I realise how little I used to take part.'
'I feel a lot more comfortable now, coming to talk to Joanna [practitioner], if I've got any problems.'

(PEAL practice examples: Stop, Look and Listen. www.peal.org.uk)

Many settings extend learning into the home by sharing equipment through book and story bag loans, listening libraries, and maths, play and toy libraries. This approach is most effective when matched to an individual child's level of development, and a system is established for regular written or verbal feedback with the key person. Other settings share observations using sticky notes on notice boards, home–school diaries, digital photographs, or video footage.

Example: Using video

Thomas Coram Children's Centre makes use of video to share children's nursery experiences with parents. While practitioners have been privileged to learn a little more about the child's family life from the home visit – perhaps seeing a child they have thought of as quiet showing confident fluency in their home language – parents watching a video of the child's day in nursery will often be struck by the ways in which their children are different in the setting – passing food around at lunchtime, for instance, might be something they've never done at home. In this way the child's two worlds are brought together, with the adults in each having a greater understanding of the child's experiences in the other.

A wide range of practice ideas can be viewed at www.peal.org.uk.

Reaching out

Combinations of factors can sometimes make it harder for practitioners and parents to work together. Some parents find it hard to engage because of pressures of time and social and economic circumstances, often compounded by ill-health or practical limitations such as languages spoken, transport or perhaps childcare provision. Certain assumptions, professional attitudes and organisational inflexibility can also create substantial barriers. These factors can lead to families being labelled as 'hard to reach', or considered to have little interest in their children's education.

In reality, services are often very hard for many families to locate, understand and access, but when a leadership team commits to the provision of a good range of options to engage parents and they are warmly and consistently welcomed, the vast majority of parents grasp the opportunity enthusiastically. Parents' own experience of early education – where they have had any – has sometimes been very different from what is provided for their children and they are surprised and delighted by the quality and range of the provision on offer.

Example: Involving parents

Pen Green begins with the firm belief that all parents are interested in the development and progress of their own children. Parents are offered a wide range of ways to get involved. As well as day-to-day chats these include weekly study

(Continued)

(Continued)

groups, open evenings, family group meetings, sessions to explore key child development concepts, child observation diaries, receiving and making video of their children, home visits and joining trips to the Science Museum. Group sessions are offered at flexible times to suit working and family patterns. Evening meetings have, for instance, been particularly effective in attracting fathers, who are invited through personal invitations.
(Whalley and the Pen Green Team, 2007)

In **Oldham and Sheffield,** families needing more confidence to engage are involved in the Making it REAL (Raising Early Achievement in Literacy) project, inspired by the successful outcomes for children in the original Sheffield REAL research (Nutbrown et al., 2005). The families welcome a short series of home visits to enhance their children's opportunities and interaction with print, books, rhyme and mark making, and are supported in how they model literacy practice and recognise small steps in their children's progress. They develop trusting relationships with practitioners, more confidence to attend literacy events and outings, and to talk about their children. The practitioners are often surprised at the parents' positive response: 'They are all so keen for new ideas – they are thirsty for knowledge about how to help their children.'

Referral to help with parenting

Because parents trust practitioners, they are particularly well placed to refer parents when they need help with the parent–child relationship. A Parental Opinion Survey (DfE, 2010) reported that just over two-thirds of parents said they would like more information and help from practitioners. Parents often see nursery staff as experts on the parenting role, but since most have not been trained for this work, they can feel nervous and inadequate when faced with questions from a distressed or confused parent. Rather than attempting to deliver parenting support sessions themselves without the necessary training, practitioners can have a brief training in how to refer appropriately and encourage parents to take up parenting support.

What kind of topics are likely to be included in a typical parenting programme? These will probably include:

- how to listen to children and young people
- how to talk so children and young people listen
- encouragement or praise
- avoiding positive or negative labels, for example 'the quiet one' or 'Mr Grumpy' rather than describing the behaviour
- building the self-esteem of children, young people and parents
- helping parents to look after themselves

- setting and maintaining limits
- goal setting
- celebrating achievement.

If the pre-school setting has the contacts and the facilities for adult group activities, it is really useful to arrange an introductory parenting education session open to all parents. Some parents have said to parenting service providers that they were really surprised by the collaborative nature of the sessions, which was the opposite of the school-based, top-down, expert model they had dreaded. Ideally the sample session should be done at a time the children are being looked after by the early years staff, since otherwise childcare duties may prevent one parent from attending. It is highly desirable for both parents to attend the parenting education sessions to avoid the risk of one parent seeing themselves or being perceived as the 'parenting expert'. Experienced parenting service providers also advise organisers to use a venue with adult-size furniture and to offer drinks and snacks.

Working with fathers

Increasingly fathers and other male relations feel welcome in early years settings and staff are more confident in encouraging them to be involved. Research underlines the importance of father involvement in their children's upbringing. Buchanan and Flouri's 2002 study was clear that if fathers are involved with their children at 7, both boys and girls will achieve higher educational attainment when they are 20.

We know that fathers are keen to be involved from the results of the Parental Opinion Survey (DfE, 2010) which covered a representative sample of 2,319 parents with resident or non-resident children aged 0–19 in England. Some 30% of fathers said they would be likely to attend a local group specifically for fathers to discuss parenting issues. Enthusiasm was highest among non-white fathers (61%) and fathers where English was not their first language (55%).

Positive male influence is not limited to biological fathers, but can apply to adoptive and foster fathers, stepfathers, grandfathers, uncles or older male siblings. Ideally invitation letters from the early years setting should be addressed by name to the father and should quote research that emphasises the importance of father involvement in their children's upbringing. Care needs to be taken in ensuring the correct postal address for the father, especially where he does not live with his child(ren).

There is now a range of helpful publications to support father-inclusive services. The Fatherhood Institute's *Toolkit for Father-Inclusive Practice* (2007) helps managers and practitioners meet policy requirements. The

Pre-School Learning Alliance website has useful references to research and offers a range of materials and publications, such as *Where's Dad?* (2010).

Early years service providers report that arranging parent meetings on Saturdays or at another convenient time is often more successful in ensuring the attendance of fathers. It can also help if the decor in the early years setting reflects male influence.

Bilingual children

Children whose parents speak only a language or languages other than English have a wonderful opportunity to grow up bilingual, an ability that will enhance their learning potential. *Raising Bilingual Children* (Sorace and Ladd, 2004) makes the point that

> Many people are ready to believe that handling two languages at the same time is too much of a burden for the infant's brain, or that the languages compete for resources in the brain at the expense of general cognitive development ... these [are] false beliefs ... If they [the children] are exposed to two languages in varied circumstances with different people from the moment they are born, and if they need both languages to communicate with the people around them, they will learn both.

A key study in the 1960s (Peal and Lambert, 1962) found that the ability to speak two languages does not restrict overall development. On the contrary, when controlling for other factors that might also affect performance, such as socio-economic status and education, they found that bilinguals outperformed monolinguals in 15 verbal and non-verbal tests. Parents will appreciate the acknowledgement that in fact their children have an advantage in this opportunity to grow up bilingual rather than feeling inadequate because they themselves may not speak English fluently. Supporting parents in this is also about handing over knowledge to them about how using home languages helps learning – how it gives children greater cognitive flexibility, greater social skills and understanding of others, and strong self-identity – all factors that help children learn more as they progress through school. The National Literacy Trust has produced a helpful leaflet with a summary, which is available at: www.literacytrust.org.uk/assets/0000/0804/FAQsonbilingualism.pdf.

Where parents speak limited or no English, it will be necessary to arrange professional interpreting for events where parents are invited to take part. Local authorities where there are large numbers of speakers of languages other than English usually provide a free interpreting service but this will need to be booked well in advance. For example, Lambeth Interpreting Service offers interpreting in 34 languages, including British Sign Language.

Benefits for parents and practitioners

When partnership is in place, parents feel respected and valued and grow in confidence. They sustain involvement in learning beyond the early years, have clearer expectations of schools and teachers and articulate these more powerfully. They often welcome the chance to develop themselves as individuals. Involvement can release untapped potential with enrolment on courses leading to further and higher education, or volunteering and employment in the setting leading to childcare and education qualifications. Greater involvement in groups and events also brings parents together, reducing isolation and helping to build support networks and cohesion in the wider community.

For practitioners, working with parents adds a new dimension to their work, making the role more interesting, enjoyable and satisfying. Practitioners can sometimes assume that their own experience of family life is the only way it can be, and working with parents from diverse communities widens views as differences are shared, respected and explored. Practitioners appreciate the increased knowledge about their families and children and enjoy friendlier relationships; they gain greater awareness and understanding of some of the difficulties families face, and develop more confidence in communicating with parents. They appreciate seeing both children and parents making progress as they use knowledge from home to make connections and support learning.

Safeguarding considerations

Safety concerns can sometimes discourage early years staff from enabling parents to be more involved in the work of the setting. Clarity about expectations and people's area of expertise will enable parents to benefit from the range of information, encouragement and support which early years staff are ideally placed to offer and will enable the early years staff to benefit from the parents' input and enthusiasm. There is a need to have clear policies and systems for volunteer parents in line with other volunteer policies. Safeguarding considerations apply of course to women as well as men. They are considered at greater length in Chapter 14.

Skills and knowledge for working with parents

'How we work with parents is as important as what we do' is how David Quinton sums up his research findings (Quinton, 2004). Parents who were interviewed by Ghate and Hazell for their 2002 study reported feeling undermined rather than supported. Studies such as these underline the importance of appropriate training and support for people who undertake work with parents around the parent–child relationship. The National Occupational Standards for Work with Parents (2005; revised 2010) set down the skills and knowledge needed for the work. They include for example how to engage with parents in an open, clear and honest manner that engenders mutual respect, how to identify common barriers which may prevent parents engaging in parenting services and how they may be overcome.

The Nutbrown Review (2012) calls for working in partnership with parents to be a much stronger strand in all early years qualifications, including teaching. As Professor Nutbrown points out, 'having impressive knowledge of child development and ability to identify individual needs and support a child will count for little if that information cannot be shared effectively with parents and carers'.

Parent governors

Inviting parents to make a contribution to governance can help them to feel involved in the services provided for their children and to raise awareness of managers and staff to the perspective of local parents and the local community. Some parents will be ready to contribute to decisions about the running of the early years facility, to staff recruitment and financial decisions, some might wish to make a strong contribution but lack the necessary experience and will need help.

Parents with little or no experience of committee work can be helped by a member of staff or an experienced parent governor explaining the protocol and talking them through the committee papers in advance on the first two or three occasions. It makes a great difference to the confidence of the parent and to the contribution they are able to make to the proceedings.

Key points to remember

- All parents are interested in the development and progress of their own children.
- 'At-home good parenting' has a significant positive effect on children's achievement and adjustment even after all other factors shaping attainment have been taken out of the equation.
- Children whose parents speak only a language or languages other than English have a wonderful opportunity to grow up bilingual, an ability which will enhance their learning potential.
- Parents and professionals each function in their own world and learn to know and respect each other's sphere of action. The children move between these two worlds.

Points for discussion

- Do all parents make and share observations on their own children's learning and development regularly?
- What do you think is the most useful approach to reassuring parents?
- Why is it worth making an effort to enable fathers to visit the early years settings and to feel at home?

Reflective tasks

- Can you think of a situation you have been in where you felt out of place and not sure of what was expected of you? Why did you find yourself in such a situation? What helped you to deal with it?
- Which aspect covered in your training have you found most helpful in enabling you to develop a good relationship with parents? From the point of view of this relationship, is there anything you wish had been included in your training?

Notes

1 Subsequently called Parenting UK and in 2012 merged with Family Lives.
2 PEAL was commissioned by the Department for Education and Skills (2005–9) and developed by the Early Childhood Unit at the National Children's Bureau in partnership with Coram and the London Borough of Camden. The training and resources support practitioners to work with parents to enhance children's early learning and development.

Further reading

Miller, S. (2010) *Supporting Parents Improving Outcomes for Children, Families and Communities*. Maidenhead: McGraw–Hill Education/Open University Press.

Miller, L. and Hevey, D. (2012) *Policy Issues in the Early Years*. London: Sage.

Sylva, K., Melhuish, E., Sammons, P., Siraj-Blatchford, I. and Taggart, B. (eds) (2010) *Early Childhood Matters: Evidence from the Effective Pre-School and Primary Education Project*. London: Routledge. ch. 4.

Whalley, M. and the Pen Green Team (2007) *Involving Parents in Their Children's Learning*, 2nd edn. London: Paul Chapman.

Wheeler, H. and Connor, J. (2009) *Parents, Early Years and Learning. Parents as Partners in the Early Years Foundation Stage: Principles into Practice*. London: National Children's Bureau.

Useful websites

www.education.gov.uk/publications/.../DFE-RB061.pdf For information on Parents, Early Years and Learning (PEAL) training options and resources and examples of practice in working with parents to support young children's learning, visit: www.peal.org.uk.

Parentinguk.org provides up-to-date information and resources for people working with parents around the parent–child relationship; advertises job opportunities and events.

www.scotland.gov.uk/Publications/2009/01/13095148/1 – Describes the Scottish government's vision and commitment to services for children and parents.

www.childreninwales.org.uk/areasofwork/earlyyears/index.html – This is a voluntary organisation which works with 22 local authorities in Wales providing a wide range of services for under-8s and their parents.

www.real-online.group.shef.ac.uk/ – Information about REAL, its underpinning research and ORIM Framework. Practical examples of early literacy work with families.

http://www.literacytrust.org.uk/talk_to_your_baby – Talk to your baby resources and information to support practitioners' and parents' understanding of early language development.

http://www.literacytrust.org.uk/assets/0000/0804/FAQsonbilingualism.pdf – Provides a useful discussion of the benefits of children speaking more than one language and responds to frequently asked questions on this topic

To access a variety of additional web resources to accompany this book please visit: **www.sagepub.co.uk/pughduffy**

References

Buchanan, A. and Flouri, E. (2002) *Fathers' Involvement and Outcomes in Adolescence* (end of award report). London: ESRC study based on NCDS.

Department for Education (DfE) (2010) *Parental Opinion Survey 2010*. London: DfE. DfE RB061.

DfE Press Release (2011) 'Supporting Families in the Foundation Years': Sarah Teather, Minister of State for Children and Families, and Anne Milton, Parliamentary Under-Secretary of State for Health. Department for Education.

Department for Education (DfE) (2012) *Statutory Framework for the Early Years Foundation Stage 2012: Setting the Standards for Learning, Development and Care for Children from Birth to Five*. Runcorn: DfE Publications.

Department for Education (DfE) (2013) *CANparent Trial Evaluation: first Interim Report*. www.gov.uk/government/uploads/system/uploads/attachmentdata/file/190980/DfE-RR280.pdf (accessed 7 June 2013)

Department for Education and Skills (DfES) (2007a) *Every Parent Matters*. Nottingham: DfES Publications.

Department for Education and Skills (DfES) (2007b) *The Early Years Foundation Stage: Setting the Standards for Learning, Development and Care for Children from Birth to Five*. London: DfES (revised 2008).

Department for Education and Department of Health (DfE/DH) (2011) *Supporting Families in the Foundation Years*. London: DfE/DH.

Department of Health (DH) (2011) *Preparation for Birth and Beyond: A Resource Pack for Leaders of Community Groups and Activities*. www.gov.uk/government/publications/preparation-for-birth-and-beyond-a-resource-pack-for-leaders-of-community-groups-and-activities. Gateway ref. 16509. (accessed July 2013)

Desforges, C. and Abouchaar, A. (2003) *The Impact of Parental Involvement, Parental Support and Family Education on Pupil Achievements and Adjustment: A Literature Review*. Research Report 433. London: Department for Education and Skills.

Fatherhood Institute (2007) *Toolkit for Father-Inclusive Practice*. www.fatherhoodinstitute.org/2007/toolkit-for-father-inclusive-practice/. (accessed July 2013)

Ghate, D. and Hazel, N. (2002) *Parenting in Poor Environments*. London: Jessica Kingsley Publishers.

Home Office (1998) *Supporting Families*. London: HMSO.

Hutchings, Judy and Bywater, Tracey (2010) *The Evidence for the Incredible Years Programme in Wales*. School of Psychology, Bangor University.

Moran, P., Ghate, D. and van der Merwe, A. (2004) *What Works in Parenting Support? A Review of the International Evidence*. Research Report 574. London: Department for Education and Skills.

National Occupational Standards for Work with Parents (2010) www.family matters.org.uk/work-with-parents/national-occupational-standards. (accessed July 2013)

Nutbrown, C. (2012) *Foundations for Quality. The Independent Review of Early Education and Childcare Qualifications: Final Report* (Nutbrown Review). London: Department for Education.

Nutbrown, C., Hannon, P. and Morgan, A. (2005) *Early Literacy Work with Families: Policy, Practice and Research*. London: Sage.

Peal, E. and Lambert, W. (1962) *Psychological Monographs*, 76, 27, 1. Montreal: McGill University.

Pre-School Learning Alliance (2010) 'Where's Dad?'. www.pre-school.org.uk/practitioners/research/351/where-s-dad-exploring-the-views-of-children-fathers-and-mothers-on-involving-fathers-in-early-years-settings. (accessed July 2013)

Pugh, G. (ed.) (1980) *Preparation for Parenthood*. London: National Children's Bureau.

Pugh, G. and De'Ath, E. (1984) *The Needs of Parents: Practice and Policy in Parent Education*. Basingstoke: Macmillan.

Pugh, G. and De'Ath, E. (1989) *Working Towards Partnership in the Early Years*. London: NCB.

Pugh, G., De'Ath, E. and Smith, C. (1994) *Confident Parents, Confident Children*. London: National Children's Bureau.

Quinton, D. (2004) *Supporting Parents: Messages from Research*. London: Jessica Kingsley Publishers.

Rutter, M. and Madge, N. (1976) *Cycles of Disadvantage*. London: Heinemann.

Sammons, P., Sylva, K., Melhuish, E., Siraj-Blatchford, I., Taggart, B., Grabbe, Y. and Barreau, S. (2007) *Influences on Children's Attainment and Progress in Key Stage 2: Cognitive Outcomes in Year 5*. London: DfES and Institute of Education, University of London.

Sheridan, M. (1994–5) *Canadian National Longitudinal Study of Children and Youth* [conducted every two years on behalf of the Canadian government]. http://www.tes.co.uk/article.aspx?storycode=80380 (accessed July 2013).

Siraj-Blatchford, I. and Manni, L. (2007) *Effective Leadership in the Early Years Sector: The ELEYS Study*. London: University of London, Institute of Education.

Siraj-Blatchford, I., Sylva, K., Taggart, B., Sammons, P., Melhuish, E. and Elliot, K. (2003) *Intensive Case Studies of Practice Across the Foundation Stage*. Technical Paper 10. London: University of London, Institute of Education, DfES.

Sylva, K., Melhuish, E. C., Sammons, P., Siraj-Blatchford, I. and Taggart, B. (2004) The Effective Provision of Pre-School Education (EPPE) Project: *Technical Paper 12 – The Final Report: Effective Pre-School Education*. London: Department for Education and Skills/Institute of Education, University of London.

Sylva, K., Melhuish, E., Sammons, P., Siraj-Blatchford, I. and Taggart, B. (2012) Effective Pre-School, Primary and Secondary Education 3–14 Project (EPPSE 3–14). *Final Report from the Key Stage 3 Phase: Influences on Students' Development from Age 11–14*. London: Department for Education.

Sorace, A. and Ladd, B. (2004) *Raising Bilingual Children*. Washington, DC: The Linguistic Society of America.

Tickell, C. (2011) *The Early Years: Foundations for Life, Health and Learning. An Independent Report on the Early Years Foundation Stage to Her Majesty's Government* (Tickell Review). London: Department for Education.

Tunstill, J., Meadows, P., Akhurst, S., Allnock, D., Chrysanthou, J., Garbers, C. and Morley, A. (2005) *Implementing Sure Start Local Programmes: An Integrated Overview of the First Four Years*. NESS Summary SF010. London: Department for Education and Skills.

Whalley, M. and the Pen Green Team (2007) *Involving Parents in Their Children's Learning*, 2nd edn. London: Paul Chapman.

Wheeler, H. and Connor, J. (2009) *Parents, Early Years and Learning, Parents as Partners in the Early Years Foundation Stage: Principles into Practice*. London: National Children's Bureau.

CHAPTER 14

Safeguarding Children in the Early Years

Harriet Ward and Rebecca Brown

Chapter contents

- The impact of abuse and neglect on early childhood development showing why early intervention is important
- The role of early years practitioners in identifying and responding to maltreatment, in preventing its recurrence and mitigating impairment
- Complementing the skills and interventions of social workers

---

Introduction

The most recent study of the extent of child abuse and neglect in the United Kingdom was conducted by the NSPCC in 2009. It showed that 2.5% of children aged under 11 and 6% of young people aged 11–17 had experienced some form of maltreatment from a caregiver within the previous year (Radford et al., 2011). However, only a relatively small proportion of these children receive support from social workers, for many are never referred to the statutory services, and many referrals are not assessed as being sufficiently severe to be taken up as ongoing cases.

Statistics relating to those children who *do* receive support from social services show that very young children are particularly vulnerable to maltreatment. Children under the age of 1 are nearly three times as likely to be identified as likely to suffer harm from physical abuse as older children, and over twice as likely to receive services in response to evidence of neglect. If a child dies or is seriously injured, the Local Safeguarding Children Board is required to undertake a Serious Case Review in order to identify what lessons can be learnt to prevent such cases in the future. Almost half (45%) of all Serious Case Reviews in England involve a child under 1, and children of this age face around eight times the average risk of child homicide (Cuthbert et al., 2011).

Early years practitioners are well placed both to detect possible signs of maltreatment in very young children and to complement the work of children's social services in offering preventive and protective services that safeguard and promote their welfare and support their families. This chapter explores their role in this area.

Why is early intervention important?[1]

Over the past 10 years or so there have been significant advances in our understanding of early childhood development. Recent research has explored the role the infant's environment plays in shaping the development of the brain and central nervous system, and has focused particularly on how this affects the child's ability to negotiate the key developmental tasks of impulse control, trust and attachment. At birth human infants are dependent on their primary caregivers (usually their mothers) for survival, and it is this relationship which forms the most significant part of their early environment.

Human infants are born with very immature brains. The brain develops very rapidly in the first two years of life, but because so much development takes place after birth, the baby's social environment has a particularly strong influence. Very early interactions with the primary caregiver through touch, face-to-face contact and stimulation through conversation (or reciprocating baby babble) provide the positive experiences necessary to the construction of a rich network of neural connections in the brain that form the basis for cognitive and social development.

It is through early interactions with their primary caregivers that babies and very young children also learn to regulate their emotions. When infants feel their survival is threatened, through hunger, cold or discomfort, they experience stress, and this triggers a specific physiological response: 'the adrenal glands generate extra cortisol to generate extra energy to focus on the stress and to put other bodily systems "on hold" while this is being dealt with' (Gerhardt, 2004: 59). Infants cannot regulate their own stress response systems; they are dependent on their caregivers to respond to their signals of discomfort, and to re-establish their equilibrium through tending to their needs and soothing them by, for instance, mirroring and defusing their distress, and by touching, holding and rocking (Hofer, 1995). The manner in which the caregiver responds to the infant's needs lays the foundation for the construction of the child's internal working model of how the world of the self, others and relationships seem to work. Children who experience 'sensitive, loving, responsive, attuned, consistent, available and accepting care' become securely attached to their caregivers. They are able to regulate their emotions, and they develop internal working models in which they see themselves as loved, likeable and socially effective and other people as positively available (Howe, 2005).

Impact of abuse and neglect on early childhood development

Improved understanding of early childhood development has also shown what happens when children do not receive the type of sensitive, loving care that stimulates the growth of the brain and promotes the establishment of secure attachments. Studies of American children who have experienced gross neglect show that severe sensory deprivation inhibits the growth of the brain (Perry, 2002). At a less extreme level, poor stimulation and social deprivation in early childhood are associated with developmental problems such as language delay, fine and gross motor delays, attention difficulties and hyperactivity (Perry, 2002).

Early childhood development is shaped as readily by negative experiences of parenting as by positive experiences. While children who receive sensitive, loving care that is responsive to their needs are likely to develop secure attachments and positive internal working models, those whose interactions with their caregivers are inadequate or damaging are more likely to develop insecure attachments and to see themselves as neither loved nor loveable.

Children who experience their caregivers as frightening, dangerous and/or frightened may develop disorganised attachments. They may be fearful of approaching their caregivers because they cannot predict whether they will be shouted at or cuddled. These children develop highly negative internal working models and see other people as not to be trusted. Up to 80% of children who experience abuse or neglect in their early years develop disorganised attachments (Van IJzendoorn et al., 1999). Because their caregivers are unable to respond appropriately to their basic needs, these children experience persistent and chronic stress. Such stress results in the brain being flooded by cortisol for prolonged periods and can have particularly toxic consequences. These can include damage to areas of the brain high in cortisol receptors, thereby impeding the development of capacities such as planning, impulse control and language comprehension and an eventual lowering of the threshold for arousal, with the result that these children have difficulty in regulating their emotions. High cortisol levels are related to a range of psychopathologies in adulthood; they can affect the brain's ability to think and manage behaviour, and have a negative impact on physical as well as mental health (see Gerhardt, 2004).

Children who experience physical abuse, particularly in the early years, may be permanently disabled or indeed may die as a consequence. They may also experience long term adverse psychosocial consequences. Young children who experience sexual abuse may also be physically harmed, as well as emotionally damaged. The more recent research on the development of the brain and nervous system demonstrates that emotional abuse and neglect also have long term, negative consequences for all areas of children's physical, cognitive, emotional and social development. Moreover the evidence shows that emotional abuse and neglect can compromise children's development from earliest infancy, indeed before birth if they are subject to alcohol or substance misuse *in utero*. Because such rapid development takes place within the first two years of life, and because we now know more about how it can be compromised, there has been a particular emphasis in recent years on the development of policies to prevent abuse and neglect and to intervene early when maltreatment occurs (see Field, 2010; Marmot, 2010; Allen, 2011). Two major reviews, of the child protection system (Munro, 2011) and the family justice system (Norgrove, 2011), both stress the importance of early intervention, an issue that also lies behind recent government initiatives to speed up the process and increase the number of children placed for adoption (DfE, 2011a). Policies designed to promote early intervention often have a double meaning: safeguarding children is important in the early years, because of the speed with which the brain and central nervous system develop; it is also important to intervene when maltreatment first occurs, as the more entrenched it becomes, the more difficult to eradicate and the harder for children to overcome the consequences.

Protecting and safeguarding children from abuse and neglect outside the early years setting

Recent government policies have emphasised the point that 'safeguarding children is everybody's business' and that agencies should work collaboratively to ensure that all children are properly protected from abuse and neglect and their consequences. It should be clear from the evidence discussed

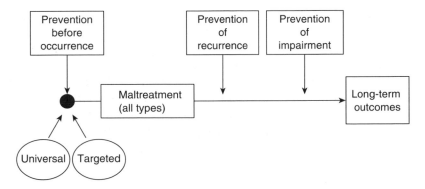

Figure 14.1 Framework for intervention and prevention of maltreatment. (Reproduced with permission from Barlow, J. and Schrader McMillan, A. (2010) *Safeguarding Children from Emotional Maltreatment: What Works*, London and Philadelphia: Jessica Kingsley Publishers. p. 41)

above that practitioners in early years settings have a particular role to play in ensuring that children are safeguarded from harm.

Figure 14.1 has been used by a number of commentators to illustrate the difference between preventive services, designed to reduce the likelihood of children being abused and neglected, and therapeutic interventions aimed at preventing recurrence and/or mitigating the consequences of abuse for children and families. The left-hand side of the diagram indicates that preventive services can be universally provided (i.e. available to everyone) or targeted at particularly vulnerable groups in a population; interventions offered after maltreatment has occurred (on the right hand side of the diagram) are generally more specialist and are designed to prevent long term impairment to the child's health and development.

The role of early years professionals in identifying maltreatment

Because almost all families will make use of universal services such as GP surgeries and schools, practitioners who work in them are most likely to be the first professionals to see the early signs of vulnerability in a family. In fact, failure to register with a GP or to send one's children to school are well-known indicators of the presence of more deep-seated problems. Moreover professionals who work in universal services tend to see a very wide range of families and are in a better position to identify children whose appearance and behaviour stands out from the norm than those who work more exclusively with families in need, who may see so much evidence of abuse and neglect that they become desensitised to indicators of maltreatment.

Thus within the early years workforce health visitors, early years practitioners and primary school teachers are in a particularly strong position to identify those families who may require additional support in order to prevent abuse and neglect from occurring or escalating. However, in order to do this they need firstly to be aware of the evidence detailed above that shows how abusive and neglectful parenting can have a long term detrimental impact on early childhood development and that clearly demonstrates the importance of taking early preventive action. They also need to be aware of the types of situations in which maltreatment is more likely to occur, and of a range of key indicators that suggest that preventive action should be taken.

A wide body of research has attempted to identify the risk factors that compromise parenting capacity and make it more likely that children will be harmed, and the protective factors that may reduce their impact (see Jones et al., 2006, for further details). For instance, mental illness, alcohol and drug misuse, learning disability and domestic violence are all known to reduce parents' capacity to meet their children's needs, particularly when they occur in combination; however, having a supportive partner, extended family or friendship network, or accessing effective services can mitigate their impact and ensure that children are adequately protected (see Cleaver et al., 2011 for further information). Families that show multiple risk factors and no evidence of protective factors are extremely unlikely to develop the capacity to safeguard a baby within an appropriate timeframe (see Ward, Brown and Westlake, 2012); early years practitioners need to be aware of this when deciding whether or not to refer to children's social care.

The *Statutory Framework for the Early Years Foundation Stage* (DfE, 2012) lists the following signs that early years practitioners may encounter which indicate that children could be experiencing abuse or neglect:

- significant changes in children's behaviour
- deterioration in children's general well-being
- unexplained bruising, marks or signs of possible abuse or neglect
- children's comments that give cause for concern
- any reason to suspect abuse or neglect outside the setting, for example in the child's home; and/or
- inappropriate behaviour displayed by other members of staff, or any other person working with the children.
  (DfE, 2012: para 3.6)

Research programmes and reviews of research tend to identify more specific indicators, such as any sign of bruising on a baby (Cardiff Child Protection Systematic Reviews); sudden weight loss in a small child (Wooster, 1999); or inconsistent or sporadic attendance at nursery (see Ward, Brown and

Maskell-Graham, 2012). A recent overview of findings from 15 new research studies on safeguarding children sets out a number of indicators that should raise concerns amongst early years practitioners in health and education (see Davies and Ward, 2012: ch. 2). However, information is constantly changing in this area as new research findings are disseminated, and no list can be thoroughly comprehensive. Practitioners need to take up opportunities to attend training sessions organised through the Local Safeguarding Children Board both to explore their role in safeguarding children alongside other professionals and to keep up to date with new research findings.

Referrals to children's social care

All early years practitioners should be aware of the procedures they should follow if they have concerns that a child may be being maltreated (see DfE, 2012). However, even if a referral is made, concerns may not be considered sufficiently serious for the family to be offered social work support. Health visitors and primary school teachers often find themselves frustrated by the high thresholds for access to social work support, and by what they regard as a poor and sometimes inappropriate response to their referrals (see Ward, Brown and Westlake, 2012; Ward, Brown and Maskell-Graham, 2012). On the other hand, there is evidence that many practitioners, in early years as well as other services, are reluctant to take direct action other than to make a referral (Daniel et al., 2011). In part this is an understandable response to the intense negative media interest engendered by high profile tragedies such as those of Victoria Climbié (Laming, 2003) and Peter Connolly (Haringey LSCB, 2010), where professionals failed to identify abuse or prevent a fatal outcome. In the three years following the public outcry caused by the death of Peter Connolly, referrals to children's social services rose by 14% (DfE, 2011b); however, this does not necessarily mean that children were better safeguarded. In the inner city areas in particular, children's social services departments are often overloaded, resulting in high caseloads, social worker exhaustion and rapid staff turnover. All agencies with responsibilities for children have a part to play in making sure that they are adequately safeguarded. As numerous inquiries have found, working alongside other services including children's social care is more likely to provide better protection than referring on and assuming that another agency has taken over responsibility (see for instance Laming, 2003, 2009).

The role of early years practitioners in preventing maltreatment and its recurrence

Early years practitioners therefore have an important role to play not only in identifying abuse and neglect but also in preventing its appearance or recurrence. They should be familiar with the Common Assessment Framework (CAF), a shared assessment and planning framework for use across all children's services and local areas in England. The purpose of the CAF is to facilitate the early identification of children and young people's additional needs and promote the provision of coordinated services to meet them. An early research study that preceded its introduction showed that almost all practitioners working in children's services shared a common understanding of children's needs and agreed on those areas that indicated a cause for concern but that children and families were poorly served by overlapping assessments, fragmented services and unnecessary referrals to children's social care (see Ward and Peel, 2002). The CAF was introduced to: ensure that all practitioners adopted a common approach to assessments where families appeared to have additional needs; to reduce duplication; and to promote the development of a team around the child, with a lead professional acting as a family's key point of contact, while other members of the team provided preventive, family support services that were jointly planned and carefully coordinated. Early years practitioners may well form part of the team around the child or act as lead professionals; at least some practitioners in every service should be equipped to undertake a common assessment (Children's Workforce Development Council, 2009).

Early years practitioners also have a role to play in delivering services designed to strengthen parenting capacity and prevent abuse and neglect in families that are known to be vulnerable. Diminishing resources have increased pressures to demonstrate that costly interventions are effective, and in recent years there has been a move towards the introduction of standardised, evidence-based programmes that have been subject to formal evaluation and proven to produce better outcomes than other alternatives (for further details see Davies and Ward, 2012: ch. 5). The Triple P – Positive Parenting Programme is one of the best developed of a number of evidence-based parenting programmes designed to 'prevent severe behavioural, emotional and developmental problems in children by enhancing the knowledge, skills and confidence of their parents'. There is both a standard version, for all parents, and an enhanced version, with additional modules aimed at teaching parents 'a variety of skills aiming to challenge the beliefs they hold regarding their own behaviour and the behaviour of their child, and to challenge any negative practices they currently use in line with these beliefs' (see www.triplep.net). In Glasgow, for instance, the Triple P programme is offered free to all parents with young children through health visitors, schools and nurseries on a one-to-one, seminar or group basis. Some health visitors have been specially trained to offer the enhanced version to families where there is a high risk of maltreatment or its recurrence (see http://glasgow.triplep-staypositive.net/contact).

The role of early years practitioners in preventing impairment

Early years practitioners also have a part to play in programmes designed to prevent impairment after maltreatment has occurred. An example is the development of nurture groups, which have been introduced by many schools in areas of high deprivation in the United Kingdom to meet the needs of children whose poor nurturing experiences in early childhood have meant that they are not ready to meet the social and intellectual demands of formal schooling. Nurture groups aim to address the consequences of insecure attachment and compromised development typically seen in children who have experienced emotional abuse and neglect, discussed earlier in this chapter. Most nurture groups have high staff–child ratios; they are usually led by a trained teacher supported by additional staff with early years' experience or training.

A study of nurture groups in Scottish primary schools found them to be effective in helping build resilience, confidence, self-esteem and ability to learn in some of the most vulnerable children. A particular strength is their focus on the development of those language and communication skills that are essential for both social interaction and educational progress and are often poorly developed in children who have been severely neglected in infancy. However nurture groups are also often poorly integrated into the mainstream school and into other services for vulnerable children (see Education Scotland, 2008).

Poor integration and lack of communication can reduce much of the value of an effective intervention. For instance, acting outside nurture groups, individual primary school staff sometimes personally offer exceptionally high levels of care to children who appear to be neglected or abused; but although these may be beneficial in the short term, unless they form part of a strategic, inter-agency plan, initiatives that are taken in isolation from other services may come to an abrupt end when a child moves class or a staff member leaves, and may also mask evidence of deteriorating home circumstances that require a swift response from children's social care (see Ward, Brown and Maskell-Graham, 2012). National policies that are designed to increase the autonomy of schools may inadvertently reduce incentives for integrating services that form a necessary part of ensuring that children are adequately safeguarded.

Working alongside social workers

It should be evident from the above that children are best protected from harm when all those who have responsibility for their welfare can work closely together. This means that, where there are safeguarding concerns, early years practitioners will almost always need to collaborate with social workers; practitioners from both disciplines have much complementary expertise to bring to this relationship. For instance, we have already seen that practitioners in universal services are sometimes better able to identify children whose delayed development or abnormal behaviour marks them out from the crowd. While social workers should, through their training and experience, have greater expertise in issues concerning child protection, early years practitioners might expect to have a more detailed understanding of normative childhood development. Moreover, social workers are involved with a much wider range of age groups, and they may not necessarily have extensive experience of working with very young children. Secondly, early years practitioners may well be able to provide greater continuity than social workers, who may not be able to retain responsibility for a family as their case is moved from one team to another. Recent research has identified an urgent need for practitioners in less intensive services, such as health visitors and early years practitioners in Sure Start children's centres, to provide ongoing preventive family support both for children whose families are labouring under the types of stresses that may lead to maltreatment, and for families where child protection issues have been addressed and the social work case file is now closed. There are particular concerns about inadequate procedures for 'stepping down' from an intensive intervention, so that families with extensive additional needs who have experienced high levels of social work support may find themselves unable to cope if this is suddenly withdrawn without continuing, less intensive involvement from other services (see Davies and Ward, 2012). The case study of Simon illustrates these points.

Case Study 14.1 📁

Simon's mother was several months pregnant when she told her GP she was an extensive crack cocaine user. She was referred immediately to children's social care. Although Simon was made the subject of a child protection plan before his birth, his mother continued to use crack cocaine throughout the pregnancy. Because she was unlikely to meet his needs he was expected to require permanent placement, probably with his maternal grandmother. However, once Simon was born, his mother became determined to come off drugs and change her lifestyle. A residential parenting assessment, made when Simon was a few weeks old, was positive and Simon and his mother returned home with the added support of the grandmother who came to live with them. When Simon was 1, the original, Interim Care Order was replaced with a Supervision Order; shortly after he was 2, children's social services ceased to be involved with this family because there were no continuing concerns. When Simon was 3 he was showing signs of emotional and behavioural disturbance, possibly related to his extensive exposure to drugs 'in utero'. His mother was having difficulty in managing his behaviour, and both the nursery and his health visitor had raised concerns about his defiance and his tendency to be disruptive when in a group of children; they helped his mother access specialist help through 'positive play' sessions arranged through the local Sure Start children's centre. Simon was 5 when last visited by the research team. He was still living with his mother who continued to receive substantial support from her extended family, and had remained free of drugs since his birth. He and his mother had responded well to the play sessions and his behaviour was no longer a cause for concern.

(Simon is currently being followed in a longitudinal study of infants suffering or likely to suffer significant harm. Parts of his case history have previously been published in Ward, Brown and Westlake, 2012; Ward, Brown and Maskell-Graham, 2012).

Simon's case illustrates how early years practitioners can work together effectively with social workers and professionals from other services to promote long term significant change when they succeed in complementing one another's skills and expertise. The team around Simon were the social worker, the health visitor and the substance misuse worker, and each provided separate, but complementary support. For the first two years of his life, the social worker took the lead in ensuring that Simon was safe, but his mother also received extensive support from her health visitor and the substance misuse worker. In the early months, Simon's health visitor and social worker coordinated their visits, to ensure that at least one professional saw him every week. As so frequently happens, the social worker had an exceptionally heavy caseload, and once she was sure that Simon would be kept safe, she turned her attention to other cases, and the health visitor took increasing responsibility for these visits, on the understanding that she would contact the social worker should the situation deteriorate. After social services closed the case, the health visitor continued to visit for at least another year, offering less intensive, stepped down support, and advising on normative childhood development and appropriate eating, sleep patterns and behavioural management, areas in which she had specific expertise. Simon's mother regarded this support as helpful, and it allowed the health visitor to build up a good relationship with her. Simon's mother was well aware that he had come close to being permanently separated from her at birth; like many other parents in her situation, when difficulties later arose she was reluctant to contact the social worker, for fear that Simon would be removed. However the good relationship with the health visitor meant that, when Simon's behaviour began to cause concern, his mother felt able to discuss her worries with her and the nursery staff, both of whom had independently identified difficulties and were able to help her access specialist support. Although in Simon's case maltreatment ceased when he was born and there has been no recurrence, the early years practitioners were aware of his previous history and able to identify any signs of further problems, as well as offering appropriate continuing support to prevent them from recurring. Simon's mother was lucky in that the social worker was able to retain responsibility for his case throughout social services involvement, but it was the health visitor who could offer the long term supportive relationship that she needed to develop her capacity as a parent.

Protecting and safeguarding children from abuse and neglect within early years settings

While the majority of abuse and neglect occurs within the family, providers should also be alert to the need to ensure the safety of children within early years settings. *The Statutory Framework for the Early Years Foundation Stage* (DfE, 2012) sets out mandatory safeguarding and welfare requirements concerning issues such as the designation of a practitioner with lead responsibility for safeguarding children and liaising with the Local Safeguarding Children Board; appointment and vetting of staff; staff training in safeguarding and child protection; staff supervision; procedures concerning complaints and allegations against staff members; the role of key workers; staff to children ratios; and behaviour management. There are good reasons why these standards are set out in such detail, for there is ample evidence of what can happen when procedures designed to ensure that children are properly safeguarded are not followed and agencies fall short of their duty to protect the children in their care. The example of Nursery Z emphasises how women can become sexual abusers as well as men, and demonstrates how lax procedures can create a culture in which the abuse of small children can go unrecognised and unchecked for lengthy periods. This case only came to light by chance, when police searched the computer used by the male perpetrator and found images that linked him indirectly to the nursery.

Example: Nursery Z

In October 2009 a female member of staff, 'K', at Nursery 'Z' in Plymouth was found guilty on seven counts of sexual assault and six counts of making and distributing indecent pictures of children. She had been arrested after photographs of a sexual nature, in which Nursery Z was identified, were found on the computer of a 39-year-old man in the North of England.

The Serious Case Review found a number of factors at individual, agency and strategic levels that might have prevented abuse from happening at the nursery or led to its early identification.

At an individual level K had been demonstrating increasingly sexualised behaviour over the previous 6 months. Other staff had become concerned about her crude language, her discussion of extra-marital relationships (in some of which she apparently exchanged sex for money) and her showing them indecent images of adults, stored on her mobile phone. These behaviours were evidently inappropriate, yet no one felt able to challenge her.

K was described as an emotionally vulnerable woman who had been working in an environment where she was able to supply images of sexual abuse of children to further her on-line relationship with a predatory man. At an agency level it became evident that the nursery was run very informally, with boundaries between staff and parents blurred by friendship networks, and with senior staff forming a clique that made it difficult to question them. Lax recruitment procedures, a lack of supervision, poor access to safeguarding training, and a failure to provide clear procedures for intimate care of children or for complaints about individual members of staff had all led to a situation where risks were not identified and the nursery's capacity to provide a safe environment for children compromised.

At a strategic level, Nursery Z's status as an unincorporated institution had led to insufficient arrangements for governance and accountability; there was also insufficient integration with other services such as children's social care, and too little communication between Ofsted and the Early Years' Service so that concerns were not adequately shared or progress monitored.

(see Plymouth Safeguarding Children Board, 2010)

The Serious Case Review into events at Nursery Z demonstrates why staff in early years settings need to remain vigilant when caring for young and vulnerable children. Incidents such as those described above are, thankfully, relatively rare, but all early years practitioners need to be aware that paedophiles will target places where children are to be found. Of more common concern, however, are those staff who have difficulty in responding to children's needs with the type of sensitive, nurturing care that is necessary for successful development. This is a particular issue in contexts such as day nurseries, where staff are required to fulfil many of the routine parenting tasks, and is a further reason why rigorous recruitment processes and clear policies for behaviour management are so important.

Conclusion: Implications for training

Finally, this chapter concludes by considering how the issues discussed above have implications for training. Safeguarding children is not the main focus of early years training, but it should form a thread that runs throughout it, for the need to ensure that children are safe should be at the forefront of every practitioner's mind. This means that training needs to raise awareness that abuse and neglect are common experiences for many thousands of children and that they cause both immediate distress and long-term, negative outcomes. Basic training on normative childhood development should also incorporate discussion on how this can be compromised by abuse and neglect, and why there is a need for preventive services and timely intervention in the early years. Training should also be informed by the principle that safeguarding children is everyone's responsibility and explore what this means in early years settings; in particular it should equip practitioners with the skills to identify and work with parents who may not recognise certain practices as abusive or who may be resistant to change (see Fauth et al., 2010). Training on assessing learning and development through watching and learning (see Chapter 8) should incorporate information on key indicators of abuse and neglect, which should become apparent in the process of analysing what has been observed. More specialist training on these issues should be undertaken at post-qualifying level through the inter-agency training sessions run by Local Safeguarding Children Boards. All early years practitioners with responsibilities for safeguarding children should attend these sessions, which should not only provide access to up-to-date information, but also opportunities to develop collaborative relationships with other professionals including social workers, which form the bedrock of ensuring that children are safe.

Key points to remember

- The evidence concerning the impact of abuse and neglect on early childhood development demonstrates why prevention and early intervention are so important when there are indications that children may be at risk of harm.
- Early years practitioners have an important role in identifying potential maltreatment and in responding through programmes designed to prevent its recurrence and/or mitigate the consequences.
- They need to develop complementary relationships with social workers so that children and families can benefit from their combined skills.
- They also need to ensure that children are protected from harm both outside and within early years settings.

 Points for discussion

- Is safeguarding children everybody's business? To what extent and why?
- What are the factors that facilitate or obstruct successful working relationships with social workers?

Reflective task

- Reflect on your interactions with children, parents and colleagues throughout the previous day and write down any incidents which indicate that children might be better safeguarded. How might you use this information to develop your work with individual children? Are there any implications for procedures within your agency?

Note

1 For a full discussion of the material in this and the following section see Gerhardt, S. (2004) *Why Love Matters: How Affection Shapes a Baby's Brain*. London: Routledge.

Further reading

Davies, C. and Ward, H. (2012) *Safeguarding Children Across Services*. London: Jessica Kingsley Publishers.
Gerhardt, S. (2004) *Why Love Matters: How Affection Shapes a Baby's Brain*. London: Routledge.

Useful websites

The Department for Education is responsible for the development of policy and practice concerning safeguarding children from abuse and neglect. Key policy documents can be downloaded from: www.education.gov.uk/childrenandyoungpeople/safeguardingchildren.
Research briefs and other documents from the Safeguarding Children Research Initiative including a free download of the Overview (Davies and Ward, 2012) are located at: www.education.gov.uk/researchandstatistics/research/scri/b0076846/the-studies-in-the-safeguarding-research-initiative.
Short summary papers showing findings from systematic reviews focusing on specific issues concerning child abuse and neglect are available from: www.core-info.cardiff.ac.uk.

To access a variety of additional web resources to accompany this book please visit: **www.sagepub.co.uk/pughduffy**

References

Allen, G. (2011) *Early Intervention: The Next Steps*. An Independent Report to Her Majesty's Government. London: Cabinet Office.
Cardiff Child Protection Systematic Reviews. www.core-info.cardiff.ac.uk/ (accessed July 2013).

Children's Workforce Development Council (2009) *Early Identification, Assessment of Needs and Intervention: The Common Assessment Framework for Children and Young People: A Guide for Practitioners*. www.education.gov.uk/publications/standard/publicationdetail/page1/IW91/0709 (accessed July 2013).

Cleaver, H., Unell, I. and Aldgate, J. (2011) *Children's Needs – Parenting Capacity: Child Abuse: Parental Mental Illness, Learning Disability, Substance Misuse and Domestic Violence*, 2nd edn. London: TSO.

Cuthbert, C., Rayns, G. and Stanley, K. (2011) *All Babies Count: Prevention and Protection for Vulnerable Babies*. London: NSPCC.

Daniel, B., Taylor, J. and Scott, J. (2011) *Recognizing and Helping the Neglected Child: Evidence Based Practice for Assessment and Intervention*. London: Jessica Kingsley Publishers.

Davies, C. and Ward, H. (2012) *Safeguarding Children Across Services*. London: Jessica Kingsley Publishers.

Department for Education (DfE) (2011a) *An Action Plan for Adoption: Tackling Delay*. London: DfE.

Department for Education (DfE) (2011b) *Referrals, Assessments and Children who were the subject of a Child Protection Plan (2010–11)*. London: DfE.

Department for Education (DfE) (2012) *Statutory Framework for the Early Years Foundation Stage 2012: Setting the Standards for Learning and Development and Care for Children from Birth to Five*. Runcorn: DfE Publications.

Education Scotland (2008) *Developing Successful Learners in Nurturing Schools: The Impact of Nurture Groups in Primary Schools*. www.educationscotland.gov.uk/inspectionandreview/Images/ingps_tcm4-712899.pdf (accessed July 2013).

Fauth, R., Jelecic, H., Hart, D., Burton, S. and Shemmings, D. (2010) *Effective Practice to Protect Children Living in 'Highly Resistant' Families*. London: Centre for Excellence and Outcomes in Children and Young People's Services. www.c4eo.org.uk.

Field, F. (2010) *The Foundation Years: Preventing Poor Children Becoming Poor Adults. The Report of the Independent Review on Poverty and Life Chances*. London: Cabinet Office.

Gerhardt, S. (2004) *Why Love Matters: How Affection Shapes a Baby's Brain*. London: Routledge.

Haringey Local Safeguarding Children Board (2010) *Serious Case Review: Child A, March 2009*. London: Department for Education.

Hofer, M. A. (1995) 'Hidden regulators: implications for a new understanding of attachment, separation, and loss', in S. Goldberg, R. Muir and J. Kerr (eds), *Attachment Theory: Social, Developmental, and Clinical Perspectives*. Hillsdale, NJ: Analytic Press.

Howe, D. (2005) *Child Abuse and Neglect: Attachment, Development and Intervention*. Basingstoke: Palgrave Macmillan.

Jones, D., Hindley, N. and Ramchandani, P. (2006) 'Making plans: assessment, intervention and evaluating outcomes', in J. Aldgate, D. Jones, and C. Jeffery (eds), *The Developing World of the Child*. London: Jessica Kingsley Publishers.

Laming, Lord (2003) *The Victoria Climbié Inquiry: Report of an Inquiry by Lord Laming*. Cm 5730. London: TSO.

Laming, Lord (2009) (HC 330) *The Protection of Children in England: A Progress Report*. London: TSO.

Marmot, M. (2010) *Fair Society, Healthy Lives. Strategic Review of Health Inequalities in England Post 2010* (Marmot Review). London: Department of Health.

Munro, E. (2011) *The Munro Review of Child Protection: Final Report. A Child-Centred System*. Cm 8062. Norwich: TSO.

Norgrove, D (2011) *Family Justice Review: Final Report* (Norgrove Report). London: Ministry of Justice.

Perry, B. D. (2002) 'Childhood experience and the expression of genetic potential: What childhood neglect tells us about nature and nurture', *Brain and Mind*, 3, 79–100.

Plymouth Safeguarding Children Board (2010) *Serious Case Review Overview Report Executive Summary in Respect of Nursery Z*. Plymouth SCB.

Radford, L., Corral, S., Bradley, C., Fisher, H. et al. (2011) *The Maltreatment and Victimisation of Children in the UK. NSPCC Report on a National Survey of Young People's, Young Adults' and Caregivers' Experiences*. London: NSPCC.

Van IJzendoorn, M. H., Schuengel, C. and Bakermans-Kranenburg, M. J. (1999) 'Disorganized attachment in early childhood: Meta-analysis of precursors, concomitants, and sequelae', *Development and Psychopathology*, 11, 225–49.

Ward, H. and Peel, M. (2002) 'An inter-agency approach to needs assessment', in H. Ward and W. Rose (eds), *Approaches to Needs Assessment in Children's Services*. London: Jessica Kingsley Publishers.

Ward, H., Brown, R. and Maskell-Graham, D. (2012) *Young Children Suffering, or Likely to Suffer, Significant Harm: Experiences on Entering Education*. Loughborough: Centre for Child and Family Research, Loughborough University.

Ward, H., Brown, R. and Westlake, D. (2012) *Safeguarding Babies and Very Young Children from Abuse and Neglect*. London: Jessica Kingsley Publishers.

Wooster, D. (1999) 'Assessment of nonorganic failure to thrive: infant–toddler intervention', *The Transdisciplinary Journal*, 9 (4), 353–71.

PART 3

Workforce

CHAPTER 15

Training and Workforce Issues in the Early Years

Pauline Jones

Chapter contents

- The early years workforce
- Workforce quality matters
- Workforce quality costs
- The early years workforce: part of the children's workforce?
- Early Years Professional Status
- Level 2 and 3 early years qualifications
- The way forward

Introduction

This book is *for* the early years workforce[1]: part 1, policy and research, reflects on the context in which practitioners work, and part 2, on aspects of their practice. This chapter, however, is *about* the workforce itself. It will reflect on achievements for and with the workforce over the past decade, dilemmas that have arisen and challenges that still need to be addressed.

The early years workforce

Table 15.1 Workforce characteristics

Setting	% of (paid) workforce	% 40 years or older	% male	% BME	% at least level 6	% at least level 3	Average hourly pay (£)
Full daycare	50	32	2	10 17 in CCs	11	84	7.80 11.30 in CCs
Sessional	14	58	1	6	8	78	7.90
Maintained schools	24	50	2	6	40	83	14.50
Registered childminders	12	66	2	9	3	59	3.80 per child per hour

Source: Adapted from DfE (2010 and 2011) *Childcare and Early Years Providers Surveys*

Notes: Approximately one-third of places for under 5s are in maintained schools.
Full daycare has the greatest proportion of staff under 24 years.
Between 2010 and 2011 the national average hourly wage for UK employees rose by 1%, from £14.65 to £14.76.
BME, black and ethnic minorities; CCs, children's centres.

For the purpose of this chapter, the early years workforce includes those who work in the four categories of settings identified in the workforce characteristics data in Table 15.1 (DfE, 2010 and 2011). These categories mask the full extent of the fragmentation of this workforce because within and across each category there are significant differences, which affect practitioner roles and responsibilities including:

- setting size;
- whether the setting is maintained, for profit or not for profit; and
- the setting's main purpose, i.e. early education or childcare.

Comparison of roles and responsibilities across setting types is difficult because even within one setting category there is little consistency in the use of job titles. Efforts to categorise practitioner roles and responsibilities across the workforce in England have been largely unsuccessful, unlike Scotland where the Scottish Executive (2006) set out a group of Core Responsibilities, outlined the broad expectations of each category of workers in relation to these responsibilities, and has subsequently specified the qualifications acceptable for each category.

In her report *Foundations for Quality* (2012: 45), Professor Nutbrown suggested that:

> we need to move towards a greater sense of professional roles and identities and ensure that early years staff have clear and intelligible roles, responsibilities and status, which are understood and adopted across the sector.

It is not clear however, how this laudable aim can be achieved across such a fragmented workforce. It is one thing to articulate a career path and another to implement change, even with increased regulation, as the Scottish experience has shown.

Obtaining and analysing accurate up-to-date early years workforce data and information is difficult. The Childcare and Early Years Providers Survey, commissioned by the Department for Education (DfE), is most often cited and the data in the workforce characteristics table is taken from the 2010 and 2011 survey results, but there is a significant time lag between data collection and publication and the collection methodology has changed over time. Nonetheless, it is possible to identify trends.

Some characteristics of the workforce have hardly changed over the past ten years and there remains a fault line between maintained schools and other settings, particularly in pay, conditions and level 6 qualifications. Although from 2006 to 2011, the total number of paid staff overall across all early years settings rose by 23% to 406,500, it is still an overwhelmingly female workforce. A very low proportion of practitioners are disabled (between 1 and 2%) and practitioners from black and minority ethnic (BME) groups are under-represented in most settings. Professor Nutbrown suggested that DfE should conduct research on the number of BME staff at different qualification levels, and engage with the sector to address any issues identified.

From 2007 to 2010 the number of childminders decreased significantly (by 21%). Some argued that this was due to a cumbersome regulatory system and some of the lowest staff to child ratios in Europe making the hassle-factor high and the rewards limited for childminders, without necessarily guaranteeing quality. However, the downwards trend came to an end in 2011 when 48,800 childminders were active, marking an increase of 3% on the 2010 figure of 47,000. The 2011 survey suggests that childminders were the most optimistic of all the childcare providers when it came to future growth, with 16% saying they planned to expand their provision in the next year.

In 2011 a majority of the workforce in full daycare (84%) held at least a level 3 qualification, which the survey classed as relevant (this is not exactly comparable with full and relevant for the purposes of registration and regulation). This was a significant increase from the figure of 72% in 2007 and marked progress from the 2010 figure of 81%. The proportion of childminders with a level 3 qualification increased, from 41% in 2007 to 59% in 2011.

The proportion of the workforce with no qualifications has decreased and the proportion of the workforce holding at least a level 6 qualification has increased. In 2011 11% of staff in full daycare settings had a relevant level 6 qualification, an increase from 5% in 2007 and 7% in 2009. This represents significant progress, albeit from a low base line.

Qualification levels in maintained schools are typically higher than those in other settings and they are required to provide a 'school teacher' for each early years class, both nursery and reception. Eighty-three per cent of staff held at least a level 3 qualification in 2011, while 40% held at least a level 6 qualification. However, unlike other providers, there has been no real change in these figures since 2007.

Despite increases in qualification levels, early years workers' salary levels in full daycare and sessional settings remain substantially lower than average salaries. In addition, in 2011 the long term trend for their wages to increase more rapidly than those in the broader national economy came to an end. Between 2010 and 2011 average pay in maintained schools remained essentially flat.

Workforce quality matters

Following a decade of evidence-based policy implementation it is now widely accepted that the 'quality' of the workforce is a significant determinant of the quality of early years settings, which in turn is a significant determinant of improved outcomes for children.

Research evidence has highlighted the relationship between qualifications and the quality of early years provision, as well as differences in quality between maintained and private, voluntary and independent (PVI) settings. According to the *Quality of Childcare Settings in the Millennium Cohort Study* (Mathers et al., 2007) the childcare qualifications of staff observed were an important predictor of quality and were most strongly related to those aspects of provision that foster children's developing language, interactions and academic progress. The study concluded that although the mean qualification level of staff working with the children was the strongest predictor of quality, the percentage of staff members unqualified was important (and was negatively related to quality). The presence of a qualified teacher was particularly important for educational quality. The qualification levels of the centre manager/ head teacher were positively related to quality of provision and, in particular to provision for personal care routines. Weak but significant relationships were also found between the qualifications of the managers and the quality of provision for interactions, language and reasoning skills and literacy.

Reform of the workforce was one of the five key themes of the *Every Child Matters* Green Paper (DfES, 2003). *Choice for Parents, the Best Start for Children: A Ten Year Strategy for Childcare* (HM Treasury, 2004) identified the workforce as the single biggest factor determining the quality of childcare and suggested that if the system was to develop into one that is among the best in the world, a step-change was needed in the quality and stability of the workforce. Working with pre-school children it suggested should have as much status as a profession as teaching.

Quality, however, is a complex multi-dimensional concept. The introduction of the *Early Years Foundation Stage Framework* (in 2008) was seminal, providing the workforce with a set of common principles and commitments to deliver quality early years experiences to all children in England and out-lining regulatory requirements, e.g. regarding staff:child ratios. But the *Quality Wheel* (DfE, 2011a), which illustrates what quality looks like, rightly includes other dimensions including workforce characteristics such as quali-fications and aspects of practice such as warm responsive relationships.

Different stakeholders have different perspectives about the relative impor-tance to workforce quality of the EYFS framework, qualifications (or 'Status') as well as particular Standards or aspects of 'pedagogical interaction' or prac-tice. According to the *Report on the Consultation with Parents, Carers and Children on the Standards for Early Years Professionals* (CWDC TA, 2006a) there were mixed views about whether a degree was essential, but:

> for all parents/carers and their children certain Standards were seen as very important. For different reasons, they all valued practitioners that worked closely and communicated openly with them. Having high expectations for and of children and safeguarding and protecting them, was seen as crucial by all those interviewed. Children felt that listening to them was a real skill and some-thing that all Early Years Professionals should be able to do well.

As well as influencing the quality of a setting, the quality of the workforce is also influenced by it, and what a practitioner can do in a setting is determined to a large extent by their 'agency' within it, or what they are enabled to do. Over the last decade local authorities have invested significant resource in sup-porting and challenging settings to enable practitioners to be reflective, lead and manage and engage in continuing professional development. This support typically involved providing dedicated qualified advisory teachers and Early Years Professionals to work directly with non-maintained settings in an area. With resource constraints it is increasingly difficult for local authorities to pro-vide this support, let alone to ensure as recommended by Nutbrown that newly qualified practitioners starting in their first employment have mentoring for at least the first six months. Even if government does bring together a suite of online induction and training modules it is unlikely that they will be accessed by everyone working in early education and childcare as she recommended, unless there is support and challenge within the system.

The status of the early years workforce, particularly in non-maintained set-tings, remains low. Developing parental and societal understanding of the significance of early childhood and how young children interact and develop and raising expectations of the quality of the workforce remains a challenge.

According to the Evaluation of the Graduate Leader Fund (Mathers et al., 2011), staff qualifications were not amongst the primary reasons for parents selecting a setting, with only 26% citing this as one of their top three factors. Parents exhibited a limited awareness of the presence of an Early Years Professional (EYP), and of qualifications more generally within their child's setting; only 25% in EYP settings knew that their setting had an EYP in place. Forty per cent of parents did not know what the highest qualification held by staff was and parents saw staff experience as more important than qualifications.

The United Kingdom has a well-established and effective tradition of early education, based on nursery schools and classes linked to the rest of the education system. The focus of efforts to improve the quality of the workforce over the last decade has been on PVI settings, but government has utilised the skills, knowledge and experience of early years teachers, as consultants and advisers to support new developments, such as the introduction of the EYFS. A National Strategies Early Years Team was deployed to ensure that these consultants and advisers worked in a systematic way with settings to improve quality and outcomes for children. The evaluation of the Graduate Leader Fund found that external advice and support from early years advisers, who were seen as experts in the delivery of high quality provision affected settings' abilities to successfully implement improvements in practice. Early years teachers are a requirement in children's centres and many led the way in achieving Early Years Professional Status and Advanced Teacher Status.

As the case study illustrates, early years teachers have a complex role, which is not always recognised within, as well as outside the education system. The Training and Development Agency for Schools was responsible for the initial and in-service training of teachers and other school staff in England until April 2012 when their work transferred to the Teaching Agency. During this period they did not instigate any major changes, so there are still no Initial Teacher Education routes covering the birth to 3 years age range. Nutbrown's recommendation for early years specialists with Qualified Teacher Status (QTS), covering birth to 7 years was not accepted. Instead Early Years Teachers specialising in birth to 5 years but without QTS will be introduced.

Case Study 15.1

The role of the early years teacher in schools is a complex one typically involving both leadership of the play and learning in the outdoor area and classroom, and leadership and management of a team of other professionals.

There is a unique challenge to the new teacher taking on a new class and a perhaps very established team. It is not simply a matter of qualifications but of recognising the professional capacity and perspective of each unique adult in getting to know the 'unique child'.

An experienced but 'new' reception teacher in an inner London school led a bold change in assessment practice by asking his 'established' team to abandon their sticky notes and copious written observations and instead 'get to know the children'. Through his leadership and daily professional dialogues with support staff each of them learned to relax and really look at and talk with children and understand the learning processes that they were going through rather than simply and frequently writing down what they do.

As a result the knowledge of each child's attainment became deeper (as was apparent when reviewing and moderating the judgements made for the children in relation to the Early Years Foundation Stage Profile) and their pedagogy became stronger. The team had an agreed and joint view on the children and this has become the key starting point in development of the Reception class and early years unit because the adults respect each other's point of view and have a clearer understanding of the needs of the children in it.

However the leadership role of the early years teacher remained. Whilst other qualified and unqualified staff had been successfully deployed in building relationships with the children, observing them and assessing them by getting to know them as unique individual learners, the reception teacher retained the key accountability for the attainment and progress of each child.

So in this case, it was the range of qualifications and the range of professional perspectives that this brings to a team that contributed to the very effective observation and assessment practice. However it was the leadership of an early years teacher that gave each individual confidence in their unique role and perspective.

Workforce quality costs

Over the last decade there has been unprecedented political interest in the provision of care and education for young children and the government has made significant financial investment in the early years workforce. From 2006 £250 million was made available through the Transformation Fund for local authorities to develop a graduate-led workforce in PVI settings, and between 2008 and 2011 a further £305 million through the Graduate Leader Fund to support full daycare PVI settings in employing a graduate or EYP to help professionalise the early years workforce and to deliver the *Ten Year Strategy for Childcare* (HM Treasury, 2004).

Although some of this money was used to subsidise wage costs, government did not think it appropriate or feasible for them to 'interfere further in workforce pay and conditions'. They argued that improved qualifications would, in time, lead to higher status and remuneration. Practitioners, however, argue that the low status and pay of the early years workforce militates against professionalism and quality in the workforce. *Pay, Progression and Professionalism in the Early Years Workforce* (Cooke and Lawton, 2008) summarised interviews with 53 early years staff and identified trends in staff views on pay and status including:

- The early years sector was seen as not just low paid, but underpaid, especially in relation to the responsibility practitioners had for children and their development.

- They thought their work had a low status in society and this impacted on their sense of self-esteem and professionalism. This was also linked to the perception that working in early years was 'women's work'.
- They also stated that it led to low motivation and impacted on their work with the children due to the stress of living on the breadline.

Quality Costs: Paying for High Quality Early Childhood Education and Care (Daycare Trust, 2009) identified the necessary elements required for early childhood education and care to be of 'high quality', and costed a high quality model for England. The key findings included the following:

- Full daycare and sessional settings need substantial increased investment to enable them to meet the requirements in the high quality model, whereas 'maintained' settings require less additional investment as their staff are generally more highly qualified.
- Current staff:child ratios are adequate for high quality provision in the majority of settings when combined with well qualified staff, although higher ratios may be required in disadvantaged areas.
- If fees were increased overnight to cover the costs of better qualified, better paid staff, parents would have to increase their contribution from £2.6bn per year to £4.9bn per year.
- Without reform of government subsidies for childcare it is highly unlikely that parents could afford these levels of increases.

In the same week that Professor Nutbrown's final report was published, recommending that government consider the best way to maintain and increase graduate pedagogical leadership, the Prime Minister announced a childcare commission to look into the cost of childcare. According to the *Daycare Trust's Annual Childcare Costs Survey* (2012), nursery costs had risen by nearly 6% and 44,000 fewer families were getting help with childcare costs since tax credits were cut in April 2012. The Daycare Trust maintains that the high cost of childcare in the UK is the result of a fragmented market with few economies of scale, and a complicated government funding model.

Interestingly, only Nordic governments spend more on children under 3 than the UK, which spends more than France, the Netherlands, Germany and the United States. Yet costs to parents in the UK are the second highest in the OECD (the highest is Switzerland, where childcare take-up is low), with parents spending 27% of their income compared to the 11% Dutch or German parents spend.

Put simply, there is a cost to a more highly qualified workforce and unless settings bear the cost, or government increase subsidies, that cost has to be passed on to parents through increased fees. In their response to the Nutbrown Review, government proposed increasing the ratios of children to early years practitioners in order to reduce costs (DfE 2013). This was strongly opposed by parents, early years providers and academics, and the proposal has been dropped.

The early years workforce: part of the children's workforce

Every Child Matters: Change for Children (DfES, 2004) outlined the government's very ambitious long term vision, which included 'services provided by better qualified staff'. Following consultation, *The Children's Workforce Strategy: Building a World Class Workforce for Children, Young People and Families* (DfES, 2005) was set in the context of the then administration's overall plans for system-wide change in children's services This strategy situated the early years workforce firmly within the wider children's workforce. The four key strategic challenges it outlined were to:

- recruit more people into the children's workforce, ensuring the work is attractive and promoting more flexible entry routes;
- develop and retain more people within the children's workforce, improving their skills building on the Common Core of Skills and Knowledge and creating a single qualifications framework;
- strengthen inter-agency and multidisciplinary working, and workforce re-modelling;
- promote stronger leadership, management and supervision.

In Spring 2005 the Children's Workforce Development Council (CWDC) became operational to translate the strategy into reality on the ground. It was set up by government, but with a level of 'independence', as a company limited by guarantee, a partner in the Sector Skills Council 'Skills for Care and Development'. It was re-classified in April 2008 as an Executive Non-Departmental Public Body.

   CWDC achieved much for and with parts of the children's workforce and in support of an integrated workforce. However, as a delivery agent of the DCSF, which invested around £500 million through it, its priority for the early years workforce was delivering government policy. Promise of a single 'integrated' qualifications framework for the children's workforce was abandoned when it proved unlikely to achieve its purpose and the Qualification and Credit Framework[3] (QCF) was launched, with the potential to support career pathways across related occupations.

   Late in 2010 the new administration announced its decision to no longer fund workforce development activity through CWDC, to remove its Non-Departmental Public Body status and from April 2012 to take ongoing key functions into the DfE and the Teaching Agency (TA), which became operational from April 2012. The TA is responsible for three key areas of delivery:

- supply and, with others, retention of the workforce;
- the quality of the workforce; and
- regulation of teacher conduct.

The agency also fulfils some 'sector body responsibilities' with regard to staff who support teaching and learning. From April 2012 CWDC's 'sector body responsibilities' with regard to the early years workforce in England were taken up by Skills for Care, a partner in the Sector Skills Council 'Skills for Care and Development'.

Early Years Professional Status

The government's response to the 2006 *Consultation on the Children's Workforce Strategy* set out its aim to develop a new Early Years Professional role. CWDC worked in partnership with TDA and early years stakeholders to develop a new 'change agent' role to improve practice. Because of the nature of government funding this had to be done to a very tight timeline and in 2006 it published the *Early Years Professional Prospectus* (CWDC TA, 2006b), which set out the approach to the award of Early Years Professional Status (EYPS). Thanks to a partnership with experienced early years training providers and the legacy of early years foundation degrees, the first candidates to achieve EYPS did so in January 2007 and up to 2012 about 10,000 candidates had achieved the Status. The speed of development of EYPS meant that beyond the training providers and candidates involved in it, the assessment process was not well understood.

Whilst recognising the dilemmas that arose and the challenges that remain with EYPS there are now many more graduates in PVI settings working directly with children and leading and supporting other staff (in 2011 32% of non-LA settings employed at least one EYP). According to the Evaluation of the Graduate Leader Fund (Mathers et al., 2011), settings that gained a graduate leader with EYPS made significant improvements in quality for pre-school children (aged 30 months to 5 years) as compared with settings that did not. Gains seen in overall quality included positive staff-interactions; support for communication, language and literacy; reasoning/thinking skills. EYPs provided added-value over and above gaining a graduate in terms of overall quality and provision to support literacy/language development. Improvements related most strongly to support for learning, communication and individual needs and EYPs were most influential on the quality of practice in their own room rather than setting-wide.

However, EYPs are tasked with leading practice across the full age range from birth to the end of the EYFS and in contrast to these positive findings there was little evidence that EYPs improved the quality of provision for younger children (birth to 30 months). The low number of EYPs working in these rooms meant that firm conclusions on the potential impact of EYPs on provision for infants and toddlers could be drawn and the evaluation concluded that further research is needed to establish the most effective ways of raising quality for under 3s, through workforce development.

While EYPs have been dissatisfied with their lack of parity with those who hold QTS many are disappointed by the removal of EYPS and its replacement with Early Years Teacher (DfE 2013). Nutbrown suggested that having qualified teachers leading early years practice would raise the status of the sector, increase professionalism and improve quality. This resonates both with society's view, where the role of teacher is widely understood, and practitioners who aspire to the pay and conditions associated with being a teacher. However, the new early years teachers will not have QTS or the pay and conditions linked to it. There will continue to be early years teachers with QTS in maintained schools and at least initially two roles with very similar names and the same entry requirements but very different pay and conditions. Lumsden, (2012), argues that what is actually needed is a new 'integrated' professional model, a new professional space with flexible borders at the intersection of education, health and social care.

Level 2 and 3 early years qualifications

The vocational qualifications system in England is multi-layered and complex. *The Government's Response to the Wolf Review of Vocational Education* (2011) acknowledges that although there are examples of excellence within the system, they do not add up to an excellent system. Within this system the DCSF asked CWDC to rationalise the plethora of early years qualifications and clarify what is full and relevant for the purposes of registration and regulation.

CWDC reviewed the criteria that qualifications must meet in order to be deemed 'full and relevant' and mapped over 300 against these criteria. In 2008 they developed the Qualifications List for those delivering the EYFS. As well as listing 'full and relevant' qualifications, the Web-based tool also lists qualifications that, together with accredited additional learning, enable a practitioner's package of accredited learning to be viewed as 'full and relevant'.

In 2008 CWDC brought together seven awarding organisations, and supported by an expert group, developed the QCF Level 2 Certificate and Level 3 Diploma for the Children and Young People's Workforce (Early Learning and Childcare Pathway). Given awarding organisations' vested interest, this was a significant achievement, but in its *Monitoring Report on the Level 3 Diploma for the Children and Young People's Workforce* (2010), Ofqual found that with the roles and responsibilities of awarding organisations and CWDC in the lead, development and accountability of the qualification had become confused. Nutbrown did not think the Level 3 offered the fundamental content and pedagogical processes necessary to work effectively with babies and young children.

The core of skills, knowledge and understanding that is common across the children's workforce was incorporated into the Diploma to offer learners the opportunity to move between occupational areas without having to repeat learning. However, Nutbrown felt that the birth to 19 age range covered by these qualifications was too broad to be meaningful and was persuaded that qualifications for early years staff should be specific to the early years age group.

It was DfE and CWDC's intention that from a 'specified date' all new learners who wished to achieve a qualification deemed to be full and relevant for the purposes of registration and regulation would need to undertake these qualifications. This deadline however, was postponed a number of times, finally pending the outcome of the Nutbrown Review of Qualifications, which made four recommendations:

1 Government should continue to specify the qualifications that are suitable for staff operating within the EYFS, and the TA should develop a more robust set of 'full and relevant' criteria to ensure qualifications promote the right content and pedagogical processes. These criteria should be based on the proposals set out in the report.
2 All qualifications commenced from 1 September 2013 must demonstrate that they meet the new 'full and relevant' criteria when being considered against the requirements of the EYFS.
3 The previous plan to move to a single early years qualification should be abandoned.
4 The government should consider the best way to badge qualifications that meet the new 'full and relevant' criteria so that people can recognise under what set of 'full and relevant' criteria a qualification has been gained.

However, stipulating qualification content, i.e. what should be learned and taught, is not sufficient to ensure competent practitioners. CWDC's *Analysis of the consultation on the implementation of Level 2 Certificate and Level 3 Diploma for the Children and Young People's Workforce* (CWDC TA, 2011) identified the quality of training provision and teaching and learning as the key (yet also the most variable) factors in ensuring that qualifications produce competent practitioners. Employers maintained they could tell which training provider learners and practitioners had or were training with, by reference to their practice and attitude. This was confirmed by responses to the Nutbrown Review consultation, and led to the following recommendations:

• Tutors should be qualified to a higher level than the course they are teaching.
• All tutors should have regular continuing professional development and contact with early years settings. Colleges and training providers should allow sufficient time for this.

Awarding organisations have a crucial role to ensure consistent outcomes across learners undertaking the same qualification with different training providers, in specifying and verifying assessment and in standardisation and moderation of qualifications. Ofqual's regulation of awarding organisations and their qualifications, coupled with funding agencies addressing the perverse incentives inherent in their funding methodology, are as crucial as the content of qualifications and the quality of teaching and learning.

The government currently regulates the early years workforce in England through minimum qualification requirements, which are laid down in the *Statutory Framework for the Early Years Foundation Stage* (2007). In recognition of the progress made in raising the proportion of the workforce with a level 3 qualification, Nutbrown recommended that the EYFS requirements should be revised so that to count in the staff:child ratio

- by September 2022, all staff must be qualified at level 3
- from September 2013, a minimum of 50% of staff in group settings need to possess at least a 'full and relevant' level 3
- from September 2015, a minimum of 70% of staff in group settings need to possess at least a 'full and relevant' level 3.

Nutbrown also recommended that level 2 English and mathematics should be entry requirements to level 3 early education and childcare courses. This received more publicity than her other recommendations, possibly because it resonates more with the general public.

The way forward

In relation to the workforce, *Supporting Families in the Foundation Years* (DfE, 2011a), which set the new administration's vision, stated that working closely with partners, employers and sector bodies, the government would:

- review how best to strengthen qualifications and career pathways in the foundation years;
- explore how to improve the gender balance of the early education and childcare workforce;
- continue to invest in graduate-level training in early education and childcare;
- make early years education professionals a central part of the remit of the new Teaching Agency; and
- support the development of strong system leadership including through funding 10 'Early Years Teaching Centres', testing an extension of the specialist leader of education role for the foundation years and reviewing the National Professional Qualification in Integrated Centre Leadership

In 2011 the government established an early education and childcare workforce co-production group to work with them to implement the long term vision for ensuring the quality and diversity of the early years workforce. In doing so they will need to address the 'thorny' underlying issues of whether to strengthen regulation and how to implement change across a fragmented workforce and continue to raise quality without increasing costs for parents.

Notes

1 In this chapter the term 'early years' is used generically to refer to the workforce in the full range of maintained, private, voluntary and independent Early Years Foundation Stage settings in England. The original author's terminology is used when quoting or paraphrasing another source.
2 Skills for Care and Development is a partnership made up of the Care Council for Wales, the Northern Ireland Social Care Council, the Scottish Social Services Council and Skills for Care England.

In Wales the Care Council for Wales works closely with the Welsh Government and maintains the *List of Accepted Qualifications for the Early Years and Childcare Workforce in Wales*.

In Scotland, 'daycare of children' workers are required by the Scottish Government to register with the Scottish Social Services Council who stipulate which qualifications are acceptable for the categories of functions they have identified.
3 The Qualification and Credit Framework is a way of recognising achievement through the award of credit for the achievement of units and qualifications. It provides a simple and rational organising framework that presents learner achievement and qualifications in a way that is easy to understand, measure and compare. It gives individuals the opportunity to learn in a more flexible way and enables a wider range of organisations, including employers, to have their training recognised.

Key points to remember

- The early years workforce remains fragmented with a fault-line between maintained schools and other settings.
- There is agreement that the quality of the workforce is crucial to good outcomes for children, but there is a cost to quality.
- The previous administration's early years workforce policy was set in the context of an integrated children's workforce. The new administration's is being set in the context of 'education'.
- There remain some 'thorny' underlying issues that are likely to continue to dog progress towards a quality early years workforce.

Points for discussion

- To what extent does regulation of the workforce raise quality?
- Should there be one approach to issues across maintained, private, voluntary and independent settings?
- What are the respective roles of government and the sector in addressing the 'thorny issues' identified in the chapter?

Reflective tasks

- Reflecting on early years workers you know, how do you understand and define what makes them of high quality?
- Do the characteristics of the workforce identified in the chapter accord with those in a setting(s) known to you? What national strategy would impact positively on this setting(s)?
- How has early years policy implementation affected you and your colleagues?
- What brought you to the early years workforce? What are your aspirations for the future? What might affect the realisation of those aspirations?

Acknowledgement

The author would like to thank Rob Nicholson for the case study in this chapter and his expert advice and guidance on the role and responsibilities of staff in maintained school settings.

Further reading

Lumsden, E. (2012) 'Early years professional status: a new professional or a missed opportunity?', PhD thesis, University of Northampton.

Miller, L. and Cable, C. (eds) (2008) *Professionalism in the Early Years*. London: Hodder Arnold.

University of East London, Cass School of Education and University of Ghent, Department for Social Welfare Studies (2011) *Competence Requirements in Early Education and Care: A Study for the European Commission Director-General for Education and Culture*.

Useful websites

The Quality Wheel, originally produced by Department for Education (2011b) and updated by 4Children early years team (2012), is on the 4Children Foundation

Years section of the 4Children website. It shows the relationship between workforce, practice and the EYFS content and environment: www.foundationyears. org.uk/wp-content/uploads/2012/04/quality-wheel-HIRES-High-resolution-DfE-ready-2011.pdf.

The Scottish Social Services Council provides information about qualification requirements for different functions across the early years workforce in Scotland: www.sssc.uk.com.

The Care Council for Wales works closely with the Welsh Government to identify the qualifications that are required and recommended to practice, and maintains the List of Accepted Qualifications for the Early Years and Childcare Workforce in Wales: www.ccwales.org.uk.

The Department for Education provides information and reports about workforce policy and its implementation, including CWDC/Teaching Agency. All reports and reviews referred to in the chapter are downloadable from this site: www. education.gov.uk

Nursery World often has links to other websites when a government announcement is made and they have a forum where early years practitioners discuss many of the issues raised in this chapter: www.nurseryworld.co.uk.

All the main voluntary organisations have information about, and of use to the early years workforce. They include:
National Day Nurseries Association – www.ndna.org.uk
Pre-School Learning Alliance – www.pre-school.org.uk
National Childminders Association – www.ncma.org.uk
The Daycare Trust – www.daycaretrust.org.uk
4Children – www.4children.org.uk

To access a variety of additional web resources to accompany this book please visit: **www.sagepub.co.uk/pughduffy**

References

Children's Workforce Development Council (Teaching Agency) (CWDC TA) (2006a) *Report on the Consultation with Parents, Carers and Children on the Standards for Early Years Professionals*. Leeds: CWDC.
Children's Workforce Development Council (Teaching Agency) (CWDC TA) (2006b) *Early Years Professional Prospectus*. Leeds: CWDC.
Children's Workforce Development Council (Teaching Agency) (CWDC TA) (2011) *Analysis of the Consultation on the Implementation of Level 2 Certificate and Level 3 Diploma for the Children and Young People's Workforce*. Leeds: CWDC.
Cooke, G. and Lawton, K. (2008) *For Love or Money: Pay, Progression and Professionalisation in the 'Early Years' Workforce*. London: IPPR.

CWDC (2010) *Monitoring Report on the Level 3 Diploma for the Children and Young People's Workforce* Leeds: CWDC.

Daycare Trust (2009) *Quality Costs: Paying for High Quality Early Childhood Education and Care*. London: Daycare Trust.

Daycare Trust (2012) *Daycare Trust's Annual Childcare Costs Survey*. London: Daycare Trust.

Department for Education (DfE) (2010 and 2011) *Childcare and Early Years Providers Survey*. London: DfE.

Department for Education (DfE) (2011) *Government's Response to the Wolf Review of Vocational Education*. London: DfE. http://www.education.gov.uk/publications (accessed April 2013).

Department for Education (DfE) (2011a) *Supporting Families in the Foundation Years*. London: DfE.

Department for Education (DfE) (2011b) Quality Wheel (up-dated by 4Children Early Years Team in 2012). www.foundationyears.org.uk/wp-content/uploads/2012/04/quality-wheel-HIRES-High-resolution-DfE-ready-2011.pdf. (accessed 28 June 2013).

Department for Education (DfE) (2013) *More Great Childcare*. London: DfE.

Department for Education and Skills (DfES) (2003) *Every Child Matters*. Norwich: TSO.

Department for Education and Skills (DfES) (2004) *Every Child Matters. Change for Children*. Nottingham: DfES Publications.

Department for Education and Skills (DfES) (2005) *The Children's Workforce Strategy: Building a World Class Workforce for Children, Young People and Families*. Nottingham: DfES Publications.

Department for Education and Skills (DfES) (2007) *Statutory Framework for the Early Years Foundation Stage (EYFS)*. Nottingham: DfES Publications.

HM Treasury (HMT) (2004) *Choice for Parents, the Best Start for Children: A Ten Year Strategy for Childcare*. London: TSO.

Lumsden, E. (2012) 'Early years professional status: a new professional or a missed opportunity?', PhD thesis, University of Northampton.

Mathers, S., Ranns, H., Karemaker, A., Moody, A., Sylva, K., Graham, J. and Siraj-Blatchford, I. (2011) *Evaluation of the Graduate Leader Fund*. DFE-RB144. London: Department for Education.

Mathers, S., Sylva, K. and Joshi, H. (2007) *Quality of Childcare Settings in the Millennium Cohort Study*. DCSF-SSU/2007/FR/025. London: DCSF.

Nutbrown, C. (2012) *Foundations for Quality. The Independent Review of Early Education and Childcare Qualifications: Final Report* (Nutbrown Review). London: Department for Education.

Scottish Executive (2006) *National Review of the Early Years and Childcare Workforce*. Edinburgh: Scottish Executive.

Wolf, A. (2011) *Review of Vocational Education: The Wolf Report*. London: DfES.

CHAPTER 16

Leading and Working in Multi-Agency Teams

Carol Aubrey

Chapter contents

- Global trends
- Background and development of multi-agency teams
- Challenges of restructuring children's services
- Recent government policy
- Implementation in practice
- Ways forward

A focus on multi-agency working and integrated practice across a number of policy domains has become government priority for the past 15 years. Whilst there is still a lack of agreed terminology, the importance of inter-agency working across welfare services is generally accepted.

Global trends and influences

Globalising trends and influences in a world of political and technological complexity encourage collaboration and teamwork. Post-bureaucratic organisations evolve into international federations, networks and clusters, cross-functional teams and temporary task forces. Engeström (2008: 15) noted that the notion of 'teams' endures and remains a key feature of the 'envisioned cellular, networked, knowledge-creating company … the emphasis is on project teams, internet-worked teams, virtual teams that use information and communication technologies that enable integrated work group computing networks linking design and problem-solving teams across the globe. Teams thus become increasingly distributed in space or brought together on a temporary basis for the life of a project. There is no single linear form in which team arrangements are shaped and the term 'team' is used for an increasing variety of forms of col-laborative communities. In such communities boundaries are more fluid than has traditionally been the case. The team must adapt to high levels of technical division of labour and diversity of knowledge, allowing authority to rest on knowledge and expertise rather than status. This demands a level of questioning and reflection on established practices and brings values into public discussion. This new type of work generates mutual exchange between users, producers and product that results in new relationships and configurations, or *co-configurations*. Engeström identified what he called '*negotiated knotworking*' as an emergent way of organising work, where collaboration between partners is of central importance, formed without rigid, pre-determined rules or fixed authority. One might, of course, pause to consider how much such a view of teams intrudes into the worlds of British public-sector employees, particularly those engaged in multi-professional teamwork that supports the integrated children's services of today.

Background and development of multi-agency teams

Inter-agency team cooperation between education, health, social work, pro-bation and juvenile delinquency has developed slowly over more than thirty years. The Plowden Report (1967) recommended a social work service closely linked to schools that might identify families in need and thus inter-vene in difficulties leading to poor achievement and behaviour. The Seebohm Report (1968) reviewed local authority social services with a view to consid-ering changes needed to provide an effective unified family service bringing together children's departments, education welfare, home-help services, men-tal health social services, day nurseries and other services. Joint consultative committees were set up by the National Health Service Act 1973 to promote a joint community approach to service delivery. The Court Report on Child Health Services (1976) and the Warnock Report (1978) on Special Educational Needs both stressed the potential role of joint consultative committees in coordination and development of services for children and families.

Throughout this period and even before, the Child Guidance team of psy-chiatrist, educational psychologist and psychiatric social worker provided a service through inter-professional cooperation for children defined as 'malad-justed' but it was not until the late 1980s that inter-agency cooperation was advocated by the Report of the Inquiry into Child Abuse in Cleveland (Butler-Sloss, 1988) and the Children Act 1989. With the Act, came the obligation for statutory agencies such as education, social services and health to work together in the interests of children's welfare. Improvement in collaboration between agencies and integrated services has long been recommended but now 'joined up thinking' and 'joined up services' have become the corner-stone of professional practice.

Challenges to workforce remodelling?

Barr et al. (2005) suggested that many factors challenge relations between professions and affect the services that they provide. Most fundamental is communication. Pietroni (1992) identified that profession-specific languages and discourses reflect attitudes, values and culturally determined meanings. New entrants are socialised into disciplines, methods and discourses derived from natural science (for medicine, some psychology and health-related fields) or social science (for education and social work), reinforced through specific curricula and training, attitudes and behaviours. Basic trust and mutual goodwill between professionals however may be thwarted by organ-isational policies, bureaucratic procedures and codes of confidentiality.

Concurrent with restructuring of children's services and a requirement for an integrated qualifications framework, the number of early years profession-als has grown (Nutbrown, 2012). As specialisms increase, so too does the need to establish clear and unambiguous intra-professional as well as inter-professional relations, for example between the early years professional (EYP) and early years teacher with qualified teacher status (QTS). Reform of the workforce can cause tensions, suspicion and a reluctance to cross bound-aries. A climate of organisational change, policies and procedures focused on improved quality and delivery to specific targets increases bureaucracy and managerialism. At the same time, public expectations rise as economic resources diminish, in a context of increasing poverty, migration, destabilised family structure and an ageing population. Rivalry fed by differences in pro-fessional power, status and esteem may exacerbate territorialism and raise concerns about protecting vested interests. Acknowledging existing tensions and imbalances as well as exploring new roles, responsibilities and functions may be prerequisite to workforce reorganisation.

In this context, it is necessary to take account of additional costs of time-investment to create new strategies, common work practices and ethical procedures, exchange of information, collective ownership of child and fam-ily problems, joint monitoring and evaluation of service, as well as joint training to understand one another's professional role.

New Labour policy and multi-agency working

From 1997 New Labour resolved to reform public services for children and families as part of a wider strategy to tackle poverty and social exclusion. This reflected a belief that social and economic problems are intertwined. The concept of 'joined-up' services and 'interconnectedness' of child and family needs shaped development of inter-agency cooperation and multi-disciplinary teams in the fields of education, health and social services, in conjunction with employment, family support, housing and law enforcement. 'Joined-up services' for families with children under 4 in the 500 most deprived areas of England through the Sure Start programme initiative exemplified this period (Glass, 1999). New Labour thinking was under-pinned by key principles of high standards and accountability; devolved decision-making in service delivery; flexibility of employment in public-service delivery; and promotion of choice for users, through the promotion of private- and voluntary-sector providers (Blair, 1998). Promotion of local empowerment in a climate of 'best value' and 'what works', increased accountability, performance management, monitoring and inspection have marked public sector reform over this period.

Perceived failures in 'working together' by separate planning and service provision, highlighted by the report of Lord Laming (2003) in the field of child protection and identified as a contributory factor to the death of Victoria Climbié, prompted a barrage of legislative change. It resulted in more inte-grated service-provision for children and families that originated in the Green Paper *Every Child Matters* (DfES, 2003), *Every Child Matters: Change for Children* (DfES, 2004) and the Children Act 2004. Five outcomes underpin-ning the Children Act 2004 defined delivery of services for children in local authorities (LAs) and provided a common national framework for monitoring and inspecting them. Every LA was charged with appointing an officer responsible for coordinating children's services, developing Children and Young People Plans by 2006 and Children's Trust arrangements for allocating funding to children's services by 2008. A new post of Children's Commissioner for England was also introduced through the Children Act 2004.

To facilitate the establishment of integrated services for children, Children's Trusts were required to:

- co-locate services, such as children's centres and extended schools;
- establish multi-disciplinary teams;
- implement a Common Assessment Framework (CAF) for identifying addi-tional need of children and young people (CYP) and their families;
- set up information-sharing systems; and
- provide joint training and efficient arrangements for safeguarding children.

The implementation of CAF is based on identified need, in the context of:

- *universal* and core provision of services routinely available;
- *targeted* services for CYP identified as having additional needs; and
- *specialist* services provided for complex and high-level need, requiring additional and referral related to child protection, special educational need or health-related issues.

Targeted services are often accessed from within universal services, such as Sure Start children's centres, as well as provided directly to individual CYP. Coordinated targeted services are usually undertaken by a team around the child (TAC) and a lead professional (LP) nominated to coordinate service delivery. Despite an expectation that targeted and specialist responses from services might include training, guidance, advice and support to build capacity, at the pilot stage of introduction of CAF and LP roles and responsibilities, a number of issues were identified (Brandon et al., 2006). These included:

- the extra workload;
- uneven adoption and spread of 'holistic' assessment and direct work with parents;
- lack of clarity on implementation of CAF; and
- lack of relevant assessment skills in agency professionals.

Perceived lack of guidance could lead to frustration, conflict and loss of confidence between different agencies.

Exploration of the current costs and impact of CAF (Holmes et al., 2012: 16) suggested that both professionals and families had a positive view of certain aspects of the CAF. Parents or carers emphasised the importance of an LP working as an advocate and negating the need to 'tell their story' to a range of professionals. Professionals considered the CAF to have progressed interagency working. To work effectively, however, substantial investment of time and expenditure was required to embed the framework across agencies. After piloting a national recording system (or eCAF) and further consultation, the Department for Education (DfE, 2011) announced that this was to be decommissioned by May 2012.

Holmes et al. (2012) emphasised that without systematic collection and extraction of child level data, it was not possible to follow children's journeys through the CAF and build up a national evidence base to inform strategic planning and commissioning of early intervention and prevention services.

Coalition government policy and multi-agency working

The Coalition government set up new policy with reduced funding but continued to seek improved outcomes. It sought to focus investment in systematic preventive and early intervention services as a means to break cycles of poverty and underachievement in groups and communities in order to make long term savings (Easton et al., 2011).

A review by Marmot (2010) drew attention to social inequalities of health in many countries. He examined the case for action on social determinants of health, driven by inequalities of power, money and resources and the social gradient in health outcomes related to the conditions in which people are born, grow, live and work. This theme was picked up by Field (2010), who reviewed poverty and life chances and how to prevent poor children from becoming poor adults. He recommended giving greater prominence to the 'foundation years', covering the period 'from womb to five'. This theme runs through Allen's (2011) review of early intervention, Munro's (2011) review of child protection and the Tickell Review (2011) of the Early Years Foundation Stage.

Improved integrated working through the CAF process has been seen 'not [as] an optional extra but a fundamental building block that enables LAs and their partner agencies to work together effectively to support early intervention and prevention' (Easton et al., 2011: 3). As these authors noted, 'process alone cannot deliver the improved outcomes'. They called for an underpinning of 'specific evidence-based programmes that have been shown to be effective in working with vulnerable children and families'. A review of early intervention approaches of Easton and Gee (2012) noted the case for investing in early intervention approaches to improve outcomes for CYP and families to bring about cost savings in the longer term, now widely accepted. They cautioned that there is a scarcity of UK-based evidence on cost-effectiveness of early intervention approaches and a need to improve the evidence available to local and national decision-makers.

Despite this, a Coalition government Department for Education article of April 2012 emphasised the benefits of multi-agency working that include 'quality services … [and a] reduced need for specialist services' (DfE, 2012).

How do we implement effective multi-agency practice?

Recent policy initiatives are driving changes in structures, concepts and operations with multi-agency 'joined up' services identified as the key to effective delivery and a quality service. Whilst multi-agency working is widely regarded as an essential part of early intervention and prevention approaches, there remains the challenge of demonstrating its effectiveness and cost-effectiveness. Initial findings from the National Evaluation of Sure Start (NESS), however, showed only limited evidence of impact at 9 and 36 months (Belsky et al., 2007). By 5 five years, NESS children had better health, lower body-mass index (BMI) than non-NESS children and mothers reported better home life and learning (NESS, 2010). They were, however, reported to be less likely to visit children's schools for meetings and no differences emerged on seven measures of cognitive and social development.

Restructuring children's services requires professionals to work in new ways. As noted, it is necessary to take account of additional costs of time investment and resource to create new strategies, common work practices and ethical procedures, exchange of information, collective ownership of child and family problems, joint monitoring and evaluation of services, as well as joint training to understand one another's professional roles. The lack of evidence for effectiveness and cost-effective multi-agency working should therefore come as no surprise. The NESS revealed that staff contracts impeded the smooth running of programmes. These included short-term attachments, temporary transfer from one agency to another in secondments and recruitment of staff from a variety of backgrounds, including parents and other community members, trained as 'befrienders' and managed by other professionals. The challenge of 'getting skills right' was complicated by workforce shortages and finite resources, so local workers were developed and employment of expensive specialists took place only when essential. Loss of good staff in search of better salaries and working conditions created higher workloads for remaining staff that lowered job satisfaction and raised staff turnover.

Effectiveness of integrated multi-agency working may be associated with management and funding arrangements. Øvretveit et al. (1997) identified the need to manage the total team resources related to job descriptions, work and performance supervision or appraisal that were normally undertaken by a senior staff member. This senior staff member might provide full management and responsibility for both clinical and organisational matters, provide either one or the other, or provide neither (if the 'supervisee' remained autonomous and therefore accountable). This illuminated different types of management and supervision for multi-agency teams, where a member of staff might be managed and supervised by a team manager or a professional agency manager, or be jointly managed and supervised, or contracted back out to be supervised by the agency manager. Some case studies were undertaken to illustrate challenges to multi-agency work over the period since the Children Act 2004.

Case Study 16.1

Working in multi-agency teams

The first case study (Aubrey et al., 2005) aimed to capture the development phase of multi-agency working in four Sure Start Local Programmes (SSLPs) before they gained children's centre status between 2003 and 2006. They were gathering together teams of midwives, health visitors and speech therapists,

(Continued)

(Continued)

teachers and community development workers, librarians, and care and welfare workers. The goal was to enhance the life chances of young children and their families by improving services in areas of high deprivation. This was regarded as innovative in having freedom to try different ways of working, with deprived communities where public provision had been poor.

Those who took part were active in holding the programme together through organisation and planning, communication and facilitation of teamwork.

Questions to be addressed by a related survey were:

- *How much do we know about effective multi-agency working?*
- *What are the factors contributing to their success and what kinds of challenges are raised?*

A semi-structured interview schedule was then designed to probe ambivalent and conflicting responses identified by the survey, using open-ended questions. A total of 69 questionnaires were returned from 159 staff and partnership board members, including four from the leading agencies. This gave a 50% response rate.

Regarding LA structures and boundaries, views on whether these constituted a facilitating factor or hindrance were mixed. Factors thought to facilitate multi-agency working related to being able to utilise systems and people already in place.

Working relationships within teams, and with parent agencies and other voluntary and statutory agencies, were seen as both facilitative and a force for development. The need to understand the roles and responsibilities of others was emphasised by the majority. Several described adopting roles with SSLPs as 'blurring the edges of your role to take on new responsibilities and work in a new way'. Practical factors thought to hinder multi-agency working were different terms and conditions, holiday allowances, pay-scales, policies and procedures. Respondents' views on the effect of professional and agency culture on practice were mixed, with nearly two-thirds feeling that specific policy and practice differences hindered shared practice. Different data management systems affected information-sharing and impacted on shared practice.

The majority thought resources in the form of staffing arrangements and time investment to be facilitative of multi-agency working. Staff had high expectations of working as a multi-agency team, though the development towards a fully-integrated team had been slower than desired. This was due to several factors, such as staff not being clear about their roles within the team. Concern was expressed about staff who remained managed and supervised by the parent agency and the tensions that this caused.

Development of multi-agency working has been slow. 'Baggage' brought by the SSLP members and, in some cases, professional management being maintained within statutory agencies needed to be overcome.

Aims and objectives of local programmes were regarded by the vast majority as facilitative of multi-agency working.

A number of agencies in the area would not get together formally if it were not for the SSLP.

Respondents were less certain of whether or not aims of specific agencies competed with local SSLP aims. This they attributed to different agencies working to different government targets and different emphases in the workplace of different professionals. Some were working to provide specialist services, others providing targeted services accessed from within universal services. Others felt that targets of different agencies should be seen as complementary and not in competition. Still others felt that such tensions arose from existing work cultures. Several respondents expressed the view that the ethos of all agencies was changing and becoming more prevention-focused.

'There is a general move towards preventive work which places SSLP at the heart of the government's agenda and which all agencies are beginning to recognise'.

Views concerning confidentiality and information-sharing strategies between various agencies were mixed, with the need expressed for common systems and protocols to reduce the amount of time wasted on this matter. The accountable body was highlighted as a hindrance.

'Lack of information-sharing has ground to a halt several very positive procedures that we have tried to put in place, mostly on behalf of the accountable body'.

A need to develop a common language across professional groups was felt by the overwhelming majority and there was a strong sense that language used should be accessible to parents. The majority also felt that poor communication within and between agencies created problems for those working at different levels within agencies. Successful multi-agency work could also be undermined by poor communication between different LA departments. Several respondents highlighted that, despite problems at strategic level, the SSLP teams were delivering services in a multi-agency manner.

Views regarding the challenge that budgets and financial arrangements posed to multi-agency working were again mixed. Problems specifically between the lead agency and accountable body, and their respective responsibilities were emphasised. Establishing 'good agreements' between the two, to reduce possible conflicts of interest, was also emphasised. The majority of respondents also felt that non-financial resources created a challenge. This resulted in a less effective delivery of services than otherwise might be the case. Areas emphasised were allocation of time, provision of staff, and physical space in which to work effectively.

By contrast, the majority of respondents felt that leadership or drive of individual SSLP managers demonstrated clear strategic direction, and the tenacity to overcome obstacles to progress and bring together the multi-agency SSLP team to effect change. Respondents were very positive about leadership of the SSLPs. In terms of management strategy, the vast majority felt that multi-agency working was strongly supported and promoted at SSLP management level to remain credible at delivery level. A majority felt that SSLP strategy encouraged 'like-minded individuals who sought new ways of working in order to meet shared goals and work across existing management structures'.

(Continued)

(Continued)

Key themes were then explored in interviews with 34 respondents. Representatives of the leading agencies acknowledged a 'lack of capacity' and hence delay in prioritising support for SSLPs at the strategic level. This resulted in the finance team being employed on temporary contracts. Understanding of and acquaintance with leading agencies by partnership board representatives varied and their views on its effect on multi-agency were very mixed. Team members' views were similarly mixed and while they acknowledged strategic commitment of the leading agencies, it was felt that once they developed more effective ways of working, things could be achieved 'more quickly and efficiently'.

In respect of roles and responsibilities, representatives of leading agencies identified their priorities at strategic and operational levels, but realised having two leading agencies 'added complexity' and hence a challenge to multi-agency working. The accountable body was described as having a less than positive effect on SSLPs in terms of time taken to make decisions: 'operational issues of one leading agency created particular challenges'. Partnership board members' views on the roles of leading agencies were again mixed, with some uncertainty expressed as to whether SSLP services duplicated or complemented those of their parent agencies. Team participants were sceptical about the complementary nature of the aims of partner agencies and SSLPs.

Regarding staffing, resources and workspace, representatives of leading agencies acknowledged problems arising from placing staff on temporary contracts and lack of office space. Partnership board representatives and team participants both highlighted recruitment issues and problems of locating staff while suitable premises were being secured.

Data protection and information-sharing were acknowledged as a problem by all three groups. Reluctance of different agencies to share information was emphasised along with lack of data procedures and protocols for data storage and information exchange. It was also acknowledged that the strategy for sharing confidential information was being reviewed.

Finally, with respect to communication, multiple channels were advocated by all groups of respondents, with improved IT networks, regular team meetings, direct telephone contact between locations, daily transfer of internal post, along with informal chats and social events. Problems arose at the strategic level in the LA from lack of communication of decisions when made and by Sure Start Unit's constant policy change.

Despite the real enthusiasm of SSLP respondents, effective multi-agency working had not been easy to achieve. What emerged was the impact of leading agencies' line management of SSLP managers who had overall control of strategic management, financial arrangements and 'contracting-in' of the services of different professionals. Staff with different backgrounds and skills strove towards common goals and shared values, despite barriers to effectiveness and efficiency in the form of constantly shifting policies, LA structures, lack of space and split sites, and challenges to data – storing, information-sharing and communication. Though staff clearly had an appetite for the new and 'hybrid' professional being thrown up, problems arose from joint management by SSLP managers with continuing employment by the parent agency that provided both professional leadership and supervision. Navigating LA structures and constraints, in the context of shifting internal organisational changes such as these 'formed and reformed' multi-agency teams in response to changing requirements in a changing environment, has been described by Engeström as 'knotworking'. Given the very recent report by Holmes et al. (2012) on the working of the Common Assessment Framework (CAF) it would appear some of these early problems remain. Whilst the CAF may be considered to have progressed inter-agency working, the substantial investment of expenditure and time to embed such practice across agencies remains an issue and the national system for data-sharing that professionals have recommended throughout this period will not now proceed. With the current cutbacks in funding and staffing, the task of 'getting skills right' will remain.

Case Study 16.2

Leading multi-agency teams

Our second case study (Aubrey, 2011) focused on 25 early childhood leaders and middle leaders from a range of early years settings that included nursery schools and classes, private and voluntary daycare and Sure Start children's centres (SSCCs). They were asked what leadership meant in their settings, about factors that facilitated and hindered its effectiveness, about staff-training needs and how capacity could be built in the field. Focus groups of leaders stressed that their central goal was valuing learning and that commitment to ongoing professional development was important to this aspiration. Fundamental was recognition of the profession's multi-disciplinary nature. They felt that commitment to continued professional development and support of staff contributed to successful leadership. Lack of relevant knowledge, however, was characteristic at all levels in the LA and lack of available training was a further hindrance.

New knowledge, skills and capacity, it was thought, should be brought into the sector through trainers who knew the field, and setting up networks and mentoring systems across the sector was also recommended. Freeth et al. (2005) noted that much inter-professional learning is serendipitous, happens by chance in unplanned and perhaps unacknowledged ways during interactions in the course of everyday work. Such learning is likely to be more effective, however, when it becomes planned, recognised and accessible. Much learning may remain casual, incidental and hidden from view. The latest in a series of Cochrane reviews on the evidence of the extent to which different healthcare professionals work together can affect the quality of healthcare, found that in three out of five studies that identified demonstrable improvement in patient care, one showed

(Continued)

(Continued)

no impact and the other had mixed outcomes. So far, none of the healthcare studies investigated has been able to show effects of high quality professional collaboration on patient outcomes. Joyce and Showers (2002) have studied the effect of training on educational outcomes for decades and emphasised that good training should try to accomplish targeted outcomes on pupil groups through identified stages of teacher development:

- *acquisition of knowledge or awareness of educational theories and academic content;*
- *positive attitude change towards the teacher's own role and the group of children;*
- *development of skill (or change in behaviour);*
- *transfer of training and executive control, generating consistent use in the classroom (that is, change in organisational proficiency that is of benefit to the pupil group).*

To establish change in client groups, training in inter-professional working thus needs to stimulate development at a number of levels from theory, attitude and skill through to modelling and coaching to transfer to the workplace setting. This alerted us to the need to ask our leaders about their professional development and to observe what they actually did in the workplace.

Firstly, perspectives on early childhood leadership were surveyed. Asked to rank aspects of the leadership role, there was broad agreement that the most important aspect of the role was to deliver a quality service, and there was a correlation between the quality service-delivery and professional development. A principal components analysis of a rating of personal characteristics of effective leaders revealed that leadership meant different things to practitioners with different qualifications and professional heritages.

- *Those with postgraduate qualifications favoured what we called leaders as guides, being warm and knowledgeable and providing coaching, mentoring and guiding.*
- *Those with 'other' qualifications, for instance, those from community development, health, library services or social work, favoured leaders as strategists.*
- *Those with NVQs favoured leaders as motivators, who empowered or motivated.*
- *Those with post-graduate qualifications also favoured economic competitiveness, business awareness and risk-taking.*

Despite confirming unanimity on the importance of valuing learning and provision, the survey also revealed that practitioners with different initial qualifications, following different routes into the early childhood sector, held different views about early childhood leadership and different attitudes towards this role.

Secondly, conversations with leaders and staff pursued themes that emerged from the survey. Common themes in leadership were raising children's enjoyment and achievement, personal, social development and well-being, and staff performance in providing quality care. Understanding the local community was another common theme. In terms of decision-making, it was felt that organisations were 'hierarchical at the strategic level and collaborative at the operational level'. Top-down decision-making reflected LA line-management of leaders that contrasted with collaborative decision-making at team level. This matched a finding in Case Study 16.1 that, whilst SSLP leaders pursued shared goals and worked across management structures, LA structures and representatives of leading agencies lacked capacity and failed to prioritise support for SSLP at the strategic level.

In terms of training, staff had had no experience of leadership training, mentioning 'role models and nuggets … what people said about leadership'. Books, studying and first-hand experience were also mentioned. Leaders talked about formal qualifications, short courses, internal training and meeting. They also stressed contact with other professionals and reading but thought that 'experience was more useful than theory'. SSCC leaders had gained a National Qualification in Integrated Centre Leadership (NPQICL) or, in one case, a Masters degree in Business Administration.

Finally, leaders were followed into their workplace settings. Leaders of multi-agency SSCCs reported and demonstrated a rich and varied range of activities that included meetings, paperwork, telephone calls, staff interactions, communications with parents and children, training and visiting other establishments. Some events were planned, others not. There were observed differences between those SSCC multi-agency leaders who were working indirectly with children and families through those at the 'front line', and those who were more tightly 'coupled' to children's learning, development and care through close mentoring and coaching of individual staff. What distinguished SSCC leaders' activities was their observed coordination of multiple tasks, staff teams and projects, and their sharing of decisions related to operational matters or delegating decision-making to project leaders. The multiple domains of their activity demanded multiple leadership function. SSCC leaders who were located within a wider LA organisation were observed on occasion to have their own decisions about staffing, finance or equipment overturned. As one leader mused – 'Who leads the leaders?' The traditional 'vertical' and hierarchical decision making of the LA contrasted with the more flexible decision-making that took place in close contact with children, parents, community and other stakeholders that made for a flatter and more 'distributed' model of leadership among individuals, groups and networks.

The challenge of change and growth at the time was ever present, with major new building work being planned and carried out. Leaders found themselves taking on major operational tasks, with a demand for financial management and technical expertise for which they had received no training, and hence were learning 'on the job'. The need for new skills and understanding, and hence

(Continued)

(Continued)

training reform across the sector was another feature of the video highlights. Celebrating new NVQs, welcoming trainees on work placements and new entrants to the profession also marked the new pathways being created into early childhood work.

When leaders met to share successes and problems and shared their video highlights, they marvelled at their capacity to respond to the changing national childcare strategy in the local context. They experienced changed LA structures in terms of increased bureaucracy, and felt that LAs were not moving as fast as SSCC leaders to create new dynamic patterns of relationships between individuals, teams and partners in order to create 'collaborative advantage', the ability to create and sustain fruitful collaborations and more productive relationships (Huxman, 2003).

Ways forward?

New cluster models of Sure Start children's centres are emerging that work together on strategic goals and with different patterns of management and responsibility, or co-locate with other organisations such as schools or merge with national chains (Sharp et al., 2012). The Coalition government's decision to remove ring-fenced funding for SSCCs in Spring 2011, and introduce funding through the Early Intervention Grant, stimulated a further period of work-intensification, outsourcing and change. The NPQICL content and format is being refreshed, with efforts to make it more flexible, more widely available and modular in approach. From April 2010, the Office for Standards in Education (Ofsted) has evaluated SSCC's effectiveness and this was revised in 2013. This has included the quality of partnership working, with health, adult training and employment, other centres and other partners who provided essential services.

Meanwhile, a recent study of forty SSCC leaders working in a large Midlands city (Atkins, 2011) indicated that multi-agency working was facilitated by a shared focus by agency services, good partnership arrangements and a strong commitment from staff. Leaders were able to identify challenges that they faced and constraints to multi-agency working and its success. Leaders were also able to articulate many aspects of the changing and developing agenda for SSCCs that included increased accountability and the need to demonstrate the impact of services.

Their own strategic area leaders also identified in interview a number of different challenges and issues involved in developing integrated services, such as a lack of adaptability, fear of challenge and unwillingness to set aside status and 'professional hierarchies'. Strong leadership was essential to the success of multi-agency teams, they averred, and this required a more open way of leading and shared learning across professional boundaries. Integration did not happen by chance, however; it took effort, understanding and a commitment on the part of all involved. As noted by Holmes et al. (2012), integrated team working resulted in increased professional awareness of the range of services available and brought professionals together in new contexts. Barriers to inter-agency working still included differences in agency culture and information sharing.

In conclusion, to work effectively multi-agency team working requires substantial investment in terms of expenditure and time to embed practice across the range of agencies.

Key points to remember

- Multi-agency working and integrated service delivery was central to New Labour policy but it is less prominent in current Coalition government thinking.
- Evidence for effective integrated service delivery has not been easy to demonstrate.
- There have been variations in implementation of multi-agency working at regional (LA) and local (e.g. SSCC) level.
- Investment in terms of time and resources is required to implement successfully.

 Points for discussion

- Evidence for effectiveness of multi-agency working processes and outcomes has been difficult to demonstrate. Why should this be the case?
- Initially only SSCC leaders and deputies are eligible for the NPQICL. Should other groups be eligible and why?
- What type of training would be useful to further multi-agency work?
- Do coaching and mentoring have a role to play?

Reflective task

- Holmes et al. (2012: 9) concluded that despite increased professional awareness, barriers to inter-agency working were still identified, including 'differences in agency cultures and information-sharing protocols along with perceived tensions between "CAF professionals" and those from children's social care'. Consider some reasons why multi-agency team working has been so difficult to achieve and what remedies that might ease the situation.

Further reading

Aubrey, C. (2011) *Leading and Managing in the Early Years*, 2nd edn. London: Sage.

Gasper, M. (2011) *Multi-agency working in the early years: challenges and opportunities*. London: Sage.

Atkinson, M., Doherty, P. and Kinder, K. (2005) 'Multi-agency working', *Journal of Early Childhood Research*, 3 (1), 7–17.

Useful websites

There is a 2012 DfE website on multi-agency working that will date and change, and a link to a paper in *Journal of Early Childhood Research*, vol. 3, 1 by Angela Anning, of 2005.

Please also see the following link for further articles relating to key points within this chapter: http://ecr.sagepub.com/content/3/1.toc

To access a variety of additional web resources to accompany this book please visit: **www.sagepub.co.uk/pughduffy**

References

Allen, G. (2011) *Early Intervention: The Next Steps*. An Independent Report to Her Majesty's Government. London: Cabinet Office.

Atkins, C. (2011) 'Children's centres, a time of change and evolution', unpublished Master's dissertation, University of Warwick.

Aubrey, C. (2011) *Leading and Managing in the Early Years*, 2nd edn. London: Sage.

Aubrey, C., Dahl, S. and Clarke, C. (2005) *Multi-agency Working in Sure Start*. Coventry: University of Warwick.

Barr, H., Koppel, I., Reeves, S., Hammick, M. and Freeth, D. (2005) *Effective Interprofessional Education. Argument, Assumption and Evidence*. Oxford: Blackwell.

Blair, T. (1998) *The Third Way: New Politics for the New Century*. London: The Fabian Press.

Belsky, J., Barnes, J. and Melhuish, E. (eds) (2007) *The National Evaluation of Sure Start Projects: Does Area-Based Early Intervention Work?* Bristol: Polity Press.

Brandon, M., Howe, A., Dagley, V., Salter, C. and Warren, C. (2006) 'What appears to be helping or hindering practitioners in implementing the Common Assessment Framework and Lead Professional working?', *Child Abuse Review*, 15, 396–413.

Butler-Sloss, Rt Hon. Justice E. (1988) *Report on the Inquiry into Child Abuse in Cleveland 1987*. Cmnd 412. London: HMSO.

Court Report (1976) *Fit for the Future: The Report of the Committee on Child Health Services.* Cmnd 6684. London: Department of Health and Social Services.

Department for Education (DfE) (2011) National Pilot for eCAF. www.education. gov.uk/childrenandyoungpeople/strategy/integratedworking/caf/a0072820/ national-ecaf.

Department for Education (DfE) (2012) *Multi-Agency Working.* General article. London: DfE. www.education.gov.uk/childrenandyoungpeople/strategy/integrated working/a0069013/multi-agency-working (accessed July 2013).

Department for Education and Skills (DfES) (2003) *Every Child Matters.* Green Paper. Cm 5860. Norwich: TSO.

Department for Education and Skills (DfES) (2004) *Every Child Matters: Change for Children.* Nottingham: DfES Publications.

Easton, C. and Gee, G. (2012) *Early Intervention: Informing Local Practice.* Slough: National Foundation for Educational Research (NFER).

Easton, C., Durban, B. and Teeman, D. (2011) *Early Intervention using the Common Assessment Framework Process and its Cost Effectiveness: Findings from LARC 3.* Slough: NFER.

Easton, C., Featherstone, G., Poet, H., Aston H., Gee, G. and Durbin, B. (2012) *Supporting Families with Complex Needs: Findings from LARC 4.* Slough: NFER.

Engeström, Y. (2008) *From Teams to Knots: Activity-Theoretical Studies of Collaboration and Learning at Work.* Cambridge: Cambridge University Press.

Field, F. (2010) *The Foundation Years: Preventing Poor Children Becoming Poor Adults. The Report of the Independent Review on Poverty and Life Chances.* London: Cabinet Office.

Freeth, D., Hammick, M., Reeves, S., Koppel, I. and Barr, H. (2005) *Effective Interprofessional Education: Development, Delivery and Evaluation.* Oxford: Blackwell.

Glass, N. (1999) 'Sure Start: the development of an early intervention programme for young children in the UK', *Children & Society*, 13, 257–64.

Holmes, L., McDermid, S., Padley, M. and Soper, J. (2012) *Exploration of the Costs and Impact of the Common Assessment Framework.* Research Report DFE – RR210. London: Department for Education.

Huxman, C. (2003) 'Theorizing collaborative practice', *Public Management Review*, 3, 401–423.

Joyce, B.R. and Showers, S.B. (2002) *Student Achievement through Staff Development*, 3e. Alexandria, VA: Association for Supervision and Curriculum Development (ASCD) Publications.

Laming, Lord (2003) *The Victoria Climbié Inquiry: Report of an Inquiry by Lord Laming.* Cm 5730. London: TSO.

Marmot, M. (2010) *Fair Society, Healthy Lives. Strategic Review of Health Inequalities in England Post 2010* (Marmot Review). London: Department of Health.

Munro, E. (2011) *The Munro Review of Child Protection: Final Report. A Child-Centred System.* Cm 8062. Norwich: TSO.

NESS (National Evaluation of Sure Start) (2010) *The Impact of Sure Start Local Programmes on Five Year Olds and Their Families*. RR 067. London: Department for Education.

Nutbrown, C. (2012) *Foundations for Quality. The Independent Review of Early Education and Childcare Qualifications: Final Report* (Nutbrown Review). London: Department for Education.

Øvretveit, J., Mathias, P. and Thompson, T. (1997) *Interprofessional Working for Health and Social Care*. London: Macmillan.

Pietroni, P. N. (1992) 'Towards reflective practice – languages of health and social care', *Journal of Interprofessional Care*, 6, (1), 7–16.

Plowden Report (1967) *Children and Their Primary Schools*. London: HMSO.

Seebohm Report (1968) *The Report of the Committee on Local Authority and Allied Personal Social Services*. Cmnd 3703. London: HMSO.

Sharp, C., Lord, P., Handscomb, G., Macleod, S., Southcott, C., George, N. and Jeffes, J. (2012) *Highly Effective Leadership in Children's Centres*. Nottingham: National College for School Leadership.

Tickell, C. (2011) *The Early Years: Foundations for Life, Health and Learning. An Independent Report on the Early Years Foundation Stage to Her Majesty's Government* (Tickell Review). London: Department for Education.

Warnock Report (1978) *Special Educational Needs: Report of the Committee of Enquiry into the Education of Handicapped Children and Young People*. Cmnd 7212. London: Department for Education and Science.

Index

187932